The Transcendent Adventure

The Transcendent Adventure

Studies of Religion in Science Fiction/Fantasy

Edited by
ROBERT REILLY

Contributions to the Study of
Science Fiction and Fantasy, Number 12

Greenwood Press
Westport, Connecticut • London, England

Library of Congress Cataloging in Publication Data

Main entry under title:

The Transcendent adventure.

  (Contributions to the study of science fiction and
fantasy, ISSN 0193-6875 ; no. 12)
  Includes bibliographies and index.
  1. Science fiction, English—History and criticism—
Addresses, essays, lectures. 2. Fantastic fiction,
English—History and criticism—Addresses, essays, lectures. 3. Science fiction, American—History and
criticism—Addresses, essays, lectures. 4. Fantastic
fiction, American—History and criticism—Addresses,
essays, lectures. 5. Science fiction—Religious aspects
—Addresses, essays, lectures. 6. Religion in literature
—Addresses, essays, lectures. I. Reilly, Robert,
1933-   . II. Series.
PR830.S35T73   1985   823'.0876'09382   84-542
ISBN 0-313-23062-5 (lib. bdg.)

Library of Congress Catalog Card Number: 84-542
ISBN: 0-313-23062-5
ISSN: 0193-6875

First published in 1985

Greenwood Press
A division of Congressional Information Service, Inc.
88 Post Road West
Westport, Connecticut 06881

Printed in the United States of America

10 9 8 7 6 5 4 3 2 1

To all those who seek the Truth, whether scientific or religious.

Nay, be a Columbus to whole new continents and worlds within you, opening new channels, not of trade, but of thought.

Thoreau—*Walden*

Contents

Part III.   Major Authors: Individualized Treatments of Religion

Part IV.   Bibliographies

The Transcendent Adventure

Introduction

ROBERT REILLY

Before we begin to consider the reasons that lead authors of science fiction to utilize religion in their works, it may help to suggest what religion is. First, it is a set of beliefs, held by an individual or group, that serve to explain the source of order in the universe. Usually, this explanation postulates some power beyond human understanding as the source of order, as the cause of otherwise inexplicable events. Second, religion provides means by which believers can relate to the power or source of order—means such as ritual, prayer, self-abnegation, and/or principles of ethical conduct. At this level, religion becomes institutionalized, the means of relationship passing from the individual into the hands of some special group, usually a priesthood.

One can easily see that physical science can be included within the scope of this definition of religion. It uses rational means to explain order in the universe and provides a relationship (the experimental method) to the source of order. The scientists themselves are a sort of priesthood. Science fails to conform only with respect to the postulate of "a power" to explain the order.

One other point needs to be made initially. Rather than quibble over the much-debated distinction between science fiction and fantasy, I have chosen to include essays about both in this collection. Works by C. S. Lewis and Roger Zelazny may well fall into either category; adherence to any strict definition of science fiction might include some of their works and exclude others, it would certainly exclude

J.R.R.Tolkien. Because I regard such exclusions as at least somewhat arbitrary, I have chosen not to make them. When I speak of science fiction, I am including works that may also be regarded as fantasy. Those who are interested in the distinction between the genres and some of the difficulties it raises should consult the essays by Richard L. Purtill and William A. Quinn.

Science fiction has its roots in some of the same forces—a curiosity about the nature of the universe and the desire to explain it rationally—that underlie the development of modern experimental science. Science tends to regard the universe as purely material and to see itself as capable of providing rational explanations for almost anything in the universe. Early science fiction took a wholly uncritical and enthusiastic attitude toward science. Almost to a person, its authors subscribed wholeheartedly to the philosophy that claimed "progress is our most important product." Science, and the technology envisioned as a spin-off from it, consistently received positive, optimistic treatment. In the early works of such authors as Isaac Asimov, Arthur C. Clarke, and Robert Heinlein, there is a vision of the future in which scientific progress points toward some sort of utopia where technology provides for every human desire. The general consensus of works written before 1945 was that science, the key to all truth, would enable man to understand, manipulate, and thus transcend the painful reality of his ordinary existence.

After Hiroshima, the rose-tinted view of mankind's future was no longer tenable. Even those who were most firmly dedicated to the principles of pure science were forced to question man's competency to manipulate the universe solely through technological means. A wave of pessimism, bearing a whole series of holocaust novels on its crest, swept through the genre. One of these, Walter M. Miller's *A Canticle for Leibowitz* (1959), treated the holocaust motif in a religious context that raised profound ethical and moral questions about the use of science and technology.

Today authors still struggle with those same ethical and moral questions. But, because the faith in science has in large measure failed, contemporary authors have been forced to look elsewhere for means of transcending the present reality with which mankind has perennially been dissatisfied. Numbers of them have explored the way of religious transcendence.

Yet a historical and cultural change tracing the rise and failure of science as a religion helps to explain only one aspect of why authors

deal with religious themes. Another possible reason must not be over-
looked: the author's personal search for some sort of absolute truth or
transcendent reality. Such a search is best exemplified in the work of
three authors—Philip K. Dick, Philip José Farmer, and Frank Herbert.
Each of these men has written a series of works that may be regarded
as the outward manifestation of an inward search.

Even if it were possible to explain, with absolute certainty and com-
pleteness, why authors have chosen to write science fiction containing
religious themes, the question of how they use those themes would
remain an almost inexhaustible field for critical inquiry. Fiction, of its
very nature, operates by a sort of indirection. By telling a story, the
author hopes to convey ideas or emotions. Thus, it would come as no
surprise to find certain authors who use science fiction as a vehicle for
philosophical or theological discourse. Moreover, since the dominant
philosophical/theological tradition of the West is Christian, numbers of
these authors produce works that utilize or react to the Christian tradition. James Blish's *A Case of Conscience* (1958) stands as an obvious
example of this sort of novel. C. S. Lewis utilized his profound knowledge of Christian theology to produce *Perelandra* (1943). There are
exceptions. Olaf Stapledon, in his *Star Maker* (1937), has written a
work that has more qualities of theological speculation than of fiction,
but it departs completely from the Christian tradition. Nevertheless, the
dominance of this tradition cannot be ignored.

Symbolism and myth epitomize fictional indirection. With these devices an author departs as fully as possible from the literal truth, often
in an effort to apprehend some more complex or ambiguous truth.
Numerous writers of science fiction have created works in which symbolic or mythic patterns are instruments for exploring the tenets of
religion. Harlan Ellison's "Deathbird" (1975), Roger Zelazny's *Lord
of Light* (1967), and Frank Herbert and Bill Ransome's *The Jesus Incident* (1979) are representative examples. Myths of the Creation, of
the Fall of Man, or of the Fall of the Angels frequently recur in the
genre. Sometimes such patterns may be used ironically, as in Arthur
Clarke's "The Star" (1955), or in a demythologizing way, as in Fritz
Leiber's "One Station of the Way" (1968) and in Michael Moorcock's
Behold the Man (1970).

Science fiction's essential concern with the future and its preoccupation with space exploration can lead directly to the development of
religious alternatives. The future may bring some new revelation, par-

ticularly through contact with an alien race. In Philip José Farmer's *Night of Light* (1966), Fr. John Carmody finds that he has become the bearer of such a revelation.

Other religious alternatives can be found in such works as George R. R. Martin's *Song for Lya* (1976) and in James Marrow's *The Wine of Violence* (1981). Alien religions—their conception, nature, and significance—represent an area that has so far received almost no critical attention.

Both science fiction and mainstream fiction explore the political and social implications of religion. The chief difference is one of setting. Science fiction considers what religion may become under vastly altered circumstances. Leigh Brackett's *The Long Tomorrow* (1955) suggests the possibility that one religion might better prepare its followers for post-holocaust existence than others do. Kate Wilhelm's *Let the Fire Fall* (1969) takes place in a future United States swept by millennial fanaticism. Frank Herbert's Dune tetralogy examines in some depth the effects of political rule by characters who are regarded as divine.

Certainly this is not a complete list of the ways science fiction writers treat the theme of religion. But it is suggestive of a much deeper and wider interest in the theme than many have been willing to recognize. So far, literary criticism has not adequately dealt with this fact. In light of the cultural influences already mentioned, these essays, by and large, take a generally Christian and theological approach to the topic. This is by no means the only possibility, but it is a good beginning, especially as numbers of works recognized as outstanding science fiction have overtly Christian content—the works of Blish and Lewis, for instance.

The more abstract and general sort of essays are presented first, in the section entitled "Significances: Contexts for Critical Consideration." Adam J. Frisch and Joseph Martos, in their essay "Religious Imagination and Imagined Religions," deal with three ways of thinking about religion: fundamentalizing, ultimatizing, and moralizing. They explore how these modes of thought are utilized by such authors as Ellison, Blish, and Varley to produce works of a religious nature. In a somewhat similar way, Richard L. Purtill suggests that the underlying philosophic view of reality, a view that is basically religious, may serve as a means of distinguishing science fiction from fantasy. His essay, "Mind, Matter, and Magic in Fantasy and Science Fiction," discusses the works of a number of authors in light of this distinction. The third essay, perhaps more strictly theological than the other two, deals with the religious implications of an alien encounter. "Science Fiction's Harrowing of the Heavens," by William A. Quinn, explores the way authors utilize various theological systems to deal with aliens and concludes that certain systems are only compatible with fantasy. In "For Suffering Humanity," Alexander J. Butrym examines the divergent ethical positions of Frank R. Stockton, Isaac Asimov, and Walter M. Miller to show how ethical ideas contribute to or detract from literary effectiveness.

The second section, "Dilemmas of Paradise: Blish and Lewis," comprises three essays treating *Perelandra* and *A Case of Conscience*, novels widely recognized for both their literary merit and theological complexity. Andrew J. Burgess, in "The Concept of Eden," discusses the theological implication of the ways Blish and Lewis use the Garden of Eden theme. Lewis's dramatic handling of the problem of evil is the topic of Katherin A. Rogers's "Augustinian Evil in C. S. Lewis's *Perelandra.*" Diane Parkin-Speer closes this section with "Alien Ethics and Religion versus Fallen Mankind," in which she shows how two novels use the ethical dilemmas of clergymen (each confronted with a first contact situation) to satirize the secular materialism of our time.

"Major Authors: Individualized Treatments of Religion," which forms the largest part of this collection, comprises eight essays, each devoted to an author of particular importance. Patricia S. Warrick starts things off with a thoroughgoing analysis of Philip K. Dick's novels *Valis* and *Divine Invasion* (1981). She covers style, techniques, and themes as she develops his religious cosmogony. Next is "From Rebellious Rationalist to Mythmaker and Mystic: The Religious Quest of Philip José Farmer," in which Edgar L. Chapman traces Farmer's search for a "potent religious myth" from early romanticism, through mythological speculation, to mysticism. Frank Herbert's fictional answers to the question "Is there a supreme being who is qualitatively different from man?" is the topic of David M. Miller's essay. After a careful analysis of the religious ideas in most of Herbert's work, Miller finds no supreme being, but a supreme pattern. Tracing the major themes of Doris Lessing's work leads Nancy Topping Bazin to conclude that Lessing's recent science fiction novels, rather than charting a new direction, are the culmination of a long-established interest in mysticism, especially Sufism. Frank D. Kievitt then presents an interpretation of *A Canticle for Leibowitz* as a reaffirmation of traditional values in a world of technological change. In a penetrating explication of *Mockingbird*, Martha

A. Bartter shows how Walter Tevis uses an almost perfect robot—
modeled on King Kong and Milton's Satan—to exemplify the potential
for evil in irresponsible creativity. Elizabeth Allen presents an entirely
different aspect of Tolkien's work, showing how he has utilized elements
from Mithraism to develop a pre–Christian religion in *The Lord of the
Rings*. Through a careful scrutiny of a large number of Roger Zelazny's
works, Joseph V. Francavilla demonstrates the way in which his godlike
heroes in fact serve to reject religion.

The fourth section contains a bibliography of works with religious
themes and a bibliography of critical works about religion in science
fiction.

As can be seen from these brief summaries, there is a considerable
range of critical possibilities for dealing with religion in science fiction.
These essays cannot begin to deal with all the possibilities. They are a
good beginning. Much remains to be done, however, before it can be
said that the place and importance of religion in science fiction is adequately documented and understood.

PART I

SIGNIFICANCES: CONTEXTS FOR CRITICAL CONSIDERATION

1

Religious Imagination and Imagined Religion

ADAM J. FRISCH AND JOSEPH MARTOS

Writers of speculative fiction since Mary Shelley have explored many aspects of religion, and, in doing so, they themselves have exhibited some of the fundamental features of religious consciousness. Perhaps this is because there is a universality about religious consciousness that transcends differences between both religions and individuals. Perhaps it is because writers of fiction naturally portray imagined realities along the lines of familiar realities, religion being no exception. Whatever the underlying reason, those who write fiction about religion display many of the features found in the consciousness of those who call themselves religious.

This chapter focuses on three basic features of religious imagination and examines their development in selected works of recent science fiction. We have termed these three features *fundamentalizing*, *ultimatizing*, and *moralizing*; we shall look at some of the ways that these three features show up in imagined religions and in religious imaginings that, at first glance, do not seem to be about religion at all.

FEATURES OF RELIGIOUS IMAGINATION

Those who look at the world through the lens of religion often simplify the complexities of the cosmos into basic sets of realities (such as god/ devil, or creation/duration/destruction) and then think of the universe in terms of such fundamental imagery. This inclination toward reducing

reality to its most essential features is what we would like to call
fundamentalizing. Every religion has a cosmology that is comprehensive, and because it is comprehensive it has to simplify reality into a
somewhat coherent set of fundamental images describing the objective
world.

Besides the objective world "out there," religious persons are also
concerned with the subjective world "in here"—namely, the world of
thoughts and feelings, of meanings and values. Religion is concerned
with many aspects of this subjective world (such as belief and doubt,
guilt and forgiveness), but above all it is concerned with the ultimate
meaning of human existence, the ultimate value of life. For this reason,
we refer to the second basic feature of religious consciousness as *ultimatizing*, an inclination to look for and pronounce on the bottom-line
meaning and value of life.

Third, religious persons find themselves confronted with the problem
of relating these objective and subjective worlds. How should conscious
beings respond to the rest of reality? What should be their basic orientation toward themselves, toward other sentient creatures, toward
physical realities, and toward metaphysical beings? In particular, how
should they live out the ultimate meaning of their lives in the face of
the fundamental nature of reality? Such questions necessarily lead to
moralizing, understood here to mean the way religious imagination seeks
to describe the ethically good life.

These three features can be found in all the religions that have had
an extended influence on our planet, such as Hinduism and Buddhism
in the East, Judaism and Christianity in the West, and Islam in both.
This is so obvious that it hardly needs to be documented. And if one
examines less-influential religions, one finds that they all have a fundamental cosmology, anthropology, and morality that form an imaginative framework for dealing with everything that is or might possibly
be.

These basic features of religious consciousness, however, can also
be found when religion becomes trivialized into what we might term
religiosity. When religion turns into religiosity, insights into the fundamental nature of the cosmos become naive oversimplifications of
reality, gods become idols, and teachings become dogmas. In a similar
way, human life and its meaning are devalued, and in their place various
individuals and objects, rituals and traditions are invested with ultimate
value. Likewise, morality is reduced to formality, a legalistic network

of obligations and taboos in which the trivial becomes ethical and the ethical becomes trivial.

Historically, religiosity of this sort was rejected by Buddha and Jesus, even though it is still too often found in Buddhism and Christianity, and in other religions as well. It is also rejected by science fiction writers who satirize religion or some aspect of it. This is to say, what these science fiction writers dismiss as unworthy of imitation or belief is not usually religion but its parody—religiosity. Occasionally they even reject religiosity in the name of genuinely religious fundamentalizing, ultimatizing, and moralizing.

FUNDAMENTALIZING

Imaginative fundamentalizing, or rethinking the fundamental structures of reality, is frequently found in science fiction novels and short stories. It seems that the "what if?" nature of the genre readily lends itself to a reappraisal of traditionally accepted images of reality. When science fiction was still winning over its audiences during the first half of the twentieth century, it took care to avoid confronting deeply rooted public imagery, especially in the areas of sex and religion. The cross-cultural reexaminations of the 1960s relaxed such restrictions, however, and no vision became too dangerous for intrepid and iconoclastic authors to approach.

Spearheading that movement was Harlan Ellison's 1967 anthology entitled *Dangerous Visions*.[1] The first story in that collection, Lester del Rey's "Evensong," offers a good example of religious fundamentalizing with a surprising twist. Del Rey postulates an unnamed being of great power, imprisoned for centuries, who has now escaped and is attempting to outrun his even more powerful pursuers. As the story unfolds from the hunted being's viewpoint, we learn that our spontaneous affection for this underdog must be tempered somewhat by our dislike for the selfishness and arrogance that he unconsciously reveals in his narrative. The figure finally becomes a kind of Miltonic Satan seeking the cover of the Earth's shadow, pitiable in his immediate plight although finally repugnant. But del Rey turns the tables at the very end of the story by revealing that the fugitive is God himself, being pursued as if he were a naughty boy by a mankind that has at last found its rightful place in the cosmos. Is del Rey suggesting that mankind already is or is becoming greater than God, or is he creatively playing around with possibilities just for the fun of it? In either case, he shows that we do not have to face reality the way Faustus did, fearful that there are "certain things best left alone." Del Rey does not leave them alone, and no disaster befalls him or the reader who temporarily accepts this new image of reality.

Other stories in *Dangerous Visions* distort or invert the fundamental Judeo-Christian image of divine realities, most notably "Shall the Dust Praise Thee?" by Damon Knight, and "Encounter with a Hick" by Jonathan Brand.[2] But perhaps a more revealing example of how science fiction uses and alters such fundamental images is to be found in the title story of Ellison's own *Deathbird* collection. In "The Deathbird," Ellison creates, against the Genesis account of man's creation and fall, a plot in which the snake is the patient and wise guardian of a planet that, for unexplained reasons, has been turned over to a puny but insane God. Earth has been at last completely ravaged, presumably by wars that have turned it into a windswept moonscape of desolation. Now Snake, hoping to bring his weary mission to a close, has resurrected Adam in the person of his last incarnation, Nathan Stack.

> Stack found the mad one wandering in the forest of final moments. He was an old, tired man, and Stack knew with a wave of his hand he could end it for this god in a moment. But what was the reason for it? It was even too late for revenge. . . .
> And Stack came back to Snake, who had served his function and protected Stack until Stack had learned that he was more powerful than the god he'd worshiped all through the history of Men.[3]

Some might accuse the story of being an antireligious parody, and yet the structure of the universe that exists behind the facade of Genesis in Ellison's imagination is, in fact, strikingly similar to the one found in the Bible. In both accounts, good and evil are personified, but here the roles are reversed. Instead of God being man's friend and savior, it is Snake.

Although science fiction writers who deal with religious themes today twist traditional image patterns, they generally use the accepted fundamental structure to question particular items in its content. Occasionally, however, an author will examine the fundamentalizing impulse itself, especially when he feels that it has led to the kind of imaginative rigidity that we have described earlier as a characteristic of religiosity.

Thus, we might distinguish pointed probes in stories such as those by del Rey and Ellison from the more general satire in a novel such as Robert Sheckley's *Dimension of Miracles*.

Sheckley sends his protagonist, a contemporary stumblebum named Tom Carmody, on a picaresque journey across the galaxy in a broad satire against the reductionistic ways in which human beings have traditionally imagined divine power. Carmody is first taken by an alien messenger to Galactic Center to be awarded a sweepstakes prize. It turns out, however, that the Sweepstakes Computer has made an error; the real winner should have been one Carmody from Planet 73C. When this mistake is pointed out, the supposedly infallible computer argues that the error was a deliberate assertion of its own free will.

Malfunction, gentlemen, is, I submit, our means of rendering worship to that which is more perfect than we, but which still does not permit itself a visible perfection. So, if error were not divinely programmed into us, we would malfunction spontaneously, to show that modicum of free will which, as living creatures, we partake in.[4]

The machine's argument is a simple extension of the traditional philosophical debate over determinism; but put into the mouth of a computer obviously trying to escape responsibility like any other blundering bureaucrat, the response raises some disquieting questions about the whole nature of this vision of free will. If only error separates the free soul from nonspiritual creation, is the distinction a particularly ennobling one?

Sheckley's attack on such conceptualization is broadened when Carmody encounters Melichrone, a being who, along with its "extensions," is the only possible living inhabitant of its planet. "As far as this planet was concerned," notes Melichrone, "I was God. There's no sense beating around the bush about it: I was supernal, immortal, omnipotent and omniscient." Yet even with such powers, traditional human visions of what the divine must be like, Melichrone still has problems. Not only is he plagued with a propensity toward the flamboyant that makes all his entrances and exits look like "a Mexican fireworks display in Chapultepec Park on Easter," but ultimately Melichrone finds his very divinity "boring, a job for a simple-minded egomaniac."[5] He has even created both a race of beings "free" to worship him and an afterlife for their eventual reward or punishment, only to abandon the whole business as too limiting. So Melichrone the God asks Carmody the anti-hero to help him find some meaningful employment. By making this omnipotent being so helpless, Sheckley calls into question the usual vision of divine power above vs. human powerlessness below. Furthermore, if the divine is as all-powerful and all-pervading as religion has pictured it to be, what element in reality allows for free will and choice, or even for accident and chance? Many mainstream novels have attempted to answer this question, perhaps the most famous being Robert Penn Warren's conclusion to *All the King's Men*, in which the narrator's father declares that evil was merely a divine attempt to create something other than itself. But as presented in Sheckley's setting, the entire question becomes ludicrous, especially when Carmody "solves" Melichrone's problem by enlisting the powerful being's aid to find a way back to Earth. This solution depends upon the fact that Melichrone is not really omnipotent, that there is something beyond his planet-wide control, namely, Carmody and the rest of the universe. Even so, the best Melichrone can offer is to send Carmody off to the original creator of the Earth, an absent-minded engineer named Maudsley whose chief concern is cost-overrun and who once invented deterministic science in order to cover up environmental "oversights" on Earth such as deserts and tornadoes. Sheckley sends Carmody off on similar encounters with various images of divinity throughout the remainder of the novel, in each case demonstrating the inconsistencies that result from taking too literally the image of God proposed by naive religiosity.

ULTIMATIZING

If religious imagination fundamentalizes reality in establishing a coherent cosmology, it also ultimatizes certain values in establishing an orderliness within the internal world of meaning and belief. For Jesus and much of the Christian tradition, faith is more valuable than reason, for the ultimate meaning of human life is supernatural. For Buddha and much of the Theravada tradition, meditation is more valuable than action, for the ultimate goal of life is nirvana, release from activity. In most religions, life is more valuable than death, though in some a noble death is preferable to an ignoble life. The list of examples could be drawn out and filled in with great detail, but all religions face and try to answer questions about what is ultimately important in human life.

Occasionally science fiction confronts questions of this sort, especially in its more popular guise as "what can be?" scenarios that imagine reality to be wildly different from what we ordinarily assume it to be. Certainly a great deal of *Star Trek*'s popularity as a TV series resulted from the confrontation between Spock's reliance on rationality and Kirk's insistence on affectivity. Typically, the program's creators suggested that both reason and emotion are crucial, but their deliberate ambiguity about which one was the more important kept the question open and intriguing from one episode to the next.

A more thorough treatment of the importance of ultimate values can be found in the full-length version of James Blish's work, *A Case of Conscience.*[6] The novel narrates the inner turmoil of a twenty-first-century Jesuit priest, Ramon Ruiz-Sanchez, as he discovers the meaning of the alien planet Lithia and attempts to warn others of its disastrous implications for mankind.

The first section of the novel (the original novelette) takes place on Lithia itself; the planet is being explored by a preliminary party of Earth scientists to determine if the planet and its native race have any economic potential. The reptilian Lithians turn out to be a crimeless, religionless race because of a bred-in rationality that combines reason and emotion into a single basis for action. At first perplexed by the Lithians' apparently Edenic existence without any knowledge of a divine being, Father Ruiz-Sanchez pursues his biological studies of the planet alongside a theological study of a complicated interfamilial moral dilemma originally posited by James Joyce. When he finally understands that the moral puzzle can be resolved into two separate issues, he concludes that the Lithians can be, simultaneously, both Edenic and a "trap of the Adversary." His decision has painful consequences, since it involves him in the Manichaean heresy (and thus prevents him from receiving a special papal indulgence scheduled for the upcoming ecclesiastical year); it requires him to hurt his generous Lithian friend Chtexa; and it causes him to vote with his scientific enemy, Cleaver, who wants to close the planet to commerce because it offers a rich source of fusion weapons material. Nevertheless, Father Ruiz-Sanchez persists in his beliefs and returns to Earth.

The second half of Blish's novel makes clear that the Jesuit priest's decisions involve far more than some personal theological speculations. Egtverchi, the Lithian offspring of Chtexa whom the priest has transported to Earth, manages by himself to undermine an Earth society

already on the brink of complete moral and ethical breakdown and then
escape back to Lithia. All alone, with his civilization in chaos, Father
Ruiz-Sanchez continues to search for a way to fight the "Enemy." The
novel climaxes when the Jesuit priest pronounces an ancient Latin exorcism upon the planet over an instantaneous transmitter at exactly the
same moment when an ill-advised fusion experiment on Lithia by the
physicist Cleaver results in the planet's total annihilation. Father Ruiz-
Sanchez concludes that internal coherence can occur on many different
levels. For the Earth scientists, the planet's destruction will have been
the consequence of a mathematical error in Equation Sixteen; for Cleaver,
it will have been the ultimate fusion explosion; and for Father Ruiz-
Sanchez, it will have been another triumph for the Church. Although
the reader may not agree with the priest's own religious interpretation,
Blish's novel at least raises a question about the necessity for each
individual to both recognize an ultimate relationship between his or her
internal beliefs and actions, and ask whether he or she puts ultimate
trust in knowledge or faith. As Blish himself notes in his introduction
to the novel: "It was my intention to write about a man, not a body of
doctrine."[7]

Many other science fiction writers have used the resources of their
genre to explore internal worlds by looking outward at cosmic ones.
But science fiction's ability to imagine new planets and civilizations
makes it equally effective for showing what happens when religion and
other institutions try to reduce ultimate principles to a set of rules and
taboos. Very often, the institution itself, its practices, and its rituals
assume an ultimate importance, but the principles and values that the
institution purports to serve become negotiable. In this case the religious
institution becomes institutionalized religiosity, and science fiction has
done its share to show up the shallowness of such behavior. Sometimes
this is done by barbed satire, at other times it is done by means of a
parody. Parodies of institutionalized religion can be found, for example,
in Walter M. Miller's *A Canticle for Liebowitz* and James E. Gunn's
This Fortress World.[8]

Both novels imagine something like medieval Christianity that has
been transposed into the future. In *Canticle*, the future time is a few
centuries after the first nuclear holocaust; civilization has been reduced
to the level of barbarism that we associate with the fall of Rome and
the subsequent Dark Ages. In *Fortress*, the future time is some millennia
after the collapse of the Second Galactic Empire (the First Empire

already being a legend of the unremembered past) when worlds are once again fighting rival worlds in a galaxy ruled by a feudalism that is devoid of chivalry. As in medieval Europe, when Christianity was the only international organization, religion in both novels is the only universal institution. Miller represents this universality through the Order of St. Leibowitz, named after an obscure scientist whose remains (including a lunch list) have accidentally elevated him to sainthood. Gunn's interplanetary institution is the Church, whose hierarchy and liturgy are clearly patterned on those of medieval Christianity. And just as Miller's religious order reveres a scientist whose image in some ways resembles that of the original man, so Gunn's church honors the Prophet Jude, who has left writings known collectively as *The Word* and whose followers make the Sign of the Circle in a gesture of blessing. In both novels, the ecclesiastical institutions are portrayed as more interested in religiosity than religion. Their oversimplified messages of peace and consolation are narcotics for the masses who have security instead of freedom, and they give primary importance to formality and ritual rather than to the inner conversion of the individual and the moral salvation of society. Like their medieval predecessor, these organizations are legalistic, operating according to ecclesiastical laws and cooperating with established political systems with an eye toward their own self-preservation and perpetuation.

Yet, in the end, neither author is overtly antagonistic toward the institutionalized religions that they parody so convincingly. In Miller's novel, religion saves just enough truth amidst its dogmas and regulations to nurture those who are deeply committed to rediscovery and scientific development, as is evidenced in a scene in which one of the St. Leibowitz monks rediscovers electricity. For Miller, too, religion offers each person a hope for individual significance amidst a human nature seemingly forever condemned to repeat its mistakes, as illustrated most graphically in the book's concluding scene when a final confession is heard as the nuclear missiles fall once again. In Gunn's book, protagonist William Dane looks beyond the church's religiosity to a sacred core of fundamental realities and ultimate truths that lie at the heart of his religion. We are not sure how they are spelled out in doctrines, but Dane's character has certainly been molded by them, and we see their fruits in his thoughts and actions. He is concerned for the poor and the suffering, and he has a keen sense of justice. He is appalled about how cheaply others treat life, and he is convinced that the meaning of life is more than obedience to superiors, whether secular or ecclesiastical. In their treatment of organized religion, therefore, Miller and Gunn both try to distinguish external religiosity from inner religious faith, and while they overtly parody the former, they covertly praise the latter.

MORALIZING

Sooner or later, religious imagination wonders about the relationship between the inner and the outer, subject and cosmos. It asks the basic question: How should the individual live out the ultimate meaning of his life in the face of the fundamental nature of reality? Most writings that we normally identify as religious—from the parables of the New Testament to the autobiographies of Gandhi or Merton—have as their goal some counsel about how to live a morally good life. But it is surprising to find how often science fiction, a genre whose speculative nature would seem to render it antididactic, moralizes in its imaginative visions. Two very different works, Philip K. Dick's esoteric "Faith of Our Fathers" and John Varley's recent novel series *Titan*, illustrate how science fiction sometimes searches out or proposes ethical standards and behavior.[9]

Dick sets "Faith of Our Fathers" some time in the near future when the East-Asian bloc, ruled by an Absolute Benefactor, has emerged as world conqueror. Dick's protagonist, Tung Chien, is a young bureaucrat being tested for admission to the Leader's private cadre. Aware of this test, a secret organization that suspects the identity of the Absolute Benefactor manages to slip Chien an antihallucinogen to counteract the effects of the citizenry's habitual drugging from the country's water supply, thus allowing Chien to see the Leader as he *really* is. What Tung Chien discovers when he uses the drug during one of the Benefactor's private parties is that the Leader is a loathsome alien being, without solid shape or substance, who uses time itself as a sadistic weapon to torture and finally destroy human individuals. The alien reveals to Chien that it alone has been the source of all religious and political dialectics. "I founded everything. I founded the anti-Party and the Party that isn't a Party, and those who are for it and those who are against, those that you call Yankee Imperialists, those in the camp of reaction, and so on endlessly. I founded it all. As if they were blades of grass."[10]

"You are God," Chien realizes. The alien tells Chien to go home and forget its existence; after all, it assures him, there are "others worse than I" who will someday gain power over the Earth. But when Chien returns to his apartment he discovers that the creature has left a perpetually bleeding wound, a kind of diabolical stigmata, that will soon cause Chien's death. As a final act of defiance, Chien makes love to Tanya Lee, who originally brought him the antihallucinogenic drug, because, for mankind, sex is the one human thing "outside of time; it's boundless, like an ocean. It's the way we were in Cambrian times, before we migrated up onto the land; it's the ancient primary waters. This is the only time we get to go back, when this is done."[11] Only in this way can Chien, and all humanity, truly rebel against God who has created time.

"Faith of Our Fathers," like many of Philip K. Dick's works, has at its core a fear that the fundamental reality will in fact turn out to be a trivial one, such as here, where "God" is merely a sadistic being whose only motivation is to soak up as much pain and suffering as possible before something stronger replaces him. As the Absolute Benefactor says, "It is automatic; it was arranged that way."[12] The power in Dick's writing, however, comes not so much from his grotesque imaginings about the nature of the divine, but from his sincere desire to discover a course of human action that can survive even this extreme a metaphysical foundation. His answer in "Faith of Our Fathers," which advocates a kind of "good sex," like some of Dick's other responses championing "continual quest" (*Deus Irae*) or "emotional perseverance" (*Dr. Bloodmoney*), may appear rather reductionistic and jejune to many modern readers. At the same time, however, his search for a so-called bottom-line morality may well account for his avid following among a wide class of readers in the genre.

One of the more interesting science fiction responses to the question of how to behave even under extremely adverse conditions is John Varley's Titan series, which relates the adventures of a group of Earth explorers on an artificial satellite circling the planet Saturn. The novels in the series evidence a concern for bottom-line moral and ethical principles, and some of Varley's conclusions are at once convincing and unconventional.

The first novel in the series, *Titan*, describes the destruction of the exploratory ship *Ringmaster* and the capture of her crew by the strange satellite world. The story follows the ship's captain, Cirocco (Rocky) Jones, and her shipmate Gaby Plauget as they wander the satellite searching for clues to its nature and origin. During their journeys they discover several species of alien beings inhabiting the world, including intelligent races of centaurlike creatures (the Titanides) and flying angels of destruction who continually war with each other. Eventually, the two climb one of the massive cables radiating from the giant moon's center, only to discover that the entire world has been "evolved" and is being ruled by a little old lady, a Wizard-of-Oz figure called Gaea who, although some of her regions have been usurped by underling intelligences, still possesses near-omnipotence over her domains. At the conclusion of *Titan*, Cirocco decides to accept Gaea's offer to stay on as a kind of ambassador, acting as Gaea's representative to visitors and as a mediator among various elements in Gaea's own world. Varley's second novel, *Wizard*, follows Cirocco and Gaby as they attempt to carry out this responsibility, a task that eventually leads them to plot an overthrow of Gaea herself.

Aside from the fundamental questions it raises about the basic requisites for "godhood," Varley's novel series does not seem to offer a particularly religious imaginary vision, especially since it includes much that world religions have historically labeled sinful, such as homosexuality and abortion. But in a sense, its central question mirrors the speculations of philosophers such as Descartes who have pondered the image of God as Trickster. Closely connected with this issue is the question of ethics in such a situation. Given that the crew has been marooned in a hostile world without provisions or tools, what kinds of action can they undertake that will prove morally meaningful? Varley's works surpass most of the "space operas," whose plots revolve around the exigencies of physical survival, by exploring the emotional needs of the characters and the implications of the actions they pursue to fulfill those needs.

In general, Varley's characters in the Titan series discover three prerequisites for meaningful personal actions: instinctive compassion, selfless courage, and the necessity for a persistence of moral vision. These qualities seem to be essential even if the presiding deity itself turns out to be, like Gaea, prone to callousness and personal vanity. Thus, Varley's characters sometimes fall into displays of passion in so natural a fashion that they themselves are unaware of their onsets. This is especially true in many of the lesbian encounters between Cirocco and Gaby; Rocky is usually unaware of the directions of her desires until they have overwhelmed her. Similarly, Cirocco is always instinctively honest in her emotional responses, whether weeping for a fallen Titanide or getting drunk.

But if a compassionate honesty is important to Varley, so is a type of honest courage that can overcome emotional qualms whenever a genuine human need arises. The character Gaby most frequently displays this sort of courage, whether it involves killing a harmless food-beast to prevent starvation, or slaying a ferocious mudfish when crewmates' lives are endangered, or nearly killing her shipmate Gene after he has become insane and raped Cirocco. In all cases, Varley does not glorify the courageous action; indeed, the scenes are often so gruesome that even Cirocco is disgusted. Instead, Varley presents selfless courage as an occasional, usually messy necessity.

Most important in Varley's list of moral qualities is that each individual maintain his or her personal integrity, persisting in the "right" action as long as it seems correct, even if something other is more convenient or more in accord with traditional moral laws. Thus Cirocco, instead of falling back on the "Gaea is wise" attitude of the Titanides, insists on seeing her beliefs prevail, whether pursuing an abortion after she has mysteriously conceived a child, keeping Gene alive even after he has turned into an insane rapist, or climbing a 500-kilometer cable straight up through fog and blizzard. And when, in *Wizard*, Cirocco's persistence flags, Gaby maintains Rocky's vision through a long adventure within Gaea's underworld, until eventually her death rallies Cirocco into an attempt at deicide. It is significant that both novels climax with an "apology" by Gaea, the god-figure, to the novel's human protagonists, an acknowledgment of their superior moral and ethical visions.

Confronted with such clearly heroic moral behavior, it is fairly easy to contrast it with its counterfeits. Just as religiosity is a kind of imitation religion, so ethical triviality is a sort of substitute for human moral behavior. In religious institutions it often shows up as scrupulosity about rituals and taboos, sometimes to the neglect of nobler values like honesty or compassion. Jesus and Buddha, for example, both inveighed against legalism in the religious systems of their day. In nonreligious settings, ethical triviality can show up in such diverse forms as bureaucratic rigidity and amoral indifference. A number of the tales in *Dangerous Visions* deal with ethical triviality in various ways.

In "Flies," Robert Silverberg has aliens revive a dead astronaut and return him to earth minus (for experimental purposes) his conscience, but they are soon dismayed by his atypical and inhuman behavior. The implication is clear: amoral behavior is less than human. Robert Bloch and Harlan Ellison in a pair of interrelated stories ("A Toy for Juliette" and "A Prowler in the City at the Edge of the World") describe a future in which aesthetics has replaced ethics, murder has become an art form, and the population has dwindled to a handful of hedonists. At one level the stories are neither more nor less terrifying than typical Alfred Hitchcock tales; but at a deeper level they become morally disturbing when we realize that the ones taking such incongruous delight in these brutal murders are the last representatives of the human race. Coming closer to more identifiably religious morality, the ethics of those who still possess the "Faith of Our Fathers" is obviously a sham morality maintained by drugs, dogmas, and bureaucracy; it is the "faithless" ones who rise to a level of making their own moral decisions. The ethics of religiosity is parodied in Fritz Lieber's "Gonna Roll the Bones," a fantasy version of the folk tale which makes a man's eternal salvation depend on such a morally insignificant act as a roll of the dice. In "If All Men Were Brothers, Would You Let One Marry Your Sister?" Theodore Sturgeon imagines a paradisiacal world held together by benign incest, throwing into question a traditional religious taboo. David Bunch's "Incident in Moderan" and Henry Slesar's "Ersatz" depict worlds torn by war, a practice that has hardly ever been forbidden by organized religion. Other stories in the collection describe other moral atrocities, but these can suffice as a sampler. If nothing else, they show that science fiction can be concerned with morality of the lowest as well as the highest order.[13]

CONCLUSION

If religious consciousness fundamentalizes reality, ultimatizes values, and moralizes about human behavior, and if religious imagination pictures such realities, values, and behaviors in myths and parables, then it certainly seems that a good deal of science fiction is a product of religious consciousness and imagination. The visions of some authors and some stories are obviously religious (even when they often appear to be antireligious); the visions of many other authors and stories are more subtly religious (even when they do not specifically mention religion). They are concerned in some way with basic being, meaning, and goodness, and since these are essentially religious concerns we can say that science fiction of this sort is essentially religious.

Moreover, we suspect that science fiction authors who fundamentalize, ultimatize, and moralize are themselves deeply religious, or at least they have a penetrating insight into what religion is and should be about, even without formal training in religious studies. When these authors satirize religion or some aspect of it, therefore, we submit that what they are usually doing is condemning religiosity, that is, the external and shallow trappings of organized religion. The basis for their negative evaluation of religiosity is their sometimes unconsciously positive estimation of religion, at least of religion's traditional concern for the fundamental nature of things, the ultimate meaning of existence, and the ethically good life. And if this analysis is correct, science fiction's general treatment of religion can be seen to be far more constructive than destructive, far more spiritually affirming than faith-denying.

NOTES

1. Harlan Ellison, ed., *Dangerous Visions* (New York: Doubleday and Co., 1967); hereafter cited as *DV*.
2. Damon Knight, "Shall the Dust Praise Thee?" in *DV*, pp. 322–25; Jonathan Brand, "Encounter with a Hick," in *DV*, pp. 410–14.
3. Harlan Ellison, "The Deathbird," in *Deathbird Stories* (New York: Dell Publishing Co., 1976), p. 345.
4. Robert Sheckley, *Dimension of Miracles* (New York: Grosset and Dunlap Co., 1968), p. 24.
5. Ibid., pp. 43–50.
6. James Blish, *A Case of Conscience* (London; Penguin Books, 1963). The first part of this novel was published in an abridged novelette in *If Worlds of Science Fiction* in 1953.
7. Ibid., p. 9.
8. Walter M. Miller, *A Canticle for Leibowitz* (New York: Bantam Books, 1976); James Gunn, *This Fortress World* (New York: Gnome Press, 1955).
9. Philip K. Dick, "Faith of Our Fathers," in *DV*; John Varley, *Titan* (New York: Berkley Publishing Co., 1979); Varley, *Wizard* (New York: Berkley, 1980).
10. Dick, p. 199.
11. Ibid., p. 202.
12. Ibid., p. 198.
13. Robert Silverberg, "Flies," in *DV*, pp. 11–19; Robert Bloch, "A Toy for Juliet," in *DV*, pp. 115–21; Harlan Ellison, "The Prowler in the City at

the Edge of the World,'' in *DV*, pp. 125–44; Fritz Leiber, ''Gonna Roll the Bones,'' in *DV*, pp. 220–34; Theodore Sturgeon, ''If All Men Were Brothers, Would You Let One Marry Your Sister?'' in *DV*, pp. 328–66; David R. Bunch, ''Incident in Moderan,'' in *DV*, pp. 279–83; Henry Slesar, ''Ersatz,'' in *DV*, pp. 379–81.

2

Mind, Matter, and Magic in Fantasy and Science Fiction

RICHARD L. PURTILL

There is a view of the world that to many people seems obviously true, the merest common sense. According to this view, our minds can affect other minds or the world around us only through the medium of our bodies. If I want you to understand me, I cause my body to make vibrations in the air or marks on paper that affect your ears or eyes and, through them, your mind. If I want to affect nearby matter on a small scale—moving a chair, for example—I use my body directly. If I want to affect matter at a distance or on a large scale—firing a missile or operating a bulldozer, for example—I use my body to set up chains of physical causation. Thus, in this view, our minds are "insulated" from other minds and from matter apart from our body. For convenience I will call this view the *Insulated View* of mind and matter.

Note that this view does not in itself presuppose any view about what minds are. I have used ordinary language to describe the view and, rightly or wrongly, ordinary language is dualistic; it assumes that our minds are different from our bodies. But if you identify the mind and the brain you can restate the view in terms of brain and body. On the other hand, if you hold that the mind is a nonmaterial substance, you could restate the view in terms of soul and body. Dualists as well as materialists can hold the Insulated View; materialists as well as dualists can deny it. Whether the Insulated View is true is a separate question from whether dualism or materialism is true.

There are a number of views that are incompatible with the Insulated

View, but I will discuss two historically important views that are incompatible with it in rather different ways. The first of these is what I will call the *Primitive View*: Many people at many times have held such a view, and probably all of us at some time have been tempted to accept it. According to this view, our thoughts, desires, and wishes can sometimes affect other minds or the material universe directly, without the intervention of our bodies; furthermore, we can sometimes affect other minds or the material universe by symbolic means, using our bodies to speak words or perform actions that do not set up chains of physical causation, at least in any ordinary sense. The witch doctor, for example, sticks pins into the image of his enemy, hoping to give that enemy pains in the corresponding portions of his anatomy; or the witch, as another example, recites incantations hoping to blight her enemies' crops.

The rejection of the primitive view is often equated with "mental maturity" or "a realist attitude." Here are two quotations to that effect, one from Thornton Wilder's "historical fantasy" *The Ides of March*, the second from a book column by Algis Budrys in *The Magazine of Fantasy and Science Fiction*. In Wilder's book, Julius Caesar writes to a long-time friend:

> From you I learned, but slowly, that there are large fields of experience which our longing cannot alter and which our fears cannot forfend. I clung for years to a host of self-delusions, to the belief that burning intensity in the mind can bring a message from an indifferent loved one and that sheer indignation can halt the triumphs of an enemy. The universe goes its mighty way and there is very little we can do to modify it. You remember how shocked I was when you let fall so light the words "Hope has never changed tomorrow's weather."[1]

Budrys is discussing the worldview characteristic of what he calls "modern" science fiction:

> The fundamental discovery that the Universe does not care; it simply works. There is no way to repeal or amend physical laws. The rich, the poor, the holy and the unholy are all subject to hunger, thirst, pain and death. Civilization of whatever kind, is a response to the discovery that community action at least offers hope of relief to all. Most human history represents the ongoing attempt to work out a plan whereby that relief is in fact distributed to all rather than merely to some. Technological action-exploring physical possibilities and applying deft means of conveying maximum comfort to the maximum number of individuals offers the best hope, magic showing a very poor record in that

respect. (And yet how appealing it is to think that simply displaying the proper attitude might modify the Universe! It's a hope we somehow cannot bring ourselves to abandon. Hence John W. Campbell's interest in fantasy. He was a humanist.)[2]

Note that I am not calling the Primitive View "primitive" in a necessarily unfavorable sense: as Budrys's last words suggest, it may be primitive in the sense of "basic" or "ineradicable." But we need to consider one further view, a view that has also been held by many people at many times and is still held by many people today: I will call it the *Animistic View*. According to this view, there exist nonmaterial minds or spirits that can affect matter and embodied minds directly. Our minds can affect other embodied minds and affect the material universe through the intermediary of these nonmaterial minds or spirits; we affect the nonmaterial minds or spirits either by thinking or by speech or by other symbolic actions.

Notice that the Animistic View, as I have defined it, covers, at one extreme, the traditional Christian theist, praying either mentally or verbally or by some ceremony such as a Catholic Mass to a nonmaterial person, God, for good weather or peace in the Mideast or consolation for a suffering friend. At the other extreme, the Animistic View takes in the Medieval or Renaissance magician invoking devils with his spells and pentagrams to raise a storm, cause a war, or afflict an enemy. Both cases presuppose an Animistic View (in my technical sense of "Animistic," not necessarily in a dictionary sense).

At the moment I am not interested in the very important and fascinating question, which of these three views, Insulated, Primitive, or Animistic, represents the truth about the universe. For those of my fellow philosophers who are interested, I recommend a thoughtful reading of the evidence cited in the paper "Telepathy" by Stephen Braude in the philosophical journal *Nous*[3] and perhaps also some of the evidence given in Raymond Moody's two books *Life After Life* and *Reflections on Life After Life*.[4] Now, however, I am not interested in which view is *true*, but rather in the embodiment of these views in contemporary fantasy and science fiction.

In many books intended to introduce science fiction and/or fantasy to those who are not familiar with the field, there is a curious shilly-shallying about the difference between science fiction and fantasy. Typically the author starts off by stating confidently that the difference consists of the fact that science fiction deals with what is scientifically possible, whereas fantasy deals with what is not scientifically possible. Then the author loses his or her nerve a bit, because, after all, faster-than-light travel is, so far as we know, scientifically impossible, and much modern science fiction could not do without it; the solar system is now too small for science fiction. And then there is that good old science fiction theme, time travel, which may be not only scientifically impossible, but somehow logically impossible. So, the grand generalization dies away in a flurry of qualifications, and the subject is tactfully changed.

I now want to use the machinery I have just assembled to say something about the relation of science fiction and fantasy. My thesis—broadly speaking and subject to qualifications—is that science fiction is happiest with the Insulated View, can tolerate some versions of the Primitive View, and is extremely uneasy with any version of the Animistic View, whereas almost all fantasy presupposes either the Animistic View or a version of the Primitive View that is rather different from the view that is popular in science fiction. I will illustrate this theme from some of my own favorite authors, E. E. Smith, J.R.R. Tolkien, Marion Zimmer Bradley, and C. S. Lewis. But I might just as well have used another set of authors, say A. E. Van Vogt, Ursula LeGuin, André Norton, and Charles Williams.

It is the use of telepathy and other *psi* powers as themes in science fiction that makes it wrong to link ''modern'' science fiction solely with the Insulated View. And it was largely E. E. Smith who made telepathy respectable as a theme in ''modern'' science fiction. Smith was a much better writer than he is generally credited with being, and is incomparably more intelligent and original than most of his critics. Budrys, with some justice, characterizes ''modern'' science fiction as ''fueled by a pervading technological optimism and a set of ethical assumptions slightly to the right of the John Birch credo. Might was not only right, it was moral, and lesser breeds, peering in timorously from without the law had better come to an understanding that a great many things were about to be done to them for their own good.''[5] True of a great deal of ''Golden Age'' science fiction, but absolutely not true of the science fiction of Smith. His alien characters are remarkably convincing and likable and are equal partners in ''civilization.'' Smith's prestige in the classical period was great, and it kept telepathy acceptable as a theme.

If "Doc" Smith's work was not science fiction, what was? And if he used telepathy, then telepathy was acceptable in science fiction.

But in Smith's treatment of telepathy, we also have the parameters that governed the treatment of psi powers in later science fiction. Telepathy must be treated as on a continuum with physical forces: among other things, telepathy is amplified or blocked by mechanical means (the Lens is a quasi mechanism, and remember those thought-screens whose batteries were always running down?). Telepathy need not be subject to ordinary physical laws (Worsel or Helen of Lyrane can throw a thought across the galaxy: no light speed or inverse square limitations there), but it must have laws of its own; that is, it must be subject to systematic, "technological" treatment. In their own ways, Van Vogt's Slans and Jack Williamson's "psionic" robots obey these limitations.

In J.R.R. Tolkien, on the other hand, there is pure fantasy. In fantasy, "magic works" (this is practically a definition of fantasy), and the magic is that of the Primitive View, worked directly and not by means of spirits. Gandalf mutters a spell, and a fire lights at the end of his staff, or a locked door opens. Galadriel lends clairvoyance to Sam and Frodo, and it is hinted that she can read thoughts. Nobody ever tries to explain how such things work, they simply do, and no one in Middle Earth tries to technologize magic. Ursula LeGuin is one step away from Tolkien in the direction of standard science fiction; her Earthsea magic is symbolic, using a primitive notion of name-thing relationships, but it is more theoretical than Tolkien's magic.

In Marion Zimmer Bradley's Darkover novels, the background of spaceships and Terran way stations for interstellar commerce gives science fiction credibility to what are essentially tales of witchcraft and wizardry in a quasimedieval society. In *The Forbidden Tower*, for instance, characters travel outside their bodies in a Higher Realm.[6] If she had not included spaceships, Bradley would be accused of writing about the occult and drummed out of science fiction by the stalwarts of the Insulated View. Bradley even makes some use of disembodied intelligences or quasipersonal forces. It might be pointed out that even Smith has a disembodied Eddorian "mental remainder" that must be destroyed by the "mental bolt" generated by the Patrol; and in Tolkien, a disembodied Sauron flees away after his defeat. But there is a key limitation that keeps these stories inside the Primitive View; there are disembodied beings, but they do not *do* anything. Bradley transgresses this taboo here and there. She gets away with it not only because she uses spaceships, but because, by and large, she plays by the other rules— the matrixes are physical amplifiers of mental force, and psi powers are technologized as "matrix mechanics." (André Norton plays somewhat the same game in the Witch World series: a hint of machinery in the background legitimizes a fantasy world as science fiction.)

With C. S. Lewis we finally reach a fully Animistic View: The eldila of the Space trilogy (or Ransom trilogy) are disembodied spirits with some characteristics of angels and some characteristics of Neoplatonic Intelligences. Furthermore, God himself, under the pseudonym of Maleldil, plays an important role in the story. For many in the science fiction community, even the spaceship in *Out of the Silent Planet* is not enough to redeem Lewis's Space trilogy as science fiction; it has been called by one critic "anti-science fiction."[7]

It has been said that all human conflicts are basically theological. That is as true as most generalizations and truer than many. A good many attempts to draw the line between science fiction and fantasy are in fact "theological." Those who share the "scientific" materialistic view that dominates the intellectual culture of Western nations attempt to hold the realm of science fiction for that view, and to read out of the canon, as heretical, those stories that are based on Animistic Views or Primitive Views that do not pay suitable obeisance to science.

If, on the other hand, we use the distinction between those stories that assume the Insulated View and those that do not merely as a classificatory device with no value implications, it can help solve an important problem. The problem is this: It is notoriously difficult to give any adequate definition of science fiction, and this clouds efforts to theorize about the field.

One can delineate the field of science fiction by listing its characteristic themes. Science fiction often deals with the future, with space travel, with off-Earth locations, with time travel, with telepathy or other "psi" powers, with alien beings, or with discoveries or machines that are beyond the present scope of science. A "cluster definition" of science fiction can be given by saying that a story is science fiction if one or more of these themes is present to an important degree.

Fantasy can be given a similar cluster definition. Fantasy tends to deal with the distant and legendary past or past-like "alternate worlds," with magical means of travel or communication, with "other worlds," usually earth-like, reached by magical means, with magical powers and objects, and with nonhuman beings that resemble those in folklore or mythology.

When we try to give a *general* definition, however, that states a factor common to science fiction but not to fantasy—or to fantasy but not to science fiction—we run into difficulties. To distinguish *both* of those sorts of stories from "mundane" literature is not impossible: we can talk of "secondary worlds" as Tolkien did, or of "alternate worlds" as Poul Anderson did in a series on science fiction in *Destinies*.[8] The point is that the worlds of science fiction and fantasy are *structurally* different from the real world, different not just in the addition of invented characters or incidents, but in some major way.

This idea can be made sufficiently precise to serve as a delimitation of speculative fiction from mundane fiction, though there are many difficulties involved. But, to date, a further delimitation of science fiction and fantasy has suffered from the difficulty pointed out earlier: One cannot demarcate the "alternate worlds" of science fiction from those of fantasy in terms of "scientific possibility," since so many of the standard themes of science fiction (notably faster-than-light travel) would fall on the wrong side of the line.

To this dilemma the distinctions I have made here may provide an answer. An "alternate world" story is science fiction if it assumes the Insulated View; it is fantasy if it assumes the Primitive or Animistic view. This suggestion will give us intuitively satisfactory classification in most cases and at least a reasonable classification in borderline cases. On the one hand, the work of C. S. Lewis, for example, is fantasy according to the suggested classification despite the spaceships in the Ransom trilogy because it assumes an Animistic View. On the other hand, the "dragon" stories of Ann McCafferty are science fiction despite the use of some potent fantasy symbols and their echoes of some fantasy themes, because basically they assume an Insulated View.

No doubt my suggestion will lead to some counterintuitive classifications, though I cannot come up with any at this time. But it has one great virtue: Because the other two views in question are incompatible with the Insulated View, no story can assume *both* the Insulated View and one or both of the others. Thus, according to the suggested classification scheme, no story can be both science fiction and fantasy.

Let me draw one moral in conclusion. Nothing will prevent some people from using the scheme I have recommended as an evaluative device. Some will argue that since the Insulated View is true, and the other views are false, science fiction (as it is defined here) is superior to fantasy. So long as they mean by "superior" only "nearer to the actual state of affairs" and not "superior as literature" or "more valuable to the reader," then, if one grants that the Insulated View is true, it can hardly be denied that science fiction is closer to the truth than fantasy is. This criterion is a two-edged sword, of course: If our major concern is staying close to the way things actually are, we will reject all speculative literature in favor of the mundane realistic story.

But not everyone will agree that the Insulated View is, in fact, the truth, or at least the whole truth. The question is, in the end, philosophical rather than scientific, involving as it does views about the nature of reality based on an interpretation of our total experience. So, if anyone says, "I enjoy science fiction more than fantasy because I agree with the Insulated View and feel uncomfortable with stories based on the Primitive or Animistic view," that person is at least being more honest than a good many critics of fantasy. Such a person might profit from reading stories based on assumptions he or she disagrees with, if only to understand better the view that is being rejected. I agree to a large extent with John Stuart Mill about the free market of ideas: Let them all be rationally discussed and written about, and let the best ones win. We all have our own opinions as to what the best ones are, but no set of ideas should be ruled out of the great debate before they have their chance, or ruled out as subjects for the freest form of literature— science fiction and fantasy. It may or may not be true that "magic is loose in the world!" but at least let it have its run in the world of ideas and in the literature of ideas.

NOTES

1. Thornton Wilder, *The Ides of March* (New York: Harper and Row, 1948), pp. 183–84.

2. Algis Budrys, "Books," *Magazine of Fantasy and Science Fiction*, May 1979, p. 24.

3. Stephen Braude, "Telepathy," *Nous* 12, no. 3 (September 1978): 267–301.

4. Raymond A. Moody, *Life After Life* (New York: Bantam Books, 1975); and *Reflections on Life After Life* (New York: Bantam Books, 1977).

5. Budrys, p. 23.

6. Marion Zimmer Bradley, *The Forbidden Tower* (New York: DAW Books, 1977).

7. Brian Aldiss, *Billion Year Spree* (Garden City, N.Y.: Doubleday and Co., 1973).

8. Poul Anderson, *Destinies* 1, no. 1 (Nov./Dec. 1978): 273–308.

3

Science Fiction's Harrowing of the Heavens

WILLIAM A. QUINN

The thematic significance of religious matters in general to several major works of science fiction in particular has frequently been discussed—by J. Norman King, Theodore Sturgeon, Tom Woodman, Sam Moskowitz, Robert Scholes, and Eric Rabkin, to name a few. Yet the genre's occasional fusion of science and religion remains tense and intermittent at best. The vast majority of sf writers do seem either opposed or oblivious to most religious concerns. Awkward too at times seems the inclusion of any explicitly religious thought in mainstream literature—at least so say some modern "realist" sensibilities.

Such general considerations will not—cannot—receive any further definition in this essay, but they remain integrally connected to its primary focus—namely the salvation, damnation, and/or simple mortality that various authors of sf have ascribed to aliens, and the theological plausibility of such ascriptions. From various premises, different authors have argued to various conclusions. The debate that has gradually emerged in sf regarding God's covenants with the alien beings should not, however, be considered entirely new.

Numerous medieval writers confronted clearly analogous theological questions when they considered the afterlife of righteous heathens. Dante, as always, may be considered foremost among them. In English literature, the debate became particularly acute during the fourteenth and fifteenth centuries. The theological question confronting such authors was essentially this: How can an all-good God permit all *literally* unbaptized but morally good souls to be *de facto* damned? Answers to this question follow necessarily from certain theological presuppositions concerning the concepts of free will versus predestination, of the relation between good works and faith, and of the nature of God himself. But all such answers presuppose that theology, as distinguished from belief, is an essentially logical endeavor.

Many medieval thinkers argued that a more figurative understanding of "salvation only through baptism" could readily accommodate all God's chosen people, including those who had died before Christ's coming. Some extended the dispensation to include even morally good pagans. Such works as *Piers Plowman, Mandeville's Travels, St. Erkenwald*, and all the "Harrowing of Hell" pageants in the Corpus Christi cycles have been interpreted to embody this more "laxist" point of view. The fully recognized difficulty with such an expansion of the concept of baptism, however, is that it implicitly denies any compelling reason for current heathens to convert. And so Robert Mannyng, as one among many more "rigorist" voices, felt compelled to defend the moral imperative that everyone be literally baptized in *Handling Sin* (vv. 9493–9651).[1]

This debate about "non–Christians" in medieval literature can be and has been translated wholesale to an expanded consideration of "nonhumans" in contemporary science fiction. Many sf writers, notably C. S. Lewis and James Blish, have probably been fully aware of medieval precedents for the debate. But the main point to note is that differing conclusions may be *logically* achieved from differing presuppositions. The modern sf writer may be, therefore, completely traditional, thoroughly systematic, but totally amateur in the theology of his fiction. He may also be wrong.

The public debate regarding the "righteous heathen" in medieval European literature was necessarily circumscribed by its one creed. The debate about the "righteous alien" in sf has not been so restricted. But the logic of the Christian tradition remains very viable in sf and should be clarified as such. For utilitarian rather than historical reasons, the more liberal interpretation of the debate will be designated "Catholic" in this essay, whereas a more rigorous limitation of the gift of salvation will be termed "Calvinist." The continuing Catholic versus Calvinist debate is, of course, far more complex than can be satisfactorily analyzed at present; so, these designations must be acknowledged as stereotypical. But it is just such stereotypes that find expression in popular literature, whether medieval or contemporary.

Calvinist thought emphasized the revealed fact that man's salvation is a free gift; it is unearned, undeserved by any, and not guaranteed to all. God foreknows the salvation or damnation of each individual; not to acknowledge that God, therefore, foreordains such judgments seems logically implausible. Free will becomes a more or less moot consideration. In terms of sf, the Calvinist God may prove just as arbitrary in saving the "righteous alien" as he is in saving man—or just as generous.

Orthodox Catholic teaching states that man is not saved by good works alone, nor by faith alone. Both are mandatory; both, in fact, are inseparable signs of the free gift of grace. But each individual is uniquely responsible for freely accepting that free gift, and the gift of sufficient grace is made *to all*. Though no one earns salvation, everyone deserves his or her own damnation by refusing to accept the sufficient grace of God's universal salvific will.

But contemporary sf writers, who postulate this same Catholic stance, must also consider the probability that God's universe has other occupants. Whether or not they too will have immortal souls becomes the primary question. Since divine revelation is silent, agnosticism is orthodox, and it is precisely this doctrinal ignorance that permits each sf author to suggest certain theologically justifiable speculations.

Most authors, like Chaucer's Knight, finally confess, "I nam no divinistre" (*Canterbury Tales* I, 2811). There are, however, some sf writers who have claimed to be "divinistres" regarding the immortal fate of righteous aliens, and they seem not to have been confined in their speculative exotheology by the dictates of either monotheism or agnosticism. New questions have been generated in new and (for the time being) totally fictional contexts. Can God have an entirely different covenant with entirely different creatures? Can there be more than one God, if any? If alien creatures have redeemable souls, must they, therefore, be acknowledged as essentially "human"? Manichaeism, polytheism, pantheism, syncretism, and just plain old deism have all reemerged when sf writers consider the theological implications of an alien encounter.

But does anything go when a sf writer grants or denies immortal salvation to an alien soul? Are all such propositions purely speculative and, thus, equally plausible? Must we take all these fictions on faith alone? No—at least not if the medieval conception of *Theologia* as "Queen of the *Sciences*" is reasserted, as it has been by several of the following authors. Theology's applicability as a critical tool in evaluating the plausibility with which various works of speculative fiction address a religious conundrum may also be resurrected. Insofar as such *plausibility* remains the best—if not an entirely satisfactory—criterion for distinguishing sf "proper" from "mere" fantasy, the laws of such theological investigation (themselves governed by the universally applicable principles of logic) may prove to be just as significant in making the generic distinction as the more readily accepted laws of physics, mathematics, sociology, and even linguistics have proved.[2]

Though Darko Suvin has warned that "all attempts to transplant the metaphysical orientation of mythology and religion into SF . . . will result only in private pseudomyths, in fragmentary fantasies or fairy tales," this essay will defend sf's concern with neither mythology nor religion—but with the science of theology. Suvin has also offered as an axiom that "SF is distinguished by the narrative dominance or hegemony of a fictional 'novum' (novelty, innovation) validated by cognitive logic."[3] The following comments will attempt to assess only the cognitive validations that various authors of sf have presented in their discussion of alien souls.

The evaluation of each work's *novum* (in this case, the revelations of an alien faith) must and should be left to the individual reader. The proper focus becomes not the givens of an alien religion, but the implications of that religion for human theology. Though Darko Suvin would exclude any and all supernatural revelations from sf (technically defined), such visionary experiences have been made to seem plausible enough in several works (commonly called sf). It is empiricism (personal observation and direct experience—whether it be termed "subjective" or "self-evident") that underlies all such religious discoveries in sf—including the discovery that there is no God. But does empiricism, as such, provide a plausible validation by cognitive means? Can the supernatural be made to seem natural? If not in theory, then in "science fiction," a genre whose very name is a contradiction in terms?

If sf as a whole must remain doctrinally agnostic, it must also acknowledge the fictional possibility of a plot discovery providing some experiential validation for the realistic affirmation of faith in specific cases—and such a narrative possibility generates plausibility. The highly subjective, critical debate about plausibility still may continue over each and every such *novum*. Once, however, a revealed *novum* is granted as an empirically perceived phenomenon (whose plausibility seems to depend far more on art than on science), certain theological novelties, subnova as it were, result—by deduction—that often may be validated or disproved on the basis of logic alone.

MONOTHEISM, ATHEISM, DEISM, AND MANICHAEISM

Perhaps the most determined use of speculative fiction to investigate explicitly theological matters has been the second volume of C. S. Lewis's space trilogy, *Perelandra*. Whether the work should be considered sf ''proper'' or ''mere'' fantasy or just plain old allegory remains somewhat problematic. Lewis himself seemed sufficiently comfortable with the second designation and has even commented, ''I took a hero once to Mars in a space-ship, but when I knew better I had angels convey him to Venus.''[4] That hero is named Ransom.

In *Perelandra*, Ransom finds himself called upon to witness and ultimately to defend a second Eden. It should come as no surprise that Lewis, the medieval and Renaissance scholar and Anglo-Catholic apologist, argues for a rigorously orthodox thesis about the ''righteous aliens'' of Venus. Darko Suvin might find the very existence of the Green Lady, a pre-Lapsarian Eve, too fantastic, but the implications of Perelandra's own covenant with Maleldil, *as they refer to man's*, are developed by Lewis with all the logical rigor of a ''Catholic'' theologian forced to defend the given of Maleldil's ''universal salvific will.''

In chapter 13, for example, Weston, the ''Un-Man,'' would have Ransom abandon his belief in a God who will reward or punish *man's* soul. ''Perhaps your God does exist—but it makes no difference whether He does or not.... If your God exists, He's not in the globe—He's outside, like a moon. As we pass into the interior we pass out of His ken. He doesn't follow us in.''[5] What Weston argues here is not so much atheism as deism, the belief that a Supreme Being might exist, but remains indifferent to the universe.

If Ransom accepts Weston's premise, as he is sorely tempted to do, he must also accept its implications regarding man's alleged immortality. The antagonist's untheology is itself a thoroughly self-consistent, logical alternative to Ransom's own, and it must be recognized as such. ''That whole view of the universe which Weston (if it were Weston)

had so lately preached to him, took all but complete possession of his
mind. . . . Reality lived—the meaningless, the un-made, the omnipotent
idiocy to which all spirits are irrelevant and before which all efforts
were vain.''[6] It seems curious that Ransom restates Weston's apparent
deism in terms far more closely associated with existentialism. Lewis
might even be suggesting that the most logical extrapolation of Weston's
premise results in nihilism. And, as far as the question of individual
salvation is concerned, the distinctions to be made between such deism,
atheism, existentialism, nihilism, and solipsism do become purely academic. According to the rules of theological logic, Ransom must reject
such a false First Principle—as such—and does so: ''Apparently it had
all, *even from the beginning*, been a dark enchantment of the enemy's.''[7]
Only then may Ransom defend the equal reasonableness of his own
theology in terms that relate back to Tindril the Queen and Tor the
King.

The final chapter of *Perelandra*, apropos of itself, is explicitly te-
leological. The discussion of the "ends" that await both Perelandra
and Thulcandra and—by analogy—each of their respective occupants
is eventually clarified (by some unclear means) through the comments
of the eldila. The observations of the eldila are, of course, more rhap-
sodic than syllogistic, and at times Ransom thinks their voices are his
own—a confusion that conveys his own rapturous communion with
their Beatific Vision. Still, these same comments embody all the logic
of Lewis's faith:

In the plan of the Great Dance plans without number interlock, and each
movement becomes in its season the breaking into flower of the whole design
to which all else has been directed. . . and all the patterns linked and looped
together by the unions of a kneeling with a sceptred love. Blessed be He![8]

In short, if a *hnau* in Maleldil's universe is immortal, that same soul
has been offered some gift of sanctifying grace. The manner of the gift
may differ between humans and aliens (as between humans and angels),
and the gift itself may be refused, but the giving is universal and
sufficient for the salvation of all.

Historically, the most recurrent challenge to such Catholic theology
has been a type of dualism (ultimately traceable to Zoroastrianism, it
seems) that posits the existence of both good and evil as coequal divine
forces locked in eternal conflict. The proponents of this idea have, at

various times and with varying rites, been called Cathari, Bogomiles, Albigensians, or just heretics. But Christianity first recognized the theological threat of this idea and still refers to it most often as Manichaeism. Unlike polytheism, this dualism does offer a reasonable alternative to the logic of Catholic apologists. And sf's most sophisticated consideration of this theological challenge has been, without question, James Blish's *A Case of Conscience*.[9]

Blish once acknowledged the reasonableness of Lewis's faith in Maleldil's universal salvific will.[10] Indeed, at the beginning of *A Case*, Blish's own protagonist, Fr. Ramon Ruiz-Sanchez, S.J., professes the very same credo that Ransom accepted as proven at the conclusion of *Perelandra*. But in *A Case*, it is a monotheistic theology (presuming God's omnipotence) that precedes the test of Lithia: "... a paradise. It has resemblances to a number of other planets, but the closest correspondence is to Earth in its pre-Adamic period.... The resemblance ends there because on Lithia... life continued to be spent in the paradise, as it was not allowed to do on Earth."[11] If Lithia, like Perelandra, were merely pre-Lapsarian, there would be no real theological dilemma for the Chardin-like Jesuit. But Father Ruiz-Sanchez also recognizes in Lithia "a planet and a people propped by the Ultimate Enemy.... If we compromise with it in any way, we are damned."[12]

The internal, theological dilemma for Ramon (as distinct from his adversarial conflict with the novel's Weston-like physicist, Cleaver) is stated most clearly in chapter 8. The priest himself explains it in detail to Michelis, the chemist. Since Lithians are completely rational, completely ethical, and completely atheistic, only their lack of a covenant with God suggests any secret compact with the Other. But the Lithians themselves seem indifferent to all such supernatural matters.

Obviously, Ramon did not have to travel all the way to Lithia to discover proponents of such rationalism (i.e., atheism), and Ramon can reject its First Principle as such. But the very apparent perfection of Lithian society invites Michelis to ask " 'A question'... and his voice was painfully gentle. 'To set such a trap, you must allow your Adversary to be creative. Isn't that—a heresy, Ramon?' "[13]

In Book II of *A Case*, Egtverchi, the Adversary's Earth-born, only "begotten son," is described as having an "animal soul"[14] —*animal* in the Aristotelian sense of *coterminal* with the body. Furthermore, Lithians undergo complete physical recapitulation outside of their bodies—a fact that seems to argue "henceforth there is to be no more God,

but only phenomenology. . . ."[15] And, henceforth, no more *human* hope
of salvation. Q.E.D.

The triune debate of Catholic monotheism, Manichaeism, and atheism
thus pervades *A Case of Conscience*—precisely as a rational debate.
The *novum* of Lithia itself may be considered implausible by some—
by Darko Suvin and Pope Hadrian VIII, for example. But, more significantly, both Ramon and Blish recognize full well that the cognitive
validity of the Lithian's relation to God is inextricably connected to
man's own. Either the Lithians are indeed (as they seem) *good*, and
Catholic orthodoxy must yield to this fact, or the orthodox arguments
for the one God's "universal salvific will" will remain a rock against
with Lithia *must* break.[16]

Blish once professed himself to be an agnostic and, aside from the
fact that his novel seems "so damned talky," his own most serious
criticism of *A Case* was that its "ending. . .fails to be ambiguous
enough."[17] But both Blish-the-ironist and Lewis-the-apologist approached the basic question of an encounter with righteous aliens in
terms of the same specifically Catholic theology.

It is difficult (thank God) to think of an example in sf that applauds
the utter damnation of an entire and entirely good alien civilization,
even if the theologically arguable premise may have been to indicate
the uniqueness of God's gift to mankind. Of course, Godless monsters
throughout the galaxy have often been exterminated with glee. In such
cases, either the question of alien salvation is completely ignored because, as J. Norman King has suggested, "the idea of an afterlife. . .strikes modern technical man as highly improbable, even prior
to any serious consideration,"[18] or the aliens' "souls" are not damned
immortally so much as designated merely mortal. Such aliens, however
technologically sophisticated, have *animal* souls and are often
depersonalized[19]—if not slaughtered at will.

The damnation and/or oblivion that may await both BEM's (bug-
eyed monsters) and righteous aliens alike, however horrifying, seems
perfectly logical—at least from the perspective of rigorously Calvinist
theology. Why should such aliens "merit" eternal reward any more
than man? Although few, if any, sf writers have developed this premise
in order to defend it, many have attempted to attack its plausibility.
With rare accord, both Catholic theologians and atheists are quick to
indicate the apparent self-contradictoriness of a faith that posits both an
all-good and a completely arbitrary God. Theodore Sturgeon, for ex-

ample, has already considered three key opponents to such Calvinist doctrines: Lester del Rey, Arthur C. Clarke, and Marion Zimmer Bradley.[20] But the logic (if not truth) of this opposition must itself be tested against the self-consistency of Calvinist theology—taken on its own terms—in order that the narrative plausibility of these speculations themselves may be tested.

Bradley's *Darkover Landfall* may be considered a direct negation of Lewis's defense of God's universal salvific will. Bradley's protagonist, one Father Valentine, crashes on an unknown planet, "a world unknown to God" it seems. A maddening pollen on the planet *compels* the priest to commit mortal sin, and this negation of free will, of course, results in a crisis of faith. If Lewis could respond to the implications of Bradley's *novum* (not to the *novum* itself), he might observe that the atheism or agnosticism that results from such an experience seems thoroughly plausible. But he might add that Father Valentine's subsequent humanism—in which everyone should act as "priest" to everyone else (that is, as consoler)—remains logically unjustified by the premise; it is hopeful and good, but not logical.

In a far more satirical vein, Lester del Rey's "For I Am a Jealous People" posits that an arbitrary God might transfer his covenant from mankind to an alien species. Del Rey's minister-protagonist must deal with the fact that God's chosen reptiles have carried the Ark of the Covenant to victory over humanity. Harlan Ellison's anthology *Dangerous Visions* offers yet another example of del Rey's dark humor— "Evensong," in which man successfully overrules God on "the eighth day."[21] Del Rey's two stories together suggest that, come Doomsday, this author's universe will not be big enough for both God and Man; one must abandon the other. The theological challenge implicit in Clarke's "The Star" seems far more conventional, yet serious. Clarke's protagonist, another man of the cloth, must deal with the realization that the Star of the Nativity was, in fact, a supernova that destroyed an entire species of conspicuously righteous aliens.

All of these stories may be discussed in terms of the God-Is-Dead movement. More specifically, all may be considered anti-Calvinist propositions in that they all posit some (seemingly horrible) predestined event. But only del Rey's heroism and/or pessimism may be considered thoroughly consistent with his own theological system—however ludicrous the *nova* of his two stories may seem to human theologians. Bradley's priest—if he were indeed a "reformed Catholic"—should realize that mortal sin per se requires an individual's full consent. Father Valentine could theologically (if not psychologically) consider himself spiritually not culpable, though objectively guilty, of his sins. In other words, Father Valentine's crisis of faith is not itself logically compelling.

The dilemma confronted in Clarke's short story is fairly straightforward: Either the mass destruction of the alien civilization at the time of Christ's birth was a natural accident, a mere coincidence in an indifferent universe, or God did indeed intervene in cosmic affairs and became, thereby, a mass murderer. In both cases, man's own conceptions of salvation seem challenged by the indifference that obliterated such righteous aliens. Either God is brutally arbitrary in his predestined plans, or God's Plan is itself a delusion. Clarke, thus, offers in this fictional dilemma a direct parallel to the questions that historically have surrounded the "Slaughter of the Innocents" by Herod. How could God not just permit, but foreordain such slaughter to accompany the birth of his son? Calvinist theologians could offer the same answers in terms of Clarke's righteous aliens that they have already offered in terms of human experience. The real question is not the corporal death of so many bodies, but the fate of their immortal souls, and that fate is a gift.

In short, both Bradley and Clarke have invited their protagonists (and readers) to deny a God who would deny man's free will by interfering with "natural" events. Both, therefore, presuppose a Calvinist conception of God in order to challenge the presupposition. But neither argues *within* the theological system of Calvinism itself. Both offer experiential, not necessarily logical, arguments to suggest the apparent indifference of the universe. Such indifference may free man's will again, but it concomitantly denies his immortality. Nevertheless, such "a-theism," whether the denial of God's concern or of God himself, remains—as it has always been—more compelling psychologically, rather than theologically, in its opposition to Calvinism.

Del Rey, by contrast, does not ask us to deny the existence of an interfering God, but to fight his interference. Del Rey's theology does not challenge the existence of Calvin's God, just his omnipotence. If mankind wins, as in "Evensong," mankind becomes—by definition— God. If mankind loses, as in "For I Am a Jealous People," del Rey knows full well that the joke was on del Rey. But blasphemy presupposes a God to blaspheme. So, del Rey's theme seems more *anti*-theism than atheism; it is an act of human will that does not even attempt to disguise itself as an act of logic.

The examples of various exotheological stances that have been considered so far may all be considered sf's reactions to or extrapolations from the "mainstream" theological systems. Monotheists (whether Catholic or Calvinist) would accommodate the souls of righteous aliens to the judgments of a common God. Contrariwise, human atheism seems the most recurrent theme in sf that considers alien religions at all. The objective distance with which the genre itself permits its readers to review alien religions often invites a retrospective recognition of the fiction in human beliefs as well. J. G. Ballard has gone so far as to assert that sf is "totally atheistic."[22] Since such atheism precludes a consideration of salvation—whether human or alien—except in the negative, it will be discussed no further. But it can be noted that atheism itself may be considered a very conventional and, on its own terms, a "theologically" plausible system.

POLYTHEISM AND SYNCRETISM

In *Perelandra*, the eldila seemed at first to Ransom's eyes, "the gods." And, indeed, they provide Lewis's novels with a sort of *divine machinery*. But, theologically, there is never any doubt that these preternatural beings might be confused with the Supernatural. They are immortal, but they are not self-created, nor are they self-judging. The covenant of the eldila with Maleldil, thus, duplicates Lewis's conventional conception of God's covenant with the angels. Many another author of speculative fiction, however, has been free—that is, not restricted by his vocation as an Anglo-Catholic apologist—to conceive of such beings as gods in their own right, removed from their *gradus* in a monotheistic hierarchy.

Ancient human mythology has been tapped at will by numerous authors of speculative fiction in order to resurrect such gods.[23] But few of these works have much relevance to a consideration of the righteous alien's salvation (or lack thereof) precisely because polytheism properly defined presupposes the immortality of the gods *as gods* in contrast to the mortality of man. By this definition, the questions that have surrounded the immortal destiny of righteous aliens in terms of monotheism become completely void whenever such aliens are conceived to be not divine but, like man, merely mortal.

The proposition that certain preternatural aliens may serve as a "substitute God-figure and father figure,"[24] however, poses more substantial problems for both human logic and belief. The *novum* of such alien beings has been made to seem plausible enough by several sf authors. Roger Zelazny, for example, uses mutation to validate elements of Greek folklore and myth in *This Immortal*. Analogously, the "Who Will Mourn for Adonis?" episode of *Star Trek* employs von Daniken's theory (however dubious in itself) to explain the Olympian gods as extraterrestrial travelers. And one need not look far to discover the full vitality of most other myth systems in speculative fiction.

Suvin is by no means alone in designating all such speculative fiction "mere" fantasy. And such fantasy's customary dependence on magic as opposed to science (however "rubber") has frequently been proposed as the key distinction between these two genres. But, in order to address the apparent plausibility of several works of sf "proper" that do seem validly to present such "gods" *as metaphor*, it first seems necessary to distinguish the *vehicle* of this mythology from the *tenor* of true polytheism.

W. H. Auden once observed: "Art is compatible with polytheism and with Christianity, but not with philosophical materialism; science is compatible with philosophical materialism and with Christianity, but not with polytheism."[25] The science of physics might balk at sf's use of the vehicle of mythology insofar as the apparent immortality of such divinities seems a violation of the law of entropy. But, even granting the plausibility of such a *novum*, the science of theology would then object to the proposition that such immortals should be thought of as gods by men—the tenor of polytheism.

Most often, the vehicle of mythology in sf presents a conception of the "gods" as merely natural cohabitants with mankind in an otherwise atheistic or monotheistic universe. Such aliens (for that is all they are) may be feared if hostile, or thanked if generous, but not logically worshipped. Theology separates true religion from such superstition, and much fantasy seems inherently superstitious—but not on the basis of its inclusion of immortal aliens alone. Rather, the theological responses of such fiction's *human* protagonists determines whether it be sf or fantasy. The tenor of polytheism is inherently atheological and, therefore, fantastic from the perspective of human logic. Conversely, any speculative fiction that suggests that man's encounter with such alien immortals will seriously affect human belief (or lack thereof) becomes fantasy because it lacks validation of the proposed effect (i.e., superstition) by any cognitive means. The fantasy of mankind worshipping such immortals would have more to do with humanity's alogical response than with the aliens' proposed lifespan.

In short, plausibility requires that sf "proper" deny the tenor of polytheism. It may do so simply by avoiding the vehicle of mythology entirely, as Suvin advises. Or it may do so by mutating the vehicle so that it fits some other theological context in which the question of an alien's immortality (corporal or spiritual) again becomes relevant to man. If aliens seem to be "gods," they must bow either to God or to man's denial of God. If, however, aliens have "gods" (or even just one other God), the theological viability of adopting a new or syncretic faith must then be considered as a plausible alternative for mankind.

New faiths win converts all the time, but syncretism should fail as a plausible premise in sf because, while attempting to reconcile an alien religion to human beliefs, it must also assume that the theology of one faith can somehow accept the other. If the theologies are identical, such a reconciliation is gratuitous since the distinction between such religions may be considered to have been nominal from the start. But if the theologies are in fact distinct, either the superior logic of one will convert (not reconcile) the other, or an impasse regarding First Principles will be discovered—in which case there can occur no logical synthesis of doctrines. Each will deny the other. Spock would agree with this paragraph.

Nevertheless, an incredibly popular pitch for the syncretic road to salvation has been that proposed by Robert Heinlein's Martian-reared human, Michael Valentine Smith, in *Stranger in a Strange Land*.[26] It is quite impossible to capsulize the full teaching of Michael's eclectic religion; his church offers an odd hodgepodge of Judeo-Christian-Islamic theology, Eastern mysticism, Barnum-and-Bailey gnosticism, and Hollywood hype. But in reviewing the logic of the metaphysical system implicitly proposed by *Stranger in a Strange Land* as a whole, most theologians—not fans—would agree with James Blish that "it is, to say the best of it, a shambles."[27]

Michael himself ultimately teaches a type of pantheism, which obliterates the distinction between Creator and Created; if one *groks*, one *is* God. Salvation follows from initiation into the mystery of this concept. And such gnosticism is—by definition—either self-evident or fantastic. Jubal, however, "a devout agnostic . . . rated all religions, from the animism of Kalahari Bushmen to the most intellectualized faith, as equal."[28] The impasse between faith and rationalism is not in itself a theological dilemma. Insofar as Jubal experiences *grokking*, he accepts the religion. The true dilemma of *A Stranger*, its theological fantasy, derives from Heinlein's divergent dispensations for the souls of men and Martians.

The Old Ones of Mars endure in an incorporate state on Mars itself— ghosts. Dead humans, however, "go somewhere else, location not given."[29] There also seem to be some suggestions of certain human souls' random reincarnations as "field agents." As the angelic Foster explains to the not so angelic Digby, "you don't understand the System yet. The Martians have their own set up. . . . They run their show their way—the Universe has variety, something for everybody. . . ."[30] "Variety" suggests polytheism, but Digby also mentions "The Boss," which suggests monotheism, and all the while Michael has been preaching pantheism.

Of course, Heinlein's intent is more satiric than didactic—but it is a satire based on fantasy rather than on exotheological plausibility. If the ghosts of Mars and the angels of Earth—both may be considered *alien* immortals—are completely independent of one another in "the System," there is no common system; either polytheism or atheism might allow such a concept. At the conclusion of *A Stranger*, however, Foster leaves Michael and Digby to their continuing work with the observation, "Certainly 'Thou art God'—but who isn't?"[31] As a literal (though incomprehensible) statement, Foster's sarcastic farewell may be taken, on the one hand, as a reaffirmation of pantheism. But, confronted by the discrete dispensations of Earthmen and Martians, the reader must ponder such oxymora as "pantheistic polytheism" or "polytheistic atheism": the *all* may be *one*, but not two or three, or none. On the other hand, if Foster's final statement is taken figuratively, the reader may ponder the monotheistic "System" of "The Boss," but it is a concept (unlike Lewis's "Great Dance") about which the reader has been told next to nothing in *A Stranger*. So, the reader is left—as Jubal was from the start—an agnostic rating "all religions . . . as equal" while Michael plans "a lot of changes."[32] In any event, Michael Valentine Smith's efforts at syncretism turn out to be illogical, a deliberate fraud—Heinlein's ultimate theological joke.

The invalidity of such syncretism to monotheists seems hardly note-worthy, though the human faithful, too, are permitted a certain mitigated agnosticism about the salvation of alien souls—that is, about the pre-requisite immortality of such souls. In *The Mote in God's Eye* by Larry Niven and Jerry Pournell, for example, a Motie itself explicates the theologically plausible excuse for such theistic agnosticism in response to its own question about whether Moties have souls: "It would take revealed knowledge—divine inspiration, wouldn't it? I doubt if you'll get it."[33] Such doubt, if not faith itself, prevents a reconciliation of the numerous human beliefs and more numerous Motie religions from being a theologically compelling premise. Such doubt also precludes syncre-tism from being a theologically compelling proposition to human ag-nostics conventionally defined.

In "A Rose for Ecclesiastes" by Roger Zelazny, it is implicitly acknowledged that sf's proper (i.e., theologically plausible) analysis of the human responses to alien covenants will necessitate either conversion or agnosticism—but not syncretic compromise. Gallinger, the protag-onist and narrator of "A Rose," has been sent to Mars specifically to translate its *Book of Locar*. The Martian books "said nothing of fishers on Mars. Especially of men. They said . . . that life had gotten underway as a disease in inorganic matter."[34] Gallinger presents himself with no less a challenge than preventing the extinction of these Martians who seem confirmed that their own sterile fate has been divinely ordained.

The preachings of Locar remind Gallinger of certain Buddhist texts and, especially, of the ethical implications that derive from *The Book of Ecclesiastes* with its emphasis on vanity. To convert the Martians—on a theological level, that is—Gallinger reviews for them the Old Testament analogue, "the Black Gospel according to Gallinger, from the Book of Life."[35] The fatalism of the Martians seems nothing new or alien to Gallinger. The son of a fundamentalist preacher, he has also contemplated Buddhism, "Old Peace Corps" humanism, and—if his Pulitzer Prize-winning lyrics, the "Pipes of Krishna," offer any indi-cation—Hinduism. By accepting no human faith per se, Gallinger has been able to synthesize the metaphysics of them all, and would do the same for the preachings of Locar—reason against them.

Such "syncretism," however, is eclecticism or comparative myth-ology—not theology; it presupposes, in fact, agnosticism—"free not to preach the Word" and "to try a couple of the other paths to salva-tion."[36] But Gallinger's initial skepticism, the tone of his synopsis of

Martian belief, must ultimately yield to a recognition of his own ab-
surdism; he must accept the logic of Weston's argument, which Ransom
refused.

Gallinger would have the Martian mothers save themselves by rec-
onciling their theology to human experience: "Our Locar had said,
'Why bother? What is the worth of it? It is all vanity, anyhow.' And
the secret is...he was right! It *is* vanity, it *is* pride!...It is our blasphemy which has made us great, and will sustain us, and which the
gods secretly admire in us."[37] From the start, Gallinger had conceived
of himself as a romantic or existentialist hero—"like Ulysses in Male-
bolge," "like Samson in Gaza," "Rimbaud with his hashish, Bau-
delaire with his laudanum," and so on—in short, "aloof" and "a
stranger, unafraid." But M'Cwyie, Matriarch of Mars, merely stares
at him "like Sartre's Other."[38]

The real—and tragic—theological dilemma for Gallinger stems from
his realization that the response of Martian fatalism to his agnostic
premises seems far more logically consistent than his own attempt at
heroism. Recognition of the common absurdity of both Martian and
human existence confirms Gallinger in his initial, but now pessimistic
agnosticism: "I did not believe a word of my own gospel, never had."[39]
He leaves Mars in tears.

The irony of Gallinger's reaction, however, is that it is the direct
opposite of the Martian's reaction. His attempt to refute their submission
to a divine plan only serves to reinforce it. To Gallinger, the faith in
Malaan seemed only a sort of twisted Stoicism or a mythic manifestation
of Existentialism itself. But Gallinger was unaware of "the Promise of
Locar...that a holy man would come from the heavens to save us in
our last hours."[40] And Gallinger himself fulfills that prophecy—not by
his logical arguments, but by impregnating Braxa.

The rose of Zelazny's story, Dante's symbol of salvation, remains a
gift and a given. Gallinger lacks the given of Martian faith, the hope
of salvation that justifies itself and all other human or alien efforts; he
attempts suicide, but lives, and believers in Malaan may hope for his
Messiah's own future conversion. But Zelazny has demonstrated that
the theology of a faith (whether human or alien) cannot cease to cham-
pion the exclusive rationality of its own premises without becoming
logically inconsistent to itself; the only plausible alternative to such
inconsistency remains agnosticism.

If human agnostics have not accepted the givens of so many human faiths, however, there is no logical reason why they should be converted by the theological arguments of so many alien evangelists either. Therefore, the impasses among faiths, or between faith and a lack thereof, must remain irresolvable in sf—by the dictates of *theological* plausibility. Any serious advocacy of syncretism, as of polytheism, remains mere fantasy—if "logic alone" is not itself a fantasy.

NOTES

1. For a history of the recurring debate between rigorist and laxist attitudes regarding the unbaptized, see S. Harent, S.J., "Infidèles (Salut des)" in *Dictionnaire de Théologie Catholique* (Paris: Letouzey, 1903–50).

2. A careful distinction that Walter E. Meyers makes in *Aliens and Linguists* (Athens, Georgia: University of Georgia Press, 1980) to discuss the philological plausibility of various works of sf might serve in this context as well. Faith defends what is thought to be known, but theology analyzes "what is known to be known"; the focus is on logic, not revelation.

3. Darko Suvin, *Metamorphoses of Science Fiction* (New Haven: Yale University Press, 1979), pp. 26, 63.

4. C. S. Lewis, "On Science Fiction" in Walter Hooper, ed., *Of Other Worlds: Essays and Stories* (New York: Harcourt, Brace & World, 1967); reprinted in Mark Rose, ed., *Science Fiction* (Englewood Cliffs, NJ: Prentice-Hall, 1976), p. 111.

5. C. S. Lewis, *Perelandra* (New York: Macmillan, 1944), p. 168.

6. Lewis, *Perelandra*, p. 180.

7. Ibid., p. 182; italics mine.

8. Ibid., p. 217.

9. James Blish, *A Case of Conscience* (New York: Ballantine, 1958).

10. James Blish (as William Atheling), "Cathedrals in Space: Autumn, 1953," "Afterword, 1964," and "Another Case: October, 1961," reprinted together in Damon Knight, ed., *Turning Points: Essays on the Art of Science Fiction* (New York: Harper & Row, 1977), pp. 144–52, 152–53, 154–62; p. 156.

11. Blish, *A Case of Conscience*, p. 69.

12. Ibid., p. 78.

13. Ibid.

14. Ibid., pp. 98, 104.

15. Ibid., p. 79

16. The deliberate "rock" pun of "Peter" and "Lithia" is Blish's—as it once was Christ's.

17. Blish, "Cathedrals in Space," pp. 150-51.

18. J. Norman King, "Theology, Science Fiction and Man's Future Ori-

entation," in Thomas D. Clareson, ed., *Many Futures, Many Worlds* (Kent, Ohio: Kent State University Press, 1977), p. 244.

19. One of the best considerations of the ethical implications that such depersonalization of aliens entails has been offered by Frederick Pohl, "The Day After the Day the Martians Came," in Harlan Ellison, ed., *Dangerous Visions* (Signet rpt., 1975; New York: Doubleday, 1967), pp. 21–29.

20. Theodore Sturgeon, "Science Fiction, Morals, and Religion," in Reginald Bretnor, ed., *Science Fiction, Today and Tomorrow* (New York: Harper and Row, 1974), pp. 98–113.

21. Lester del Rey, "Evensong" in Ellison, ed., *Dangerous Visions*, pp. 1–8. From the same anthology, Damon Knight's "Shall the Dust Praise Thee?" (pp. 320–25) may be taken as another example of religious satire; Knight's God, hardly omniscient, is late for his own apocalypse.

22. J. G. Ballard in *Books and Bookmen* (February 1971) as cited by Tom Woodman, "Science Fiction, Religion and Transcendence," in Patrick Parrinder, ed., *Science Fiction: A Critical Guide* (New York: Longman, 1979), p. 110. 110.

23. See S. C. Fredericks, "Revivals of Ancient Mythologies in Current Science Fiction and Fantasy," in Thomas D. Clareson, ed., *Many Futures*, pp. 50–65.

24. J. Norman King, "Theology," p. 256.

25. W. H. Auden, "Postscript: Christianity and Art," in *The Dyer's Hand and Other Essays* (New York: Random House, 1962); reprinted in G. B. Tennyson and Edward E. Ericson, eds., *Religion and Modern Literature* (Grand Rapids, Mich.: Eerdmans, 1974), p. 114.

26. Robert Heinlein, *Stranger in a Strange Land* (New York: Berkley, 1961).

27. Blish, "Another Case," pp. 156, 161.

28. Heinlein, *Stranger*, p. 134.

29. Blish, "Another Case," p. 156.

30. Heinlein, *Stranger*, p. 256.

31. Ibid., p. 414.

32. Ibid., p. 415.

33. Larry Niven and Jerry Pournelle, *The Mote in God's Eye* (New York: Pocket Books, 1974), p. 370.

34. Roger Zelazny, "A Rose for Ecclesiastes," from *The Magazine of Fantasy and Science Fiction* (1963), reprinted in Dick Allen, ed., *Science Fiction: The Future* (New York: Harcourt Brace Jovanovich, 1971), p. 190.

35. Ibid., p. 211.

36. Ibid., p. 189.

37. Ibid., p. 212.

38. Ibid., pp. 185, 187, 193, 190.

39. Ibid., p. 213.

40. Ibid., p. 213.

4

For Suffering Humanity: The Ethics of Science in Science Fiction

ALEXANDER J. BUTRYM

Idea-oriented science fiction frequently treats the ethical behavior of scientists as its major theme. To be taken seriously as literary art, these stories need to develop the theme realistically but consistently in its relation to plot and other story elements. As readers, we expect the stories fully to explore the problems or questions they raise and perhaps even to develop reasonable solutions or answers. Because we are mainly interested in ideas, we expect complete and logically consistent analysis. But because we are reading fiction, we expect also a verisimilitudinous, if not realistic, and coherent narrative that presents the ideas in an interesting way. We expect the story to contain either explicit or implicit statements of ethical postulates, and we expect to see the coherent working out of a morally right course of action.

In the analyses that follow, important works by three writers are examined to understand and evaluate literary work that emphasizes ideas or in which ideas are a major fictional given. Frank R. Stockton's work proceeds from essentially vague sentimental assumptions that morally good action springs from ''nice'' feelings. Isaac Asimov's work develops from a diametrically oppostite ''hard'' scientific materialism, and Walter M. Miller's from somewhere between the two. Miller's assumptions are perhaps best described as Western religious-humanistic generalizations. Of the works examined, Miller's is probably the most satisfactory as both literature and ethics.

I

Of Frank R. Stockton's large output, only two novels and five short
stories can be called science fiction, but these works concern scientists'
ethical responsibility for the uses made of their discoveries. His scientists
operate under purely secular ethical imperatives. His tone is Horatian—
reasonable, suave, calmly or genteelly sentimental. Stockton seems to
poke fun at sentiments that the old ways of doing things are natural,
sacred, and aesthetically pleasing. At the same time, he invests his main
characters—his mouthpieces—with moral sensitivity that stems from
that same sentiment. Over all his characters floats a cool, calm rationalism; they do not allude, even obliquely or metaphorically, to the
transcendent concerns that would underlie religious conceptions of ethical or moral behavior.

In Stockton's 1897 novel *The Great Stone of Sardis*,[1] Roland Clewe,
the main character, is a multitalented scientist-administrator-inventor
who engineers major discoveries in such ways that they cannot be
duplicated and used to upset the balance achieved by his world. In this
novel, Clewe sets out on two major projects: submarine exploration of
the Arctic Ocean with a view to discovering the North Pole, and development of an "Artesian Ray," a device that will enable him to see
deep into the earth. Clewe is less interested in the polar journey and
delegates that exploration to other people; his personal representative
is a trusted shop foreman sort, Sammy Block, who would rather stay
at home for two reasons: because he prefers his home and wife, and
because he does not trust newfangledness—a sentiment shared in some
ways by his employer.

Nevertheless, throughout the project, Clewe emphasizes the importance of the quest over its completion to the extent that he is satisfied
with the glory of designing the expedition, organizing it, and funding
it. The actual being there, the data or material substance of the discovery,
is of "slight importance" and briefly noted. This Tom Sawyer-like
attitude of Clewe's contrasts with that of his amoral competitor, the
mad Polish interloper, Rovinski, who attempts to use Clewe's program
in order to claim the North Pole for his Czarist employer in St. Pe-
tersburg, and so to secure honor for himself with relatively little effort.

On the other hand, the Artesian device interests Clewe for more than
merely personal honor and fame. Early descriptions of the ray focus on
its usefulness in making discoveries in "pure science." Stockton makes

no reference to either "developmental" work or to financial exploitation of the device. As a matter of fact, early in the tale, medical use of the device is foregone by Clewe because he wants to develop the tool in geology first. Scientific curiosity is his overriding motive; he is after the primordial secret of the Earth, nothing less. Using ever more powerful forms of the ray, he hopes to see into the bowels of the planet and determine the makeup of its core and hence the secret of its formation. Although the ray works, Clewe cannot interpret the glowing light that seems to emanate from the deepest point his ray can penetrate. Using a hole fortuitously drilled into the earth by the accidental discharge of an unstoppable artillery shell he is working on, Clewe descends to the glowing substance and discovers it is a gigantic diamond, the carbon source of all life, which lies at the core of the planet. Clewe's theory of the origin of the planet is supported by this discovery, and he is full of joy.

In the moment of his triumph, however, Clewe becomes aware of certain dangers—dangers that Stockton raises to almost symbolic meaning. When, down in the cavern, Clewe walks upon the diamond, he feels horribly insecure because although he thinks he is standing on solid rock, the surface he is on is transparent, sloping, and highly polished.[2] His circumstances, to understate the case, are precarious. In later describing the experience to his fiancée and financial underwriter, Margaret Raleigh, he expresses reluctance to return to the netherworld:

"If I were offered all the good that there is in this world, which money cannot buy, I would never go down into that cleft again. . . . In the light of my electric lamps, sent through a vast transparent mass, I could see nothing, but I could feel. I put out my foot, and I found it was upon a sloping surface. In another instant I might have slidden—where? I cannot bear to think of it!"
She threw her arms about him and held him tightly.[3]

The emphasis, given by repetition and the heightened emotional state of both Roland and Margaret during the retelling, indicates the incident is invested with more than mere literal or narrative significance. The imagery suggests that the quest for discovery can lead to a moral sliding; finding the diamond is one thing, but being taken up with it to the exclusion of the outer world is quite another and a more terrible thing. Walking on a canted, slippery, transparent surface suggests the moral insecurity of the scientist's pursuits. This vague and ultimately undefinable sentiment is cited as the spring for Clewe's decision—moral decision—to close up the access to the diamond, having salvaged enough pieces to ensure his personal wealth, to provide scientific evidence concerning the earth's origin, and to provide a symbol to be used in coronation of all the kings of the earth. Anything further to be learned about the earth's core can only be learned by looking through the Artesian Ray. Further journeys to the core are impossible, just as further journeys to the pole are unlikely.

Clewe's sentiment-based ethic is reflected in other Stockton stories. In "A Tale of Negative Gravity," the main character, a retired professional man turned tinkerer, constructs an antigravity device.[4] The problem is what to do with it? The inventor and his wife fear disruption of domestic tranquillity. They do not need the money the device will bring, and although the world will benefit from the invention, the personal turmoil of patenting the device, of forming business and legal entanglements and financial arrangements to exploit it, and other such concerns would destroy the happiness and relaxation of their retirement years. As a consequence, they decide to pass the device along to their son Herbert after they die; in the meantime, they will use the machine for "personal gratification."

Unfortunately, Mr. Gilbert, the neighbor to whose daughter Herbert is engaged, notices the odd way the inventor hops about, overloads his mules, and generally exhibits behavior unbecoming his years. Gilbert, a respectable man, breaks off the young couple's relationship without explaining why, and takes his daughter on a tour to assuage her feelings. As a solace for his broken hopes, Herbert is sent to Europe to study engineering, while his parents make the Grand Tour carrying antigravity devices for convenience. Once again, the inventor enjoys his device too thoroughly. Undertaking mountaineering and hiking outings too strenuous for his unaided aged self, he is suspected of being crazy. When he overhears a conversation between two tourists—one of whom is Mr. Gilbert, who chances to stop in the same village—he decides to explain all to Gilbert, give him a little ride on the marvelous device, then destroy the invention. The destruction accomplished, Herbert and his love are rebetrothed with the prospect of inheriting the blueprints. But, for the inventor, the "wonderful pleasure in tripping over the earth like a winged Mercury . . . is not to be compared . . . to that given by the buoyancy and lightness of two young and loving hearts, reunited."[5]

The story's half-wacky tone almost rescues it from failing because of its sentimentalilty. In having his characters assume that nice feelings and public repute govern right and wrong in scientific research, Stockton has trivialized his material. And he does this time and again.

"Amos Kilbright: His Adscititious Experiences," a story based on "psychical science," also sentimentally develops the theme that scientific experiments motivated by either hope of profit or curiosity tend to dehumanize both experimenter and subject.[6] Furthermore, such experiments are too easily perverted by greedy and inhumane scientists. In this story, Amos is a Colonial American, drowned in 1785. Rematerialized in 1887 by an unscrupulous "psychic experimenter," he is kept corporealized for so long he cannot be returned to the spirit world without the skills of a German specialist in problem dematerializations.

The ethical problems concern the spiritualists' tinkering with Amos's corporeal self without his permission or concern for either his feelings or those of his friends and family. The "researchers" hope to make money out of Amos by causing him to materialize and dematerialize on demand at seances. To let him alone would be, says Corbridge the psychic, "business suicide."[7] In the sentiment of the lawyer's wife, the psychics would exploit "poor Mr. Kilbright...as long as a dollar could be made out of him."[8] Corbridge's "conduct was not only mean, but criminal in its nature, and if there was no law against it, one ought to be made."[9]

The sentimental ethic is underscored in Mrs. Colesworthy's remark that "science is getting to be such a wicked thing..."[10] At the dénouement, Dr. Hildstein, the German specialist, promises never to attempt to dematerialize a spirit who has been corporealized long enough to make friends, and Mrs. Colesworthy remarks that he "has some heart, after all."[11]

Stockton wrote for the prosperous middle class whose ideals were respectability as much as financial independence.[12] Whenever science threatens to overcome "niceness," Stockton's scientists become frightened of their work, or Stockton's layman becomes frightened of his scientists.

Clearly the ethical implication is purely sentimental and vague: If scientists were nice, they would not be such wretchedly inhuman ogres. In displaying such overdone sentimentality, Stockton is reflecting the concerns of his audience, "Gilded Age" gentility and, at the same time, refusing to come to grips with real ethical problems.

As a consequence, Stockton's scientists devote themselves mainly to trivia. Clewe marries his financial underwriter and exults over his newest discovery, three baby birds in a rusted tomato can. The antigravity machinery is used for trivial purposes, then sent into outer space. His scientists are ambivalent; they do not want to see research solely profit-oriented or ego-oriented. But Stockton's vague, feeling-based ethical system is too weak to provide a solution to his characters' dilemma. The stories are unsatisfying.

II

Isaac Asimov's Foundation stories also involve the ethical behavior of scientists. These stories concern the failure of a Galactic Empire that rules millions of human-inhabited planets. In the beginning, Hari Seldon, a brilliant mathematician and psychologist, concludes from his newly developed science of psychohistory that the Empire has about 500 more years of life. After this period, humanity will be brutalized for 30,000 years. Using psychohistory, he formulates the Seldon Plan, to shorten the period to 1,000 years. The plan involves establishing two "foundations." The First Foundation, located on the planet Terminus at the rim of the Galaxy, has the ostensible purpose of publishing an encyclopedic summary of all human knowledge. Its real purpose, however, is to become technologically and scientifically superior to the rest of the Galaxy and a focal point for the new Empire. The Second Foundation, located at "the other end of the Galaxy," is mysterious. Its purposes are to oversee the workings of the Plan and to provide a leadership caste for the new Empire. The stories in the first volume show the First Foundation cleverly overcoming several challanges. In the second and third volumes, the stories deal with the First Foundation's attempts to learn whether there really is a Second Foundation, and where it may be.

Religious and ethical themes are developed on two levels. On the most obvious level are instances such as those in "The Mayors." A group of scientists attempts to control backward planets by offering atomic energy as a superstitious religion run by a class of priests most of whom are ignorant, superstitious, and exploited by the scientists on Terminus. References to religion, morals, or any transcendent reality are cynical. Transcendence is nonsense to Lepold of Anacreon, his evil uncle-regent Wienis, and even the chiefest "priest of the Galactic Spirit"

Poly Verisof. To them, religious commitment of any kind is superstition maintained by the self-interested fraudulence of a ruling power.[13]

Although religion is called in this story a "great civilizing influence of history," the speaker, a dissident member of the First Foundation, is impatiently cut off by his corevolutionist Sef Sermak.[14] The tone of the exchange suggests that the characters consider religion, at best, an effective means of controlling the general population; at worst, religion is a timewasting superstition whose ritual has been designed to mislead mankind.

In the third volume, *Second Foundation*, a group of First Foundation scientists attempts to learn whether the Second Foundation really exists. The group develops a science of psychology and certain tools, notably "encephalographic analysis." Homir Munn, one of these men, alludes to Occam's Razor in questioning the validity of the analysis. "It's always easy to explain the unknown by postulating a superhuman and arbitrary will."[15]

Munn calls the cultural phenomenon anthropomorphism; what he means is "creating a god." Obviously, when he refers to a more powerful and more arbitrary will, he refers to the will of a god, or of a superman. Homir Munn's allusion to Occam's Razor to question the interpretation of certain encephalographic tracings is not the issue. But the tone he uses to describe religion without calling it religion certainly sounds cynical.

The cynicism is also apparent in references to moral and ethical order. The *Encyclopedia Galactica* citation at the head of the story "The Traders" quotes the Traders' motto, which has been adapted from one of Salvor Hardin's aphorisms: "Never let your sense of morals prevent you from doing what is right."[16] The motto is described as "half serious, half mockery."

As a first step in establishing Foundation control over the planet Askone, Limmar Ponyets, a Trader, blackmails Pherl, a favorite of the Grand Master, into buying atomic gadgetry. Ponyets's colleague asks cynically whether Ponyets has a sense of morals. In reply, Ponyets refers to the Hardin aphorism.[17]

In general, then, Asimov's characters clearly express cynical attitudes toward religion and morals. Religion is superstitious; morals and ethics are described as "vague gropings of intuitive ethical systems based on inspiration and emotion."[18]

But there is another level on which Asimov's stories deal with ethical considerations. On this second level, religious and ethical motifs are expressed in Hari Seldon, the psychohistorians and psychological scientists of the Second Foundation, and the Seldon Plan. First, let us consider Hari Seldon. As the chief mathematician of his time, Seldon has used his genius to develop the science of psychohistory, by which the race's future can be read through analysis of the interactions of large social forces. His genius, his foreknowledge, and his ability to manipulate events so as to change the future make him godlike. The god in him is clearly developed and examined during his trial for treason in the first tale. He insists that he is completely free from accountability and responsibility.[19] Hari Seldon and his successors are, in effect, gods or transcendent beings from whom real order—i.e., truth—and hence moral system ought to emanate. Years after his death, Seldon appears more than once in ghostly holographic apparition to the scientists and politicians on Terminus. In these revelatory apparitions, he describes bits and pieces of the plan.

Seldon and his successors are obviously godlike, and the Seldon Plan is itself a clear analogue of the Western religious concept, Divine Providence. The plan calls for an ordered growth of human potential and destiny that, in the long run, will result in the growth of a new Empire. But this Empire will require both high technology in the physical and material spheres, and an elite ruling class in the political, social and psychological spheres. Developing the material technology is the responsibility of the First Foundation; supplying the rulers is that of the Second Foundation.[20]

Whenever the Seldon Plan is discussed, moreover, Asimov's characters use quasi-religious terms: The Plan is, for instance, an "insubstantial fabric [that] fills the enemy [the Foundation] with confidence, removes fear, maintains morale in the face of early defeats."[21] The First Foundation is described as "never defeated...protected by the Seldon Plan...destined to form a new Empire."[22]

Even though the psychohistorians are gods and the Seldon Plan is their providential care for the human race, these stories fail to strike the reader as having truly human concerns at heart. The difficulty lies in Hari Seldon's perception of the nature of truth. The first and third stories, for example, are preceded by quotations from the *Encyclopedia Galactica* emphasizing the statistical nature of psychohistory.[23] The epigraph to the third story also emphasizes the profound impersonality of Seldon's system. In it, "human conglomerates" that are "unaware" figure in "random reactions" to "social and economic forces." All these terms imply a lack of personal responsibility on the part of either the highest or the lowest human. And this impersonality is expressed over and over. Only two more illustrations will be cited, mainly as examples of the tone of these passages.

Early in the series, Hari Seldon's protégé Gaal Dornick describes psychohistory as a "statistical science that cannot predict the future of a single man with any accuracy." His lawyer replies that Dornick is wrong; Seldon expected Dornick to be arrested and, in fact, Seldon has so structured events that Dornick *would* be arrested. When Dornick expresses resentment at being so treated, Lors Avakim, the lawyer, tries to mollify him with these words: "Please. It was necessary. You were not picked for any personal reasons.... It will end well; almost certainly so for the project; and with reasonable probability for you." Dornick demands and gets "the figures": over 99.9 percent probability of success for the project; 77.2 percent probability he will come through unscathed; less than 1 percent chance he will be convicted and executed.[24] Note just how utterly impersonal the predictions are, an impersonality heightened by the lawyer's matter-of-fact exposition of the odds for Dornick's death.

Another incident, this one exuding the rich tones of murmuring in a cathedral, takes place in the lonely room somewhere on the Second Foundation planet where the prime Radiant—a device that stores and makes accessible the plan, a space age Ark or Tabernacle—is contained. The omniscient narrator describes psychohistory as the "final mathematicization" of mental science; the psychology was generalized to sociology that was also "mathematicized": "The larger groups...the billions...trillions...quadrillions...became, not simply human beings, but gigantic forces amenable to statistical treatment—so that to Hari Seldon, the future became clear and inevitable, and the Plan could be set up."[25]

The round tones combined with the heavy emphasis placed on "statistical conglomerates" tend to do more than reduce the unique importance of any individual. They almost sanctify the destruction of any basis for individual moral or ethical choice. If Truth—Capital Truth, the tone suggests—is statistical, then sheer numbers overwhelm individual commitments. Moreover, the human race is kept in ignorance of the plan because the statistical analysis is authentic only when humans react to social, political, and economic stimuli "unaware of psychohistoric analysis."[26]

Significant free will is denied to humanity in still other ways. Hari Seldon, in a holographic appearance on the fiftieth anniversary of the First Foundation, tells the assembled leaders that they have just faced a Seldon crisis and, by waiting until their actions were determined by circumstances, survived it. He provides another revelation: "You no longer have freedom of action... the path you must take is inevitable."[27] (And the assemblage seems to applaud its loss of free will!) The determinism is repeated time and again throughout the three volumes. Every person of significance except the Mule—a mutant, outside "conglomerate humanity"—is controlled, and no one objects to the control. The conditions for moral choice do not exist in Asimov's galaxy; and his scientists do not miss the freedom. But where there is no freedom to choose, there is no ethical liability.

This, of course, is the point on which the stories break down. The godlike psychohistorians attempt to cut short human suffering and ignorance. They operate on the assumption that individual human suffering and action do not mean anything or are of no consequence. Further, they assume neither religious nor philosophical responsibility when they subordinate every action to their aim—namely, shortening the period of barbarism between civilized epochs. Though they seldom resort to violence, they do lie, defraud, and maintain ignorance. Of course, the situation is a moral nightmare: Hari Seldon's Plan to reduce human suffering is actually pointless given his attitude that human life is basically determined by forces beyond free human control and hence meaningless and unimportant.

III

Walter M. Miller, Jr., deals specifically with the ethical responsibility of scientists. His novel, *A Canticle for Leibowitz* (1959), sets science and technology (represented by academic scientists and their military-political exploiters) against humanists (represented by the clergy of New Rome and the monks of St. Leibowitz Abbey). Wrestling with the question of scientists' responsibilities, the novel provides a dialectic in which the parties seem at times emotionally ambivalent toward their own arguments.

A Canticle for Leibowitz is a "post-catastrophe" novel. After a nuclear holocaust, sometime late in the twentieth century, a wave of anti-intellectualism resulted in the destruction of most of Western culture. Two questions implicit in the novel bear on ethics. Are scientists responsible for the use of their inventions? What constitutes good use of scientific and technical knowledge?

Miller assumes that humans are more valuable as individuals than as statistical items in a quasi- (not to say pseudo-) scientific enumeration. In the novel's opening pages, Miller establishes the importanace of all life, even the least iota of human life, however debased and monstrous it may seem in various circumstances. For, as the first page of the novel points out:

Who did not then know there were monsters in the earth in those days? That which was born alive was, by the law of the Church and the law of Nature, suffered to live, and helped to maturity, if possible, by those who had begotten it. The law was not always obeyed, but it was obeyed with sufficient frequency.... [28]

The novel's second section, *Fiat Lux*, introduces Thon Taddeo Pfardentrott who represents academic science. Taddeo, vain and arrogant although brilliant, seems especially single-minded. Mainly interested in relighting the lamps of learning more than 1200 years after European-American civilization died, he has no time for politicians, whose machinations he feels are beneath him. He is so concerned with the Grand Idea of a Renaissance of Science that his idealization of learning leads to an unrealistic idealization of the human race. Because the race cannot live up to his ideals, he becomes an archcynic. In one scene, Taddeo, disgusted by the sight of a filthy, stupid, and diseased peasant, reveals his blindness to the moral problems that his science, like the science of the twentieth century, generates. He cannot, he tells the papal nuncio, Marcus Apollo, believe the peasant is "the progeny of a once-mighty civilization." Calling Apollo to the window, he asks, "What *do* you see?" Monsignor Apollo's reply is so conventional as to seem almost trite and meaningless: " 'The image of Christ,' grated the monsignor, surprised at his own sudden anger. 'What did you expect me to see?' "[29]

Far from stating a mere platitude, Apollo has clearly put the individual in relation to the race. To him, Jesus Christ is not only divine, the Son of God, but he is also, as in conventional iconology that goes back to

the age of the Church Fathers, the second Adam, Arch-Man. And in
this instance, Marcus Apollo states the basic assumption of the novel's
ethical resolution: the smallest part contains the greatness of the whole
race. Taddeo's problem is that he cannot see through the concrete
manifestation of humanity in the peasant to his own idealization of the
human race. As a consequence, he cannot make the transcendent leap
that is needed before a universal moral system is possible. When Taddeo
replies to Apollo's question, he causes Apollo to make a statement that
summarizes the crux of the novel:

[Taddeo] huffed impatiently. "The incongruity. Men as you can observe them
through any window, and men as historians would have us believe men once
were. I can't accept it. How can a great and wise civilization have destroyed
itself so completely?" "Perhaps," said Apollo, "by being materially great and
materially wise, and nothing else."[30]

Miller here contrasts Taddeo's empiricism in devaluating the peasant
with Apollo's judgment on the mere materialism of technological society. He suggests that science must properly recognize the divinity in
a man—the Christ in man, to use Monsignor Apollo's words. Without
recognizing such a transcendent value, philosophical questioning becomes mere cynicism.

Miller's scientists and their ethical problems are emblems for the
whole human race and its problems. The point is developed most clearly
in the encounter between Dom Paulo, the second Abbot we meet, and
Benjamin, the Wandering Jew who by the end of the novel seems to
have been around for 7,000 years or better. Benjamin is described as
the archetype of Israel; he assumes the burden of his people and their
past: Benjamin's " 'I'was the converse of the imperial 'We.' " Recognizing this quality in Benjamin, Dom Paulo sees that he himself is also
"a member of a oneness. . . . a part of a congregation and continuity."[31]

After thus establishing the importance of each individual human,
Miller is able to argue that that individual is responsible not only for
his own deeds, but also for those of all mankind. More painfully—as
Miller seems to imply—each individual is responsible for the use that
others make of his deeds. Paulo momentarily rebels against assuming
responsibility for the actions of other members of the "congregation"
as well as his own. And yet, he transcends his rebelliousness: "Faith
told him that the burden was there, had been since Adam's time—and

the burden imposed by a fiend crying in mockery 'Man!' at man, 'Man!'—
calling each to account for the deeds of all since the beginning; a burden
impressed upon each generation before the opening of the womb."[32]
The man–Poet-in-residence at the Abbey of St. Leibowitz tells the
Thon to recognize his responsibility for the use to which his discoveries
are put. The Poet, one of whose symbols is a blue-headed—mutant—
goat, tells Taddeo that he has not been saving the animal to be used as
a scapegoat; instead the "goat is to be enshrined and honored, not
blamed! Crown him with the crown St. Leibowitz sent you, and thank
him for the light that is rising. Then blame Leibowitz, and drive *him*
into the desert. That way *you* won't have to wear the second crown.
The one with thorns. Responsibility, it's called."[33]
But the Thon does not accept this personal kind of responsibility.
His is a responsibility to capitalized, personified, and impersonal Truth.
The rebirth of technological mastery over Nature will cause a great deal
of suffering and upheaval, he admits, and he concludes, "I am sorry."
The Abbot Paulo recognizes the moral abdication in Taddeo's position:
"He had a choice: to approve of them, to disapprove of them, or to
regard them as impersonal phenomena beyond his control like a flood,
famine or whirlwind. Evidently, then, he accepted them as inevitable—
to avoid having to make a moral judgment."[34]
Fiat Voluntas Tua, the novel's third section, tells the story of humanity's self-destruction in another "flame deluge." In this section, it
becomes clear that the scientists' definition of what constitutes good
use of knowledge has failed. Nuclear science has developed weapons
that, in turn, have brought about the final holocaust. In anticipation of
the holocaust and the suffering it will cause, the political authority has
organized a plan for mass mercy killing.
The major conflict in this section is the confrontation between the
monks and the personnel of the "Green Star Mercy Camp," the euthanasia center. Dom Zerchi, the abbot of St. Leibowitz monastery at
this time, opposes Dr. Cors, the head of the local Mercy Camp. Dr.
Cors's arguments are based on expedience and sentiment. In a time of
general catastrophe, it would be difficult to arrange treatment for millions of dying people. Dom Zerchi adds sarcastically that the government
finds it convenient to herd the irradiated population into one place, then
kill them, and quickly bury them in order to prevent the spread of
disease. Dr. Cors's more appealing argument is the sentimental one:
What can one do for a person who is going to die painfully over the

next few days? What does one *feel*, hearing the screams of pain and anguish, knowing one is withholding respite?[35]

Dom Zerchi's arguments against euthanasia are twofold. In his theological argument, he maintains that pain itself is indeed evil and not pleasing to God. But "the soul's endurance in faith and hope and love *in spite* of bodily afflictions...pleases Heaven." Pain is like a temptation that leads "to despair, anger, loss of faith."[36] The morally right action in these circumstances, he insists, is to accept the pain and transcend it.

Dom Zerchi's second argument is derived from an empirical philosophical observation. From it he argues that no creature seeks death even to end a painful life. The conclusion, he says, goes back to ancient times: "Even the ancient pagans noticed that Nature imposes nothing on you that Nature doesn't prepare you to bear. If that is true even of a cat, then is it not more perfectly true of a creature with rational intellect and will—whatever you may believe of Heaven?"[37] In these arguments, Miller has developed a consistent system of human freedom and responsibility. The arguments insist on the individual's right to round off his or her life in keeping with the dignity of his or her nature, even though that nature may sometimes call for pain.

The insistence in Miller's novel on the absolute moral value of each person for the actions of all results in a leap from the small divinity in man to the transcendent capital Divinity. In its final scenes, the novel emphasizes the importance of the iota, the smallest particle of the whole, no matter how bent or monstrous. In these scenes, the tired, decrepit, and wounded Mrs. Grales, the two-headed Tomato Woman who performs abortions on the side, is transformed into the youthful, preternaturally healthy and gifted Rachel, the mother of Israel, the beginning of a new race. The least human has become the greatest.

Such a transfiguration succeeds in the novel only because Miller has developed an internally consistent and coherent set of logical relationships between the parts of his major theme, the ethics of scientific discovery and technological breakthrough.

The stories discussed in this essay fail or succeed in varying degrees because of the individual author's problems with the themes. Stockton's stories break down because theme and plot or incident do not support each other. The philosophy of genteel feeling cannot carry the rationalizing needed to make the story's structure coherent, and, as a consequence, Stockton slides into a clownish tone as a way of backing off under stress. He fails to come to grips with the ethical problems of his characters and trivializes his material.

Likewise, Issac Asimov's Foundation stories do not satisfy mature readers. His characters' cynicism and materialistic determinism limits them and makes their struggles meaningless. Scientists whose motive is to prevent or shorten periods of human suffering find themselves acting contrary to their intentions. Their professional and personal philosophic orientations do not recognize the basic dignity of the individual men who make up the generalized humanity in whose name they say they labor.

Only Walter M. Miller, Jr., weaves theme and incident together to form a richly textured pattern that shows humanity in moral relation to its works. The concatenation of plot and idea makes the story serious literature.

Science fiction is too often treated as a literature in which ideas are primary, or in which adventure or plot exists for its own sake. In fact, science fiction is primarily a form of literature. Serious criticism will develop when writers and critics begin to pull together all elements of these fictions and scrutinize these works using the classical methods of modern criticism.

NOTES

1. Frank R. Stockton, *The Great Stone of Sardis*, in Richard G. Powers, ed., *The Science Fiction of Frank R. Stockton: An Anthology* (Boston: Gregg Press, 1976), pp. 207–426.

2. Ibid., pp. 382–83.

3. Ibid., p. 391.

4. Frank R. Stockton, "A Tale of Negative Gravity," in *The Science Fiction of Frank R. Stockton*, pp. 51–82.

5. Ibid., pp. 81–82.

6. Frank R. Stockton, "Amos Kilbright: His Adscititious Experiences," in *The Science Fiction of Frank R. Stockton*, pp. 83–132.

7. Ibid., p. 97.

8. Ibid., p. 131.

9. Ibid., pp. 99–100.

10. Ibid., p. 102.

11. Ibid., p. 131.

12. Richard G. Powers, ed., *The Science Fiction of Frank R. Stockton*, "Introduction," p. viii.
13. Isaac Asimov, *Foundation* (Garden City, NY: Doubleday and Co., 1951), pp. 89–90, 102–3.
14. Ibid., p. 106.
15. Isaac Asimov, *Second Foundation* (Garden City, NY: Doubleday and Co., 1953), pp. 200–201.
16. Asimov, *Foundation*, p. 135.
17. Ibid., p. 155.
18. Asimov, *Second Foundation*, p. 101
19. Asimov, *Foundation*, p. 23.
20. Asimov, *Second Foundation*, p. 101.
21. Ibid., p. 195.
22. Ibid., p. 195.
23. Asimov. *Foundation*, pp. 3, 14.
24. Ibid., pp. 20–21.
25. Asimov, *Second Foundation*, p. 95.
26. Ibid., p, 95.
27. Asimov, *Foundation*, p. 73.
28. Walter M. Miller, Jr., *A Canticle for Leibowitz* (New York: Bantam Books, 1972), pp. 1–2.
29. Ibid., pp. 105–6.
30. Ibid., p. 106.
31. Ibid., p. 141.
32. Ibid., p. 141.
33. Ibid., p. 168.
34. Ibid., pp. 175–76.
35. Ibid., pp. 241, 244–45.
36. Ibid., p. 260.
37. Ibid., p. 261.

PART II

DILEMMAS OF PARADISE: BLISH AND LEWIS

5

The Concept of Eden

ANDREW J. BURGESS

Although the Genesis location for the primordial garden reads "eastward in Eden," recent science fiction writers have been fond of giving that Garden of Eden new space-time coordinates. These modern Edens show the beginning of rational life on imaginary planets, sometimes even managing to convey a sense of what a race's first innocence and loss of innocence might be.

Two authors who have effectively taken up the Eden motif are C. S. Lewis, in his fantasy *Perelandra* (1943), and James Blish, in the science fiction novel *A Case of Conscience* (1958).[1] Not content simply to exploit the Garden of Eden theme in a general way, as a utopia, these two men unfold their stories with a sophisticated grasp of Christian theology, and the results speak not only to literary critics but to theologians as well.

Portraying an Eden is not easy because the kind of incapacity for evil ascribed to such a state is barely conceivable. The logical issues alone are formidable, and putting an Eden into story form demands dialogues between the Adams and Eves and details about their character development, not merely an abstract definition. Lewis and Blish have taken on tough assignments, and, to the extent that they succeed, their work has more than merely literary significance. In this essay, therefore, I will examine how they tackle the Eden issues and then ask about a possible theological application of their work.

On the surface, the two novels are so different in plot and setting, except for the outer space location and the constant discussion of religious questions, that they might not seem to belong together at all. In *Perelandra* the main character, Ransom, is carried by an eldil (angel) to Perelandra (Venus), an idyllic planet covered mainly by ocean, on which float islands with delightful and delicious plants. On one of these islands Ransom meets a green-skinned woman, the Eve of the story, and a short time later a spacecraft arrives with the demon-possessed body of the scientist Weston. The center of the novel then deals with Weston's attempt to make the woman disobey Maleldil (God) and Ransom's steadily less successful struggles to thwart him, until at last Ransom attacks and kills Weston, thus preserving the woman from the threat of a continuing temptation that must eventually have succeeded.

Blish's *A Case of Conscience* also presents an innocent being on a distant planet, but in quite another way from Lewis's novel. The story has Father Ruiz-Sanchez, a Jesuit biologist, sent as part of a team of scientists to a distant planet, Lithia, to determine whether its resources should be exploited. Just before leaving Lithia, the priest-scientist has a talk with Chtexa, a member of the rational species on the planet. Father Ruiz-Sanchez learns that this species is naturally virtuous in terms of a specifically Christian ethic. Because of the way the species has evolved, these intelligent reptiles inevitably do what they consider right, so that the dream of the eighteenth-century *philosophes* holds good, in that the truths of morality are self-evident. Father Ruiz-Sanchez concludes that the discovery of this race will prove a serious, perhaps fatal, temptation for the earth's Christians who will wrongly imagine that they, too, can live as the Lithians do. This inference leads to a second—namely, because the existence of such a temptation situation directed simply and solely at Christians cannot possibly be accounted for by chance, the planet must have been created by the devil just for this purpose. The devil can create, says Father Ruiz-Sanchez, making the priest the first follower of the Manichaean heresy in more than one thousand years. In the second half of the book, Chtexa's son, Egtverchi, is brought up on earth; separated from the physical and social setting natural for a Lithian, Egtverchi loses his race's ethical restraints and becomes a threat both to Earth and to his own planet.

What ties Lewis's and Blish's novels together is not so much a set of common elements, but a shared relation to the much older Genesis story. Blish may well have read Lewis—indeed, his use of *hnau*, the word Lewis coined for "rational creature," shows that he did[2]—but that is beside the point. In determining where *A Case of Conscience* resembles Lewis, the place to check is the ancient story of Eden. Both Lewis and Blish give us temptation narratives rooted in the biblical account of a first fall by the human race. Whereas Ransom has to cope with an actual temptation by an earthling of a new and innocent race, Father Ruiz-Sanchez struggles with the possible threat to faith on earth because of the discovery of a distant planet. The situations are opposite, but the background that gives depth and force to the stories is, in each case, the same.

The similarity between the two novels and their relation to the Genesis account might strike one more forcibly than it does, if the narrator of each story did not stand outside the main action. Neither Ransom nor Ruiz-Sanchez is tempter or tempted, devil or Adam. Ransom's role in cutting off the length of the green woman's ordeal comes only after she has already vindicated herself by withstanding long testing; Father Ruiz-Sanchez's dramatic exorcism of Lithia at the end of the novel accompanies, but does not by itself cause, the destruction of that planet. The moral and physical trials that the main characters endure are real, but they take place at the edge, not at the center, of the temptation.

There is really no other way that either of these stories could be told but from the outside, because a reader cannot fully identify with a purely innocent or a purely diabolical being. A famous writer of romantic fiction remarked that she always sets her heroines in a past century because the idea of a present-day virgin would be too implausible. If that writer had been producing science fiction, she might have set her heroine in a future century or some far distant planet, to ease the strain for the cynical reader. Still, what she describes is virginity, not the kind of innocence possessed by either the green Perelandran or Chtexa. The one state everyone has experienced; the other is barely imaginable.

Blish's portrayal of Chtexa in chapters 4, 5, and 8 comes up against just this difficulty. The Lithians are a race with no antisocial behavior. In all their actions they follow blindly what they call "reason," which is in fact a set of Christian ethical principles. This unquestioning acceptance of principles was genetically bred into the race ages ago, so that they could now no more break their moral precepts than they could fly. Lithians can never be tormented by ethical indecision, while humans continually are. As Father Ruiz-Sanchez learns later, this imprinting of the moral code only works so long as a Lithian is brought up in its own carefully controlled planetary environment; within that setting the system is completely successful.

It is fitting that Blish places Lithia so distant from Earth, in that the ways of the Lithians are far removed from ours. They have no "night thoughts," Father Ruiz-Sanchez notes.[3] The difference from earthlings is profound. Lithians are at home both on their planet and with themselves; humans, however, are not. Lithians face no set of ethical choices, no alternate futures looming before them. The anxiety that the philosopher Søren Kierkegaard finds pervading even human innocence is altogether missing on Lithia.[4] Even some atheist existentialist thinkers point to this pervasive anxiety as the distinctive mark of human existence. As Christians, Kierkegaard and Father Ruiz-Sanchez go further than this in that they identify this basic anxiety as a psychological symptom of original sin.

As a paradise, Lithia is less a model for Earth than first appears. Father Ruiz-Sanchez notices that the Lithians lack some words, such as *murderer*, for which they would have no use; however, he overlooks the fact that, because Lithians do not make moral choices, they must also lack the whole battery of human words that go with ethical behavior. There can be no place in the Lithian vocabulary for *ought* or *should*, no reason for them to speak of *moral quandary* or *weakness of will*, no situation in which one could be praised for *character* or *virtue*. To admire them for behaving as they do is like admiring flowers for growing. We can indeed imagine a race of humanoids living in this way, but the language they speak when they talked about their actions would be so different from ours that communication would continually break down between them and us. As Ninian Smart noted when considering a utopia much like Blish's, "moral utterance is embedded in the cosmic status quo."[5] The ascription of moral goodness is only intelligible in a world of choice.

Lithia may be a paradise for Lithians, but it is not a possible paradise for us. At any rate, human beings cannot know it as a place where people are good, since the notion of moral goodness does not apply to the inhabitants of that planet in a way that is recognizable to us. It follows that, since the planet cannot be a paradise for humans, neither need it be quite the devil's trap that Father Ruiz-Sanchez fears. Earthlings might be taken in by the apparently ideal life led by the Lithians, and some, perhaps many, humans might be fatally tempted; but a closer acquaintance with the Lithians and a more exact study by scientists and humanists of that planet's language and culture would disabuse people of the illusory paradise. Indeed, the threat to Earth, when it arises in the second half of *A Case of Conscience*, does not come from any popular movement on Earth to idealize Lithian society, but rather from a confused and corrupted Lithian, Egtverchi, who threatens to spread a teaching of moral irresponsibility that would overthrow earthly and Lithian society alike.

Another aspect of the trap against which Father Ruiz-Sanchez warns will not stand close examination—namely, the Lithian proof of the theory of evolution. In his presentation to the Lithian scientific team, Father Ruiz-Sanchez argues that, because Lithian biology is plainly evolutionary, the news about Lithia would overthrow the Roman Catholic Church's authority by discrediting the Church's antievolutionary stance.[6] The life of each member of the Lithian dominant race is an exact recapitulation of its evolutionary history, moving from fish, to cold-blooded reptile, to warm-blooded reptile; Father Ruiz-Sanchez is convinced that this proof of Lithian evolution will persuade people to accept evolution of the human race as well. We never learn whether the priest's worries are justified because Lithia ends up in a nuclear holocaust, the product of a scientist who foolishly thinks that nuclear development is bound to be good. What we do know, however, by virtue of knowledge that Blish could not have had when he wrote the book in 1958, is that the Roman Catholic Church no longer looks at the theory of evolution with the same suspicion that it once did. The impact of the Second Vatican Council in the early 1960s has brought to the fore theologians such as Pierre Teilhard de Chardin and Karl Rahner, whose thought develops within an explicitly evolutionary framework.

Lewis's description in *Perelandra* of an innocent race is not vulnerable to exactly the same critique as that of Blish, or at least not vulnerable to the same degree. Unlike Blish's Chtexa, the green woman in *Perelandra* is faced with moral decisions; indeed, although she does not know it, she is up against a choice that will decide not only her fate, but the fate of her planet as well. When he meets her, Ransom has the impression of a precarious innocence.[7] Her purity and peace are not bred into her genes; they are not inevitable and may easily be lost.

Another avenue by which Lewis builds a bridge between the green woman and the human race is by detailing her transition from an alien

into someone recognizably close to being human. Lewis's training as
a linguist stands him in good stead here. In her innocent state, she is
simply not capable of learning words such as *pain* and *death*. Later,
Weston tries to teach her other terms as part of his strategy, but the
words that he chooses—*creative*, *intuition*, and *spiritual*, all catchwords
of the 1930s and 1940s, when the action takes place—are so alien to
her that she only laughs when she learns them.[8] The turning point in
her temptation comes when she learns, experientially, the meaning of
the term *fear*.[9] Ransom then knows that she cannot withstand Weston's
assault indefinitely and that some way must be found to stop it. Her
change in vocabulary is matched by an altered physical appearance.
When Ransom meets her, he is impressed by her strangeness. "There
was no category in the terrestrial mind which would fit her," he says.
"Opposites met in her and were fused in a fashion for which we have
no images."[10] Neither sacred nor profane art can do her justice; she
looks both like a goddess and like a Madonna. At the end of her siege
of temptation, however, Ransom comes to look upon her as a woman
with whom a human might conceivably fall in love.[11] For an instant,
Ransom sees her as one of his own kind, and the thought of what she
has lost horrifies him.

One identity between the green woman and the human race on which
Lewis trades is her childlikeness. To her, everything is new. Since she
was almost literally born yesterday, she has an appealing and often, to
Ransom, baffling naiveté; she is ignorant of things a four-year old human
would know perfectly well. Every minute in her discussions with humans she "grows older," as she puts it; indiscriminately, she turns to
Ransom or to Weston in her enthusiasm to become older as quickly as
possible.

She seems like a child, but she is not a child. Ransom's first impression of her utter strangeness is correct. Before a human child one may
feel wonder, but no child will convey the serenity and peace that the
green woman has. In an essay called "Religion and Rocketry," Lewis
once reflected on some of the issues raised for Christianity by the
existence of possible extraterrestrial beings, and he remarked that he
doubted our half-animal cunning would be able to overcome for long
the wisdom, selfless valor, and perfect unanimity of an innocent race.[12]
The green woman has this innocence, and it protects her from her
tempter's onslaughts time after time. A child also may have a certain
innocence, as it certainly has much ignorance; however, the child's

innocence is not the same kind of innocence that the green woman displays in her temptation, and the innocence she has after the temptation is something else again. As with Chtexa, therefore, the deeper one probes into the personality and language of the green woman, the further from everyday human examples she becomes. In the cases of both Chtexa and the green woman, an adroit artist has managed to make real to us personalities that are on the very boundary of human possibility or even—in the case of Chtexa—across that boundary.

But does it matter? Does it matter if these protagonists are humanly possible, so long as our imaginations can be lulled into suspension of disbelief? After all, these are only stories. The answer is that it does matter, at least in Lewis's case, just for the story to work. Chtexa does not have to be a human possibility for this to be a "case of conscience"; he only has to be a being whose possibility is plausible enough so the devil can spring his trap. But the green woman does have to be a human possibility if the plot of *Perelandra* is to take hold, and that is why Lewis lavishes such care on the portrait of his paradigm of innocence. Her gradual loss of innocence cannot be just the same as ours, but it is important for the impact of the story that the reader be able to see in the green woman's struggle part of the kind of moral battle in which each member of the human race, too, takes part.

Moreover, even apart from the story line, the theological side matters to both Lewis and Blish. These two are not alone among science fiction writers in using the medium as a way to discuss religious questions, but they must be near the top of the list in percentage of text devoted to straight theological debate. They love controversy, and the issues they take up in these two novels are among the most problematical that Christian theology has to offer. From the beginning, Roman Catholic and Protestant theology have been divided on the question of original innocence and original sin, and the opposing positions have hardened over the years.[13]

In view of this history, it is refreshing to see the context for the discussion moved from theology back to stories, the medium in which the issues were first raised. The Genesis account of Adam and Eve is, above all, a story, as the novels of Lewis and Blish are stories, and some aspects of such an account will appear cramped and out of place when the story format is eliminated. There are rules for the storyteller's art, but they are not the same as the rules for writing scholarly treatises. Whereas an academic analysis needs to be explicit and complete, a story only has to give some details, and the reader's imagination does the rest. In a story, as in life, the meaning of people's actions remains partly opaque to outsiders and even to themselves. Chtexa is an extreme example because he is of an alien race, for which the usual behavioral generalizations do not necessarily apply, but any character in a story is partially this way. The storyteller is a modest craftsman who is not ashamed of leaving descriptions incomplete and explanations fragmentary. That may be why the concept of Eden fits so well into stories but is so hard to set out in other terms. About matters from the dawn of human history or, insofar as Eden represents a general human situation rather than an historical account, about matters that deal with the nature of human life itself, we are grossly confused and ignorant. How could it be otherwise? No human being is in a position to pronounce the last word on such questions. Theology can do much to clarify and define issues, but even this boldest of the sciences has its limits. Perhaps that is the reason so many deeply religious people in every time have tended to leave the final resolution of these questions to God and have relied for the rest on the storyteller's modest art to make what sense out of them that could be made.

Perelandra itself provides a "story within a story" that illustrates just this point. In that novel, Ransom finds himself thrust into a crisis in which the only alternatives are to let the green woman's temptation continue indefinitely or else to murder Weston.[14] His first reaction is, why me? It seems absurd that a paunchy, middle-aged professor, who has been steadily failing in debate with a demonic power, should now be called upon to take center stage in the history of the planet and combat that power hand to hand. Then Ransom realizes that, although his role is critical, one could with equal justice give the central place to the woman, whose resistance thus far has been successful. Both are deciding the fate not only of Perelandra, but of a great cosmic plan that began long before each came into being and would continue long after Perelandra ceased. Yet, at the same time, neither of their roles is more central than that of countless others in the history of every planet. Every temptation is central, and every fall is a real loss. Later, in the final chapter of the novel, Ransom meets the two guardian eldila of Venus and Mars and asks them this question about the centrality of the Incarnation on earth. Their answer is the only fitting one—they tell a story. It would not be misleading to say they tell a science fiction story of the birth and death of worlds, although the antiphonal poetry in which the story is couched and the majestic sweep of the song transcends what one usually expects from that genre. Although a person would look in vain in this chapter for a conclusive answer to many perplexing questions about Earth and its destiny, its Eden and its Armageddon, the eldila's song gives an intellectual satisfaction of a powerful kind. It is by no means clear that we could comprehend the complete answers if we heard them. On such topics, there may be only one recourse—to tell a story.

NOTES

1. Many books have been written about C. S. Lewis. A major study is William Luther White's *The Image of Man in C. S. Lewis* (Nashville: Abingdon, 1969). A monthly newsletter is published containing discussions of Lewis's writings, *Bulletin of the New York C. S. Lewis Society* (466 Orange Street, New Haven, CT 06511). The April 1972 issue of *Fantasy and Science Fiction* magazine (volume 42, number 4) is devoted to James Blish and contains a bibliography of his works and a short biography.

2. James Blish, *A Case of Conscience* (New York: Ballantine, 1958), p. 103.

3. Ibid., p. 50.

4. Søren Kierkegaard, *The Concept of Anxiety: A Simple Psychologically Orienting Deliberation on the Dogmatic Issue of Hereditary Sin*, trans. Reidar Thomte (Princeton: Princeton University Press, 1980), p. 41.

5. Ninian Smart, "Omnipotence, Evil and Supermen," in Nelson Pike, ed., *God and Evil* (Englewood Cliffs, NJ: Prentice-Hall, 1964), p. 106.

6. Blish, *Case of Conscience*, pp. 77–78.

7. C. S. Lewis, *Perelandra* (New York: Macmillan, 1965), p. 68.

8. Ibid., p. 132.

9. Ibid., p. 136.

10. Ibid., p. 64.

11. Ibid., p. 135.

12. C. S. Lewis, "Religion and Rocketry," in *The World's Last Night and Other Essays* (New York: Harcourt Brace Jovanovich, 1973), p. 89.

13. A classic treatment is found in Reinhold Niebuhr's *Human Nature*, vol. 1 of *The Nature and Destiny of Man* (New York: Charles Scribner's Sons, 1964), pp. 241–300.

14. Lewis, *Perelandra*, chap. 11.

6

Augustinian Evil in C. S. Lewis's *Perelandra*

KATHERIN A. ROGERS

That there is evil in the world is one of the overwhelming facts of human existence. That evil affects everyone is a central idea of the Christian worldview. After all, God became man because people needed saving. But Christians also believe that the world and everything in it were made by God and are under his jurisdiction. One often hears it said that for every force or principle there must be an opposing one, that we could not know good if it were not for evil, and that good could not exist without evil. But the Christian cannot accept this view, the Manichaean heresy against which St. Augustine of Hippo, the greatest Christian philosopher, fought long and successfully.[1] The Christian believes that there is one ultimate principle—namely, God. God is perfectly good, everything he made was good when he made it, and he intends only good. Whence, then, is evil?

The solution that St. Augustine offered to this problem was generally adopted during the Middle Ages by thinkers in the Latin West. St. Anselm of Canterbury, the eleventh-century author of the famous "ontological" argument for the existence of God, accepts Augustine's theory of evil and, I would argue, improves upon it. Augustine and Anselm hold that moral evil comes not from God, but from the choices of free creatures. (Note that moral evil is distinguished from natural "evil." Hurricanes, tornadoes, diseases, and so forth can cause terrible difficulties for people, and hence can be called "evil," but a hurricane, most Christian thinkers would presume, is not wicked. It does not willfully disobey God.) As to the ontological status of evil, Augustine and Anselm believe that evil is "nothing." All things that exist come from God and, hence, are good. Evil is the perversion or the lack of a good that God intended for a creature. This may seem foolish. Obviously evil is something, else why would we hate and fear it? In fact, this view of evil is quite sophisticated and compelling; it is just hard to grasp. And that is where C. S. Lewis comes in.

In *Perelandra*, the second book of his space trilogy, Lewis paints a picture of the battle between good and evil. He describes Satan's attempt to corrupt the Adam and Eve of the planet Perelandra (Venus). As a Christian and a medievalist, Lewis was steeped in the Augustinian worldview. The way in which he portrays evil in *Perelandra* is clearly influenced by that worldview. By showing evil choices and evil characters in a narrative, Lewis makes the Augustinian theory understandable. He illustrates just how horrifying that nothingness which is evil really is.

There are four main questions about the Augustinian theory of evil that Lewis addresses in *Perelandra*. First, if evil is nothing, how can it be an object of choice? Second, why would anyone choose evil? The difficulties with answering this question are brought out especially clearly when the one choosing evil is free, as the Adam and Eve of Perelandra are free, from any previous corruption of sin. Third, what happens to one who chooses evil? Finally, why does God permit his creatures to make evil choices?

Anselm, following Augustine, explains that we do not choose evil because it is evil. We always choose either what is right or what we think will make us happy. Of course, if we were always clearly aware of the consequences of our actions, we would know that, in the final analysis, only right actions can make us happy, but we do not always keep this in mind. Sometimes we do what we know to be wrong, thinking that it will make us happy.[2] The object of our choice is never evil per se, for that would be nothing, but rather some good that God does not will us to choose. Anselm, in his treatise *The Fall of Satan*, explains that Satan sinned "by willing something beneficial, which he neither possessed nor was supposed to will at that time, even though it was able to increase his happiness." (That is, the beneficial thing could have increased his happiness if God had willed for Satan to choose it). By willing something that God did not want him to will, Satan willed to be God. He placed his own will above and in opposition to God's.[3]

This idea—that to sin is not to choose evil per se, but to choose the wrong good—is clearly expressed in *Perelandra*. Lewis examines two ways of willing the wrong good. One might cling to an old good, repeating and repeating it, flinching from any new good that God might offer. Or one might simply refuse the good that presents itself because one desires a different, and perhaps a lesser, good.

When Ransom arrives on Perelandra, he discovers a fruit so delicious that tasting it is like "the discovery of a totally new *genus* of pleasures." Yet he is reluctant to eat of the fruit after his thirst and hunger are assuaged.[4] He finds trees bearing bubbles that burst in a refreshing shower of sweet liquid. After his first experience of the almost ecstatic sensation, he again feels a reluctance to repeat the good. Ransom realizes that his reluctance points to "a principle of far wider application and deeper moment. This itch to have things over again, as if life were a film that could be unrolled twice or even made to work backwards. . .was it possibly the root of all evil?"[5]

When Satan arrives on Perelandra in the body of Ransom's old enemy Weston, Ransom tries to explain to the Green Lady about the sin of the fallen angel.

"You spoke yesterday, Lady, of clinging to the old good instead of taking the good that came."

"Yes—for a few heart-beats."

"There was an eldil [angel] who clung longer—who has been clinging since before the worlds were made."

"But the old good would cease to be a good at all if he did that."

"Yes. It has ceased. And still he clings.'"[6]

Clinging to a past good, insisting that it be repeated over and over, living in fear because that good might be lost, is one sort of sin. Lewis also speaks of the sin of desiring a good that is different from the good that is offered. The Green Lady explains it by speaking of having one kind of fruit in mind and finding another. There is a moment, she says, when you accept the fruit that is offered and put the image of the other fruit out of your mind. But if you wished, you might hold onto the image. "You could send your soul after the good you had expected, instead of turning it to the good you had got. You could refuse the real good; you could make the real fruit taste insipid by thinking of the other."[7]

Lewis illustrates the idea of choosing a lesser good in place of the greater good that one should choose when he has Ransom consider the desire of some to go to any lengths to ensure the survival of the species. Lewis calls this "a dream begotten by the hatred of death upon the fear of true immortality." Real death, self-negation, is the greatest evil and is rightly feared by all men. Immortality is certainly a great good. That men desire immortality is not evil, but they can desire the wrong sort of immortality. Man is offered an eternity of perfect joy in God's presence, but he turns from this, preferring the impersonal immortality of an everlasting succession of human generations. In striving to achieve this lesser good he will, Lewis says, be willing to commit acts that render him evil and so incapable of accepting the greater good, the good that was intended for all men.[8]

So Lewis, in the Augustinian tradition, holds that people do not choose evil per se. They could not, for evil is just a lack or perversion of some good. It is not any sort of "thing." But why would one choose the wrong good, that is, why would one do evil? It is not easy to explain why anyone would choose evil, and it is especially difficult to understand how a good being, not yet corrupted by sin, could choose it. St. Anselm tackles this very difficult problem in his dialogue, *The Fall of Satan*.

According to Anselm, all angels were created equally good. Some persevered in goodness, and some, like Satan, chose evil and fell. Could it be that God simply did not give Satan sufficient perseverance to hold fast to the good? Anselm will not accept this notion because then the fault for Satan's sin would lie with God. If God could have given Satan the same amount of perseverance that he gave to the good angels but simply chose not to, then the good angels can receive no credit for remaining good and Satan cannot be blamed for his failure to persevere. Anselm holds that Satan did not receive sufficient perseverance to hold fast to the good, but this was because when God offered him the perseverance he refused it.[9]

Perhaps the problem is that there was a weakness or a deficiency in Satan's will. Again Anselm must reject this solution. If Satan sinned through an inherent weakness, the fault must lie with God who created him with that weakness. Nor can one say that Satan's knowledge was deficient. He had the same amount as did the angels who remained good. Anselm holds that Satan was in every respect as capable of accepting perseverance and remaining good as were the good angels. But he chose to sin and they did not.[10]

In rejecting these possible solutions to why a good being would choose to sin, Anselm has, I think, improved on the view of his master, Augustine. Augustine will sometimes say that Adam and Satan fell because, being created from nothing, there was an inherent deficiency in them, a deficiency that caused them to sin. God could have extended the help they needed to persevere in the good, but he did not. God made them as they were and then withheld his help from them; consequently, though Augustine denies it, the real cause of Satan's and Adam's fall is God.[11]

The question remains, why did Satan will evil? Anselm finally says, "Only *because he willed*. For there was no other cause by which his will was in any way driven or drawn; but his will was both its own efficient cause and its own effect—if such a thing can be said!"[12]

In a way this is a very unsatisfactory answer. If there were no preceding causes, then Satan's fall seems unintelligible. Anselm seems to have answered the question, "Why did Satan sin?" by saying that one cannot ask the question—at least not in terms of what causes preceded the sin. One can explain what Satan hoped to gain by his disobedience, but one cannot say that anything but his willing caused him to sin. Although this answer seems unsatisfactory, it is really the only one possible. Any explanation that admits a cause preceding Satan's will must implicate God in Satan's sin.

The situation in *Perelandra* is not the same as in *The Fall of Satan*. It was Satan who "created" the spectrum of evil choices by committing the first sin. In *Perelandra* Satan is trying to spread corruption by tempting the Green Lady to place her own judgment above God's. Satan's arguments are designed to muddle her thinking and weaken her resistance to temptation. Thus, it might seem that, whereas Satan's fall must remain unintelligible, the fall of the Green Lady, had it occurred, would have been explicable; one could say that Satan caused it. But this is not quite right. If the evil choice were not truly the result of her own will, then it is hard to see how it could really be a sin. Satan can tempt her and lead her toward disobedience, but the final evil act must be truly her own. The problem of why the Green Lady would sin is really no easier to solve than the problem of why Satan sinned. And Lewis gives the same answer in her case as Anselm gave in the case of Satan. No reason can be given why she should sin, and yet she might. Ransom realizes that her purity and peace are

a balance maintained by a mind and therefore, at least in theory, able to be lost. There is no reason why a man on a smooth road should lose his balance on a bicycle; but he could. There was no reason why she should step out of her happiness into the psychology of our own race; but neither was there any wall between to prevent her doing so.[13]

So choosing sin is unintelligible. There can be no preceding causes for it. Of course, if rational beings are truly free, one can say the same of good choices. The difference is that, given a Christian universe, one can at least appreciate the rationale for being good, for that is the way to eternal joy. The evil choice is not only unintelligible, it seems crazy.

That there is something irrational about evil comes across clearly in Lewis's evil characters. Satan in Weston's body is a horrifying picture of what happens to a being who consistently chooses evil. Anselm and Augustine do not, so far as I know, address the question of what effect evil has on the one choosing it, besides, of course, some discussion of Hell. Nonetheless, their view that evil is a lack or a perversion clearly underlies Lewis's portrayal of evil. In fact, it is here that Lewis exhibits the real power of the Augustinian view.

Satan has taken possession of the body of a human being, Weston. This evil creature is thus a double negation. Weston has become a lack or a perversion of a man, a walking corpse with just a few scraps of decaying psyche still clinging to it. Ransom calls it the *Un-man*. And Satan, made by God to be supremely intelligent, to aid in the great work of creation, is a negation of the good angel he ought to have been. He has become a gibbering emptiness bent on mindless destruction.

Even the physical body of the Un-man is a negation of what a human body ought to be, for a human body ought to be the tool of a human soul. Though it is walking and talking, Weston's body looks like that of a dead man. Ransom is forced to realize that Weston is gone and that something else animates his body. Lewis emphasizes the gulf between the human body and its demonic inhabitant when he talks of how the Un-man moves.

The body did not reach its squatting position by the normal movements of a man: it was more as if some external force manoeuvred it into the right position and then let it drop. It was impossible to point to any particular motion which was definitely non-human. Ransom had the sense of watching an imitation of living motions which had been very well studied and was technically correct: but somehow it lacked the master touch.[14]

Weston's body has become a walking corpse, but the fate of his soul is even more terrifying. It has lost its rationality, lost all the traits that made it human. When Ransom glimpses Weston's spiritual remains, he realizes that Weston, a lost soul, is no longer a man at all. Over the years the will had poisoned the intellect, the affections, and finally itself, "and the whole psychic organism had fallen to pieces. Only a ghost was left—an everlasting unrest, a crumbling, a ruin, an odour of decay."[15]

But Weston was only a man to begin with and was already corrupted in the Fall of Adam and Eve. Satan was much more than a man, and so the negation of the good angel he ought to have been is that much more horrifying. The angels were created to be supremely rational beings. But Satan has abdicated reason. The Un-man is capable of cunning, but it uses intelligence only as a weapon, something external.[16]

In Lewis's universe (as in Augustine's), the angels have a special role to play, for it is through them that God creates. But Satan wants only to destroy. He is trying to destroy the Green Lady and her future children. When he is not with her, he will even tear the feathers off birds or uproot plants. No mutilation is too petty for him. Ransom first realizes what Weston has become when he finds the Un-man ripping open live frogs.[17]

Satan is a negation of what he ought to have been. He has become a mindless destroyer. Ransom realizes that the Un-man is "inside out. . . .On the surface, great designs and an antagonism to Heaven which involved the fate of worlds: but deep within, when every veil had been pierced, was there, after all, nothing but a black puerility, an aimless empty spitefulness. . . ?"[18]

So Lewis's Un-man is a perversion or negation in many ways. Weston's body has become a walking corpse. Weston's soul is a ruin, no longer human. Satan, who was created the best of angels, is a "furious self-exiled negation."[19] And what makes this picture of evil especially compelling is that irrationality, mindless destruction are precisely what characterize the genuinely evil men in the real world—the Hitlers and Stalins and Maos.

Of course, the effects of sin reach far beyond the sinner. Anselm goes so far as to say that a sinner "disturbs the order and beauty of the universe."[20] Lewis illustrates this idea when he has Ransom discover a mutilated frog.

On earth it would have been merely a nasty sight, but up to this moment Ransom had as yet seen nothing dead or spoiled in Perelandra, and it was like a blow in the face. . . . It was irrevocable. The milk-warm wind blowing over the golden sea, the blues and silvers and greens of the floating garden, the sky itself—all these had become, in one instant, merely the illuminated margin of a book whose text was the struggling little horror at his feet. . . .[21]

But if the effects of moral evil are so devastating, why does God permit it? Why did he make creatures capable of sin? One answer that Anselm gives in the case of the good angels is that, in order to merit the knowledge and happiness that God gave them, they must have refrained from sinning even though they could have sinned. So God's granting to the angels the real possibility of choosing evil was a great good, for it was what enabled them to gain merit through their own efforts. But if sin is a real possibility then some, like Satan, will choose it. Even so, it was better that the possibility should be there than that it should not.[22] (Augustine is not comfortable with this view because he feels it diminishes God's omnipotence that the good angels are able to improve themselves by their own efforts.)[23]

Another anwer, which can be nicely harmonized with the preceding one, is that God permits moral evil because he is able to bring good out of it. Both Anselm and Augustine accept this theory; the doctrine of the fortunate fall would be a classic illustration.

In *Perelandra*, these two reasons for God's allowing moral evil are woven together. The evil that Satan intends results in the great good that God planned for his people on Venus. Satan has taught the King and the Green Lady about evil that they may worship God more freely. They can better merit God's gifts because now they clearly recognize the kind of choice they are making when they choose to obey God. Furthermore, the Green Lady and the King have come to understand God's goodness better by seeing its opposite. (Though, of course, evil is not really the *opposite* of good. It is the perversion or the lack of good.) The King tells Ransom, "We have learned of evil, though not as the Evil One wished us to learn."[24] Thus, Lewis explains that, although God is in no way responsible for sin, he permits it for the time being so that he can bring good out of it.

In *Perelandra*, Lewis tackles many facets of the difficult problem of evil, and in doing so he brings to life what might have seemed to be just the dull hypotheses of long dead saints. Lewis's depiction of evil is powerful and frightening and forces one to take seriously the Augustinian theory that underlies it.

NOTES

1. Augustine's *Confessions* is largely the story of his struggle to free himself from Manichaeism. Book VII, section 2 offers a succinct refutation of the heresy.

2. St. Anselm of Canterbury, *On the Fall of Satan*, chaps. IV and XIII, in *Truth, Freedom and Evil: Three Philosophical Dialogues*, trans. and intro. by J. Hopkins and H. Richardson (New York: Harper and Row, Publishers, 1967).

3. *On the Fall of Satan*, chap. IV.

4. C. S. Lewis, *Perelandra* (New York: The Macmillan Company, 1944), p. 42.

5. Ibid., p. 48.

6. Ibid., p. 83.

7. Ibid., p. 69.

8. Ibid., p. 82.

9. *On the Fall of Satan*, chap. III.

10. *On the Fall of Satan*, chaps. III–IV.

11. See esp. Augustine's *The City of God*, book XII, viii–ix, and book XIV, xiii.

12. *On the Fall of Satan*, chap. XXVII.

13. *Perelandra*, p. 68.

14. Ibid., p. 122.

15. Ibid., p. 130.

16. Ibid., p. 128.

17. Ibid., p. 110.

18. Ibid., p. 123.

19. Ibid., p. 156.

20. St. Anselm of Canterbury, *Cur Deus Homo* in *Basic Writings*, trans. by S. N. Deane (La Salle, Ill.: Open Court Publishing Company, 1968), p. 209.

21. *Perelandra*, pp. 108–9.

22. *On the Fall of Satan*, chap. XVIII.

23. See *The City of God*, XII, ix.

24. *Perelandra*, p. 209.

7

Alien Ethics and Religion versus Fallen Mankind

DIANE PARKIN-SPEER

As a whole, science fiction is indifferent to Christianity and is optimistic in a secular, materialistic way. Indeed, some writers such as Robert A. Heinlein are explicitly and polemically opposed to the Judeo-Christian tradition. C. S. Lewis's well-known space trilogy is a notable exception as are James Blish's *A Case of Conscience* and Gordon Harris's *Apostle from Space*. These two novels explore the ethical and religious dilemmas faced by two clerical protagonists when they encounter alien beings and religions. Through the encounters of the Jesuit, Father Ruiz-Sanchez, and the Episcopalian, Father Winkler, with the inhabitants of Lithia and Elon, respectively, the reader is presented with some provocative insights into the nature of evil, the Fall, and the relation of each to an advanced technological society on Earth. Both Lithia and Elon are utopias in contrast to Earth society. With satire, both novels puncture the complacency and pride of twentieth-century secular optimism.

The underlying assumption of *A Case of Conscience* (1959) is the classic Christian definition of evil as the absence of good. Satan is the "Great Nothing."[1] This is the same assumption that undergirds C. S. Lewis's more famous space trilogy. But Blish, through his protagonist Father Ruiz-Sanchez, presents a form of the Manichaean heresy in which Satan is coequal with God in power and creative ability. The Jesuit falls into the heresy because of the Eden-like qualities of the planet Lithia and the utopian nature of the Lithians' civilization. Father Ruiz-Sanchez explains his view to his companions as they tape their recommendations to the U.N. committee. The priest characterizes the Lithian as follows:

> This creature is rational. It conforms, as if naturally and without constraint or guidance, to the highest ethical code we have evolved on Earth. It needs no laws to enforce this code. . . . There are no criminals, no deviates, no aberrations of any kind. The people are not standardized. . . . They choose their own life courses without constraint—yet somehow no antisocial act of any kind is ever committed. There isn't even any word for such an act in the Lithian language.[2]

The Lithians have no nations and, therefore, do not suffer the divisive effects of nationalism, including war. They are so rational that they have no myths, superstitions, or religion, yet they possess their high moral code.[3] Their very rational perfection without faith is what proves to Father Ruiz-Sanchez that Satan is using this world to tempt and damn humankind by showing that a utopia is possible without God and that goodness and happiness can be achieved by every individual without belief in God.[4] Michelis, the chemist, immediately recognizes that the priest is guilty of the Manichaean heresy because he has concluded from studying Lithia that Satan, "the Adversary," is "creative." This recognition by his friend increases the guilt and suffering of the Jesuit.[5] Apparently, Blish shares Tertullian's extreme view that faith is irrational or nonrational.

We might fruitfully compare the rational societies of More's *Utopia* and Swift's Houyhnhnms in part 4 of *Gulliver's Travels*. More's Utopians are eminently rational, yet they believe in a supreme being and the immortality of the soul. When Ralph Hythloday and his companions introduce the Utopians to Christianity, they immediately embrace it. Swift's intelligent horses are closer to Blish's Lithians since they, too, are completely rational and have no belief in God though they have a high moral code based on universal benevolence and friendship. Their natural adaptation to their land is similar to the Lithian's close relationship with their planet in which their electrostatic advanced technology harmonizes with nature rather than destroying it.[6] Obviously, all three writers are using their respective rational, utopian societies to satirize the irrational failure and wickedness of human society. But More seemingly shares the Christian humanist optimism that faith and reason harmonize as in the Renaissance formulation of "right reason," reason leading to ethical perception and action. Swift, the churchman,

believes man is incapable of living as rationally as the Houyhnhnms
and thinks this may be a good thing. Swift still maintains, however,
that humans should be more rational and are capable of being so.
In Blish's novel, as a result of his heretical views, Father Ruiz-
Sanchez is summoned to Rome by Pope Hadrian VIII. The Jesuit is
commissioned by the Pope to exorcize the planet.[7] Hadrian believes
with the Jesuit that Lithia is satanic, but firmly denies that the planet
shows the Adversary's "creativity." Father Ruiz-Sanchez is appalled
at the prospect of destroying the Lithians and their culture by an exorcism.[8]

Now let us turn to the denouement and examine the implications of
it for the portrayal of the nature of evil. The Jesuit is still torn with
doubt. On the one hand, as a casuist, he believes that Satan is "not
creative, except in the sense that he always seeks evil and always does
good."[9] Cleaver, the Jesuit's former associate, "was putting his hand
in the Adversary's service tottering on the edge of undoing all his work.
The staff of Tannhauser had blossomed: *These fruits are shaken from
the wrath-bearing tree.*"[10] But the priest is tormented just as he begins
to recite the words of the exorcism: "Suppose, just suppose, that Lithia
were Eden, and that the Earth-bred Lithian who had just returned there
were the Serpent foreordained for it? *Suppose it always happened that
way, world without end?*"[11] Immediately after the words of the exorcism, the human watchers see, through the lunar telescope, the planet
explode into a nova whose flash of light destroys Henri Petard's advanced telescope.[12] The denouement implies that evil is inherently negative and self-destructive. Cleaver, an agent of Satan, had hoped to turn
the planet into a weapon, and with his faulty physics, he had inad-
vertently used the chemical composition of the planet to explode it.
This cataclysmic destruction of evil by evil is similar to the ending of
Lewis's *That Hideous Strength*. Blish implies in *A Case of Conscience*
that the timing of Cleaver's experiment with the exorcism expresses
God's providence and omnipotence without negating human free will.
Through the free actions of two flawed human instruments, the excom-
municated, heretical priest and the warmonger scientist, an evil threat
to the souls of humankind was destroyed. God is a stern enforcer of
justice in the universe. Yet the reader shares with Father Ruiz-Sanchez
the grief that a fascinating race of beings, their culture, and planet have
been destroyed. The ending of the novel is both intellectually and emotionally disturbing. Only half facetiously, in a glance at the fashionable
reader-response criticsm, I might say, echoing Stanley Fish, that the

reader is "surprised by sin." Blish has made a modern version of Manichaeism very tempting while, at the same time, he has provided the corrective for the heresy.

Connected closely with the presentation of the nature of evil is, of course, humanity's Fallen nature and thus a flawed technology which leads to anomie and mass psychosis. Father Ruiz-Sanchez flirts with the idea that the Lithians are unfallen beings without the "terrible burden of original sin."[13] Their technology and culture work with nature rather than against it. By damning contrast, Earth technology and the culture it has created are unnatural and destructive of the human psyche. As a result of the nuclear arms race in the last part of the twentieth century, almost all humans live underground in "Shelter" cities. For example, the megalopolis of twenty-first century Manhattan is a "self-sufficient,"[14] closed system with recycling carried to a sophisticated extreme. However, the underground prosperity and civilization are fragile. Youth gangs roam the underground passages seeking pleasure. The morbidity and anomie affect all age groups, and the upper classes are especially prone to blind, unsatisfying hedonism. The long episode of the party given by the Countess d'Averoigne to celebrate the Lithian Egtverchi's citizenship in book two demonstrates the decadence of the "Shelter" culture.[15] Mental illness afflicts a growing portion of the society. "Apparently nearly a third of twenty-first century society loathed that society from the bottom of its collective heart."[16] Egtverchi's popular 3-V network program heightens the discontent and provides the flash point for insane riots, "the beast Chaos." The U.N. police are virtually helpless for three days.[17] Interplanetary travel has ushered in not a utopian age on Earth, but the sense of a needed new frontier. Fallen humans are trapped literally and figuratively in their self-created hell that brings death and insanity. And from the physicist Cleaver's activities on Lithia, the reader concludes that the nature-destroying human hell will spread through the universe. Earth civilization illustrates all too well the truism, "the wages of sin is death." No wonder that Father Ruiz-Sanchez concludes during the riot that "it was the God of Job who was abroad in the world now, not the God of the Psalmist or the Christ . . . the God Who made hell before He made man, because He knew that He would have need of it. That terrible truth Dante had written down."[18]

In *A Case of Conscience*, fallen humans are by definition incapable of creating a life-giving and supporting society. High technology provides no panacea. Indeed, high technology just makes possible a greater expansion of death to the human spirit and psychology. A stern Calvinist such as Jonathan Edwards would be satisfied with the novel's portrayal of the depravity of man and Jahweh's just vengeance. Both the explicit and the implicit portrayal of the theological concept of the Fall gives the novel a rigorous intellectual structure that unifies diverse plot episodes, the development of the main characters, both human and Lithian, and the planetary settings. The satire of human aspirations and their defeat in practice would have pleased Swift at his most pessimistic.

But, is there any countervision to the relentless, devastating portrayal of evil's power and human depravity? There is, first, the stern *magisterium* of the Catholic church. This order-giving institution provides the centuries-old traditional system of Christian doctrine, the order of both St. Augustine and St. Thomas Aquinas. Yet this order and guide to faith and ethics also is the inventor of the Index of Forbidden Books. When the novel opens, the Jesuit casuist is puzzling over an ethical problem posed by James Joyce in *Finnegan's Wake*. The work is on the Index, but Father Ruiz-Sanchez has special permission to study it.[19]

A second element of the novel that mitigates its pessimisim is the very personality of the Jesuit protagonist. He is a thoroughly appealing and sympathetic character. Blish presents him as a loving, tolerant person with clarity of thought and ethical fervor. He is on occasion filled with doubt as he slips into heresy, but the basic commitment to Christian thought and values remains as a witness to the sacred. One of the most striking examples of this occurs near the end of the novel as Father Ruiz-Sanchez considers the exorcism. If it is successful, Cleaver and his human companions will die unshriven. Throughout the novel, Cleaver is an enemy of the values to which Father Ruiz-Sanchez has devoted his life, but ultimately the priest shrinks from causing his damnation.[20]

Still the pessimism of the novel cannot be ignored. To do so would distort this profoundly disturbing work. Blish is questioning and wants his readers to question the comfortable post-Enlightenment secular optimism that believes in progress—not only technologically, but also morally—the optimism of those who believe the human condition is infinitely improvable if humans just try harder and harder. Blish wants to force his readers to recognize the power of evil, its cunning and attraction, and the illusion of hedonism.

A Case of Conscience, however, offers illusory black-white choices

that are logically flawed: reason or faith, submission to a papal authority
or the destruction of civilization, the destruction of life or damnation,
theological dualism or materialistic hedonism.[21] By contrast, Gordon
Harris in *Apostle from Space* (1978) envisions a universe in which reason
and faith harmonize and progress is attainable by sentient beings through
obedience to the divine law of love. This less widely known but also
provocative novel critically examines modern man's society and technology in the context of universe-wide Christian faith. In the foreword,
Harris flatly states that Earth will be visited by an extraterrestrial being.
The novel is to deal with two questions: Would God's other creatures
be in "his image," and how would humans react to the first contact
from outer space?[22] The novel, however, is not so programmatic as the
foreword would indicate. With a satiric perspective, it calls into question
twentieth-century pride in technological mastery and exposes the frag-
mented nature of human institutions that result from the Fall.

   Like *A Case of Conscience*, Harris's novel focuses on a devout and
ethically sensitive cleric, in this instance, the Reverend Jonathan Winkler, an Episcopal priest in Cocoa Beach, Florida, near Cape Canaveral.
At the beginning of the novel, after an exhausting vestry meeting, Father
Winkler goes to pray in his church and encounters the extraterrestrial
investigator from the planet Elon whom he names Peter. The emissary
was drawn to St. David's church because of his familiarity with the
symbol of the cross. Denying nationalistic security considerations, Father
Winkler conceals Peter's existence and whereabouts from the military,
the CIA, and the FBI. His religious superior, Bishop Tomlin, cooperates
in evading the claims of secular authority until he can arrange an appropriate disclosure to the president that Peter is investigating whether
human space ventures are peacefully intended. The president and his
advisers become convinced that Peter is truly an alien being who, amaz-
ingly, shares the terrestrial Christian faith. At a monastery in Wisconsin
and on a tour of U.S. space facilities, Peter is given a crash course in
English and Earth's technology and culture in preparation for the disclosure of his existence to the world and an address he will give to a
combined session of the U.S. Congress and the United Nations. Father
Winkler is torn between his duty to his parish and to be a companion
and teacher to Peter. The emissary's extrasensory perception of the
identity of a terrorist assassin saves the life of the president. Peter's
address to the combined assembly is the final revelation of the technological, cultural, and religious superiority of Elon and the other in-

habited worlds over humankind. Returning secretly to Elon, he leaves a chastened Earth whose pride has been exposed.

Apostle from Space is set in the early 1970s, the time of Apollo 16; evil as it is revealed in the novel is mundane, all too familiar. There is no cosmic dualism as in *A Case of Conscience*. Evil is what separates individuals, producing fragmentation and suspicion when Christian love is absent. The first ominous note is that the FBI has a file on Father Winkler, an eminently respectable cleric.[23] Why does the government keep files on ordinary citizens uninvolved in criminal or subversive activities? In investigating the radar sighting of Peter's ship and its traces of radiation, bitter competition emerges between the FBI and the CIA.[24] The jurisdiction of the Air Force and Florida National Guard must also be juggled.[25] In the president's circle, expediency and paranoia dominate. Tony Jackson, the president's political hatchet man, sees Peter merely as insurance for re-election—if he is truly from space.[26] The Secretary of Defense, Lloyd Reynolds, is only interested in Elon technology in order to advance the United States over the other major powers, namely Russia and China.[27] The CIA Director, Miller, cannot believe that Peter's mission is peaceful; he envisions a fleet of alien spaceships ready to invade Earth.[28] A prominent political backer, Pierre Delacourt, argues against Peter addressing a joint session of Congress and the United Nations.[29] If the emissary is a fraud, the president's political future is dim; if he is genuine, his intention may be to enslave the Earth. In his egocentrism, Delacourt never sees the incongruity of jumping, in one breath, from narrow political considerations to a doomsday vision. Even after Peter's tour of the space facilities and his conclusion that Earth lacks the technology to threaten the other peaceful worlds, CIA Director Miller cannot conceive that the Elons would not launch a first strike against Earth if Earth became a real space power.[30]

During Peter's education at the monastery and on the tour of the U.S. space facilities, the CIA manages to have him spied upon, hoping for any information to unlock the secret of Elon technological superiority. Only the president is able to rise above self-interest, provinciality, and paranoia with a serene vision based on faith and prayer.[31] On the international scene, self-interest and expediency also dominate. In crass fashion, Peter's visit is commercialized and thereby reduced in importance to the visit of a popular idol.[32] International power blocs remain locked in their own rhetoric. At the United Nations, the Russians, other communists, and third world representatives portray Peter as imprisoned by a capitalist state bent on immersing him "in capitalist religious propaganda that would turn him against popular movements."[33] The portrayal of alienation and fragmentation in response to the emissary demonstrates the pervasive influence of evil.

Harris's conception of whether the Fall is universe-wide and its effects on other planets is not very clear. The Elon received a prophecy of the incarnation, crucifixion, and resurrection of Christ. Because of the union of the infinite with the finite in Christ (a *hypostatic union*), one sacrifice is sufficient for the whole universe. Peter explains to the brothers at the monastery that Christ gave his life "for all creatures here, on Elon and other planets I have visited, and others we have never seen."[34] Apparently, some type of Fall is universal, but its effects are not as pronounced nor as severe on other planets. Christ's incarnation would not be necessary for all beings throughout the universe if a Fall were not universal in some sense. Harris's failure to clarify this major theological point weakens the intellectual structure of the novel. The explanation for the technological and moral advancement of Elon over Earth is superior obedience to the Creator's will. On Elon the Creator has spoken recently as well as in the past. Peter explains to Abbot Faircloth: "From His messages which we preserved and can hear at any time, our society developed the plan for its organization and preservation. We did this in obedience to His will. For us, His words are the law. You make laws."[35] The Elons are in an analogous position to the Old Testament Hebrews; their society is directly based on revelation. Making their own laws would be unnecessary and perverse. Elon society and technology are more advanced scientifically and ethically because with free will they have chosen to obey; humankind, blinded by pride, makes unnatural laws. Peter defines evil as "doing harm to others. We have experienced that in our planet and elsewhere. It is disobedience to His law and we eliminate it at once."[36]

This emphasis on obedience is orthodox Christian doctrine. While Harris did not take the breathtaking leap that C. S. Lewis did in *Perelandra*—namely, that the Fall did not occur on another planet—he posits that a superior technology and paranormal capacities would result from fuller obedience to God. Peter is telepathic and has telekinetic abilities that he demonstrates to the school children who visit the monastery. With the aid of unspecified waves, he is able to look at some paper, causing it to ignite, and to read one of the children's thoughts. By telepathy, he is able to identify the pro-Palestinian would-be assassin of the president. Peter's cap and body suit protect him from Earth microorganisms.[37] The Elon control the weather; there are no extremes of hot or cold or seasons because long ago they learned to "manage the relationship" between their sun and planet, keeping the sun at a constant distance.[38]

At the joint U.N. and congressional session, with the aid of his spacesuit Peter projects a huge picture on the wall of seven Elon elders who can observe the meeting.[39] His speech is a devastating critique of the limitations of an Earth technology based on using nonrenewable resources rather than, as on Elon, "light, heat and water replenished by rain."[40] He indicts the hypocrisy of humankind in prating of peace and freedom while making war and enslaving others. On Elon, individuals have freedom as long as everyone benefits; on Earth, however, people struggle for power to benefit a few. In a stroke worthy of Swift, Harris demolishes the pride of the human race: "We cannot believe that you are ready to join other peoples of His universe. I came in His name. I leave with a prayer that you will come to accept His will. When you do, we will return to help."[41] Human pride has led to a flawed technology that destroys the great material gifts that the Creator has bestowed on the earth. In addition, human competitiveness, another result of pride, disqualifies the Earth from joining the fellowship of the other planets, for they "share progress" without competition, since the Elon and other planets all live at peace.[42] Harris provides a sobering corrective to the Enlightenment vision of progress through secular science. Only an inferior, destructive science is ostensibly value free and neutral. Secular humanism tied to scientific progress is a dead end. Present science is unnatural; it is not in true harmony with universal law. Humanity's greatest capacities to develop the world and realize its highest potential including paranormal abilities can only be achieved in the context of acknowledging a divinely ordered universe and carrying out an unselfish stewardship of the plenitude of a divinely created earth. Harris holds out a vision of progress achieved through a reasonable faith that is superior to secular humanism.

In satirizing the hollowness of humanity's achievements, represented by the successful Apollo space program, Harris adapts and blends the techniques of Swift and More. Peter functions in the novel as a composite Gulliver/Hythloday figure. Like Gulliver, we follow Peter's difficult task of learning about a society and culture radically different from his own, except Peter's difficulty in understanding Earth unequivocally arises from his intellectual and moral superiority. His tutors, English professor Lawrence D'Agostino and Aileen Mullen, associate professor of History and Economics, find him a superior student, but he has difficulty with the multiple meanings of English words. From his rational standpoint he cannot understand why the language has been allowed to develop into such a confusing mode of communication; his solution would be to form different words for the multiple meanings of one term.[43] He sees and judges with the simplicity of reason. Aileen's explanation of the international power blocs and their competition is labored and unclear compared to Peter's explanation of his unitary world, untroubled by competition, nationalism, and diversity of religions. No word exists for the concept of competition on Elon, thus, Peter and the Elders on Elon, who are chosen by merit alone, have difficulty understanding Earth.[44] Like More's traveler Hythloday, Peter brings news of the existence of other, healthier cultural assumptions, in their case based on a universe-wide Christianity. Seen with the clarity and simplicity of Peter's broader perspective, the murderous tangle of Earth power politics seems tragically absurd. Peter's statement that he will "ask Him to help me understand"[45] is not simplistic or childish; it is an affirmation of a living faith in its clear simplicity.

Whereas in *A Case of Conscience* the earthly church is a rigid, hierarchical institution demanding absolute obedience, the interstellar Christianity of Elon needs no separate organization, no priesthood or hierarchy because divine revelation is continuously available to every person, and all aspects of the culture harmonize with divine revelation. No unnatural separation exists, as it does on Earth, between the secular and sacred. Elon is a theocracy without a church organization per se; thus, Peter finds the multiplicity of Earth religions and Christian denominations at first incomprehensible and unreasonable.[46] Harris avoids the authoritarianism of Blish's novel.

Whereas both Blish and Harris present dismaying portraits of humanity gone astray because of the Fall and the resultant triumph of secularism, Harris avoids the pessimistic dualism of Blish. The alien Egtverchi's corruption on Earth and the destruction of the Eden-like Lithia create an unremittingly pessimistic outlook. On the other hand, although Harris portrays the bankruptcy of secular humanism and science in the twentieth century, his novel ends on a cautiously optimistic note with the presentation of a divinely ordered universe within which humanity may evolve materially and mentally if, as Bishop Tomlin observes at the end of the novel, humans will obey God.[47] Harris's monism and his belief in the omnipotence of God enable him to present a reasonable faith. Both novels are explicitly didactic or ideological as are many other science fiction works. These novels provide a religious perspective from which to view scientific achievement and secular culture, calling into question twentieth-century pride. *A Case of Conscience* and *Apostle from Space* are prophetic novels, prophetic in the sense of ethical fervor and vision, not crystal-ball gazing. They are moving engagements with the dangerous dilemmas of both our own time and the future.

NOTES

1. James Blish, *A Case of Conscience* (New York: Ballantine Books, 1979), p. 153.
2. Ibid., p. 70.
3. Ibid., *A Case*, pp. 72–73.
4. Ibid., *A Case*, pp. 78–80. Blish stated in the foreword to the first edition of *A Case of Conscience* (London: Faber and Faber, 1959) that he was "an agnostic with no position at all in these matters. It was my intention to write about a man, not a body of doctrine" (p. 7). I believe Blish is rather ingenuous in the foreword; inevitably, the reader becomes engaged with the doctrine *and* the man, Father Ruiz-Sanchez. For discussions of the relation of Blish's beliefs to his novels, see Bob Rickard, "*After Such Knowledge*: James Blish's Tetralogy," in Cy Chauvin, ed., *A Multitude of Visions* (Baltimore: T. K. Graphics, 1975), pp. 24–34; Brian M. Stableford, "The Science Fiction of James Blish," *Foundation: Review of Science Fiction* 13 (1978): 12–43; and idem, *A Clash of Symbols* (San Bernardino, Calif.: The Borgo Press, 1979).
5. Blish, *A Case*, pp. 78–79.
6. Ibid., pp. 13, 19–20, 39.
7. Ibid., pp. 150–53.
8. Ibid., pp. 152–53.
9. Ibid., p. 178.
10. Ibid., pp. 179–80. Blish's italics.
11. Ibid., p. 179. Blish's italics.
12. Ibid., p. 180.
13. Ibid., p. 38.
14. Ibid., pp. 91–92.
15. Ibid., pp. 105–25.
16. Ibid., p. 153.
17. Ibid., p. 166.

18. Ibid., p. 170.
19. Ibid., pp. 7–8, 80.
20. Ibid., p. 163.
21. For different views of the novel see: Jo Allen Bradham, "The Case in James Blish's *A Case of Conscience*," *Extrapolation* (Dec. 1974): 67–80; Robert Reilly, "The Discerning Conscience," ibid. (May 1977): 176–80; and David Ketterer, "Covering *A Case of Conscience*," *Science Fiction Studies* (July 1982): 195–214.
22. Gordon Harris, *Apostle from Space* (Plainfield, N.J.: Logos International, 1978), p. v.
23. Ibid., p. 25.
24. Ibid., pp. 28–29.
25. Ibid., p. 42.
26. Ibid., pp. 66–67.
27. Ibid., p. 85–86.
28. Ibid., p. 86.
29. Ibid., p. 126.
30. Ibid., p. 169.
31. Ibid., pp. 126–27.
32. Ibid., pp. 105–6.
33. Ibid., pp. 109, 113.
34. Ibid., p. 157.
35. Ibid., p. 134.
36. Ibid., p. 157.
37. Ibid., pp. 154, 156, 179.
38. Ibid., p. 155.
39. Ibid., p. 181.
40. Ibid., p. 182.
41. Ibid., pp. 182–83.
42. Ibid., p. 154.
43. Ibid., pp. 119–20.
44. Ibid., pp. 167–68.
45. Ibid., p. 168.
46. Ibid., pp. 75, 168.
47. Ibid., p. 186.

PART III

MAJOR AUTHORS: INDIVIDUALIZED TREATMENTS OF RELIGION

8

Philip K. Dick's Answers to the Eternal Riddles

PATRICIA S. WARRICK

What is the origin of the physical universe? From what is it made? What laws or uniformities are everywhere present in nature? For centuries, these questions have tantalized the mind of the person given to metaphysical speculation. Philip K. Dick is one such person. He has read the answers of men like Parmenides, Plotinus, Spinoza, and Hegel and found them only partially satisfactory.

Dick asks more questions: Is knowledge of reality possible? How much of what we think we know about nature is really an objective part of it, and how much is contributed by the human mind? He turns to epistemology and reads men like Democritus, Plato, and Kant.

The questions continue. What is the nature of God? How can we explain suffering and death? Now he turns to theology, reading Judaic, Christian, Hindu, and Taoist tracts.

He is interested in all the answers he finds, but they leave him dissatisfied. So he decides to develop his own cosmogony and give it expression in the form of the science fiction novel. Does this sound impossible? Mad? Dick's answer is: Yes, but I'll do it anyway. The result is a pair of novels published in 1981 that are unlike anything he has previously written. *Valis* and *The Divine Invasion* will delight, shock, or irritate Dick's readers. They will not fulfill the expectations of those readers who are looking for more fiction in the mode of his great works—*The Man in High Castle, Martian Time Slip, and Dr.*

Bloodmoney—written in the 1960s. After a long period of relative silence in the 1970s, he again began writing and this fiction is so different from anything he has written that we can best identify it as announcing a third stage in his writing, one of radical experimentation. In his first period, in the early 1950s, he wrote a substantial body of short stories. His second period, the 1960s, yielded nineteen novels, five or six of which have become classics.

The topics he treated in his fiction during those two periods gained him a reputation as a writer of political and social science fiction. Thus, his concern with religious themes seems at first surprising. Is it the result of his devastating experiences in the drug culture that eventually led him to two suicide attempts? Are we to take seriously his visionary experience in March 1974? Charles Platt interviewed Dick in 1979, and his discussion in *The Dream Makers* of Dick's theophany is thoughtful and perceptive.[1]

My purpose in this essay is to examine Dick's fiction, not to seek biographical sources for the ideas appearing in the novels. I will not, therefore, attempt to establish connections between the events in the novels and those in his personal life except to comment that for Dick his mystical experiences are of the utmost significance.

Dick's theophany seems, at first glance, to have changed the nature of his fiction. But actually, a careful reader of Dick's extensive body of works can find seeds for the ideas that emerge in *Valis* and *The Divine Invasion* scattered throughout his fiction, in both the first and the second periods. For example, in the very early short story, "The World She Wanted" (1953), the protagonist speculates about the nature of reality and concludes that it is a private thing for each person. Dick wrote another interesting story the next year—"Jon's World," a time-travel story. It describes a disturbed child who has visions of a land in which there are green grass, fields, and people living peacefully. His vision is a sharp contrast to the war-devastated world in which he actually lives. The protagonist, Kastner, time travels to a future that grew from a past in which the bomb and other destructive devices had not been invented. This future is like Jon's beautiful vision. Kastner, fascinated with the possibilities he suddenly conceives, realizes:

This opens up whole new lines of speculation. The mystical visions of medieval saints. Perhaps they were of other futures, other time flows. Visions of heaven would be better time flows. Ours must stand some place in the middle. And the vision of the eternal unchanging world. Perhaps that's an awareness of non-time. Not another world but this world, seen outside time. We'll have to think more about that, too.

He concludes: "Let's go find some people. So we can begin discussing things. Metaphysical things. . . . I always did like metaphysical things."[2]

Philip K. Dick did think more about time and change and reality and illusion. He kept grappling, too, with the problem of evil and death. His metaphysical speculations wove through many of his novels when he turned to writing almost exclusively in that form in 1955. *The Cosmic Puppets* (1957) pictures alternative versions of reality and the struggle of Ormazd, the cosmic constructive power, against Ahriman, the de-constructor. *The Three Stigmata of Palmer Eldritch* (1964) and *Galactic Pot-Healer* (1969) also explore the question of evil in the cosmos.

Religious visionaries appeared regularly in the novels: for instance, Ignatz Ledebur in *Clans of the Alpha Moon* (1964) and Anarch Peak in *Counter-Clock World* (1967). By the end of the 1960s, death, both physical and spiritual, became almost an obsession. In a single year, 1969, Dick published three novels probing the subject—*Ubik*, *Galactic Pot-Healer*, and *A Maze of Death*. The approach of each novel to death was very different. Dick has a restless mind that seems to become bored very rapidly with any imaginary reality he creates in a novel; he never repeats himself. Over his long writing career, he has remained intrigued with the same subjects, but the answers he gives to the questions he raises on these subjects are never the same. His mind is constantly in motion.

In the 1970s, Dick began to receive considerable recognition from the critics. *Science Fiction Studies* devoted an entire issue to his fiction in 1975. But criticism focused primarily on his political interests and ideologies. Dick, if asked, would probably have disclaimed an allegiance to any ideology, but he is a quiet withdrawn man who chose not to argue with his critics. An occasional sensitive reader did recognize his deepest interests. Ursula K. LeGuin wrote in 1976: "The fact that what Dick is entertaining us about is reality and madness, time and death, sin and salvation—this has escaped most critics. Nobody notices that we have our own homegrown Borges, and have had him for thirty years."[3]

The reader of *Valis* and *The Divine Invasion* cannot fail to notice that both are about nothing else but reality and madness, time and death, and salvation. I have omitted sin from the list because it does not play a significant part in Dick's theology.

THE PATTERN STRUCTURING *VALIS* AND *THE DIVINE INVASION*

At first glance, the two novels appear very dissimilar. They share only a concern with discovering gnosis or knowledge about the nature of God and the cosmos. However, appearances are never to be trusted. This is a fundamental premise with Dick. The reader must never forget it when struggling to understand his fiction. Nothing ever turns out to be what we had assumed when we first encountered it.

Thoughtful reflection and study of the two texts will finally reveal the pattern uniting them into a single work. In summary, *Valis* portrays an anguished mind (Horselover Fat's mind) that has encountered God in a theophany. He then attempts, through reason and the intellectual process, to understand his theophany and the nature of God. After failing, Fat abandons the use of reason to build a theoretical construct explaining God's nature. In the second half of the novel, he sets out in search of the Savior. His quest succeeds briefly, but the Savior is accidently killed. As the novel ends, he is still searching to understand his theophany.

The Divine Invasion continues the story of man's encounter with God, but in this novel God seeks out man. The protagonist, Herb Asher, has fallen into a lethargy that is near spiritual death. God appears and orders Herb to assume a part in the Second Coming of the Lord. During their journey to Earth, the mother is killed, and both Herb and the divine child Emmanuel are injured; the wounds destroy their knowledge of their pasts. Only anamnesis, or recovery of what they already knew, will allow them to heal the wounds and understand who they really are. What they have forgotten and thus lost is the female aspect of the divine. The novel traces their journeys of self-discovery. They are guided in their quests by Zina, a divine presence who gives them clues. The novel concludes as Herb and Emmanuel finally awaken to, and thereby recover, their true androgynous natures. They become their own saviors, healed by their own efforts.

To briefly summarize the novels thus seems almost dishonest intellectually, suggesting, as it does, that easy comprehension is possible. Not so. The two novels are an intricate and complex maze barring any but the most determined from penetrating to the secret at the center. Dick constantly uses paradox, contradictions and reversals. His method is a dialectic of the imagination. He creates an image of assertion and then deserts it as he creates an image portraying a counterassertion. Additionally, the novels are as full of allusions—literary, philosophical, theological, mythological, musical—as the heavens are bright with stars on a clear summer night. Dick's erudition is impressive. Yet he uses the language of the vernacular to express his ideas. It is a strange combination—Gnostic theology discussed in California street language. This is the unique world of Dick—intellectual madness.

Let us push past the fascinating complexities and explore in more detail the pattern of meaning dramatized in each novel. *Valis* pictures a mind driven almost to madness by its encounter with death—not any death, but death in its most inexplicable form, death of the young. First Gloria, a young woman who is apparently lucid and rational, commits suicide. Later Sherri, another young woman, dies from cancer. Phil Dick the writer is one of the major characters in the novel. He cannot understand or accept either of these deaths and becomes suicidal himself. (We need to remember that Phil Dick is a *persona*, a character in the novel *Valis*. He should not be confused with author Philip K. Dick who is writing the novel.)

Then God reveals himself to Phil in a theophany—an hours-long ecnounter signaled by a strange pink light. The God so revealed is called Zebra and then later in the novel Valis (Vast Active Living Intelligence System). Phil's sanity is wounded by the theophany. How is an intelligent, rational man to understand such a theophany? The first nine chapters of *Valis* dramatize Phil's struggle against madness in the face of an experience that violates reason. Or is his theophany a sign that he is already mad? He is uncertain. Phil's method of coping with his crisis is to split out or project the mind that has experienced the theophany into a character named Horselover Fat. Fat's is a restless, inquiring mind obsessed with the need to understand intellectually his revelation. Phil Dick the writer gains objectivity by maintaining a distance from Fat. He listens to Fat's endless arguments and theories but he refrains generally from making a judgment. He does occasionally comment that he thinks Fat is crazy.

We have not finished with the splitting of characters. In the novel, Phil Dick the writer split himself into two. Author Philip K. Dick doubles the number and constructs a cast of four characters who are best understood as a dramatization of the inner state of a single mind. The first two characters, as we have noted, are Fat and Phil Dick. The others are Kevin, a nihilist who argues against the possibility of finding meaning in the universe, and David, who expresses the establishment position of the good Catholic. The four men endlessly debate theological questions. Primary are the questions of how one is to understand suffering and illness and death. The position from which each argues allows author Dick to cover the range of possible answers to these questions. Fat provides the energy that fires the discussions. He constantly adds fuel to the debate by tossing in passages from his private exegesis. David, the orthodox believer, and Kevin, the atheist, always attack the validity of the exegesis. Phil Dick is suspicious of its validity but generally withholds judgement.

The reader of the first nine chapters of *Valis* has become involved in a fascinating process of infinite regress. At the heart of the process is Fat, struggling to understand the meaning of that beam of pink light and the information it gave him. Phil Dick the writer watches Fat with detachment, while Philip K. Dick the author of the novel observes both Fat and Phil. The readers—provided with enough biographical information to know that Philip K. Dick is writing of personal experiences— at least in part—observes all three of the levels of the drama spread before him or her.

The death of Sherri pushes Fat to a suicide attempt, and he is hospitalized until he regains his sanity, whatever that may be. Those who are insane are out of touch with reality, but the definition of reality is uncertain. If what we perceive as reality is only an illusion (as the Gnostics and Fat maintain), then the person who believes in that reality is really insane; however, the person who rejects it is not insane. It was Fat's divine revelation that alerted him to the truth about the illusory quality of our world. And this revelation may be mere fantasy. Phil thinks it is; Fat thinks it is not. Fat decides to prove his claim by going in search of the Savior.

The last six chapters of *Valis* are a reversal of the form used in the first part of the novel. They are more powerful because they sharply contrast with the long theoretical discussions between the four men in the first half of the novel. Those conversations, like Fat's exegesis, were a mulling over of abstractions. Now the novel moves from the abstract to the particular, the California world of the present where

Kevin finds a strange underground science fiction film called *Valis* and takes his friends to see it. It offers clues that suggest a hidden meaning. That secret, when finally decoded by the men (who now call themselves the Rhipidon Society), leads them to northern California. There they discover the Second Coming has occurred. The Savior has been reborn, this time as the little daughter of Eric and Linda Lampton, rock stars; she is called Sophia (Holy Wisdom). The wound of Phil Dick is healed as soon as he finds her. Fat, the tormented part of Phil's psyche that attempted suicide twice, disappears.

Sophia instructs the little group to go out into the world and proclaim the kerygma with which she charges them. The days of the wicked are about to end. She instructs: "What you teach is the world of man. Man is holy, and the true god, the living god, is man himself."[4]

The novel has apparently reached a happy conclusion. But the reader should have known that would not happen in a world created by Philip K. Dick's imagination. The unexpected occurs—a tragic occurrence. Sophia is accidently killed by Mini, a friend of her parents who is experimenting with new electronic equipment. Fat reappears, driven back into existence by this new death and the doubts and confusion that again storm Phil's mind. He must ask all over again how he is to interpret his theophany. As the novel ends, Fat sets out in the world on another quest to find the Savior; Phil waits at home.

The Divine Invasion, as we have noted, continues the story of man's experience of gnosis, or knowledge of God. Fat temporarily achieved a paradisiacal state of joy when he found Sophia, just as the disciples of Christ had. But he lost it when she was killed in the accident. The incarnation must be repeated if mankind is to be healed.

The quest to find God in *Valis* was an intellectual quest. It did not succeed. *The Divine Invasion* dramatizes another kind of quest—the quest of love. A reversal takes place in this second novel. Herb does not search for God; God (Yah) comes to Herb and sends him on a mission to bring the Savior to Earth. Because the novel is concerned with love, not reason, its mode is very different from that of *Valis*. It is nonchronological. Its purpose is not to portray the process of ratiocination as *Valis* did, but rather to portray a transformation accomplished by love and wisdom. Consequently, this novel uses metaphor as its dramatic device. Music and poetry, not theological disputation, serve as the language through which states of spiritual awareness are presented to the reader. It is as though *Valis* had been a creation of the left forebrain in which reason and logic prevail, and now the right forebrain with its intuitive mode takes over.

The metaphor of the Black Iron Prison pictures the situation on Earth. Two oppressive authorities rule—the Christian Islamic Church and the Scientific Legate. The first is the religious establishment, and the second is the political establishment. Hand in hand, they control the population and allow no freedom. Although they give the appearance of cooperation, they secretly plot to destroy each other. This situation represents the Evil Forces that have entrapped the Earth and excluded the Godhead. The Savior, whose earlier attempts to save the Earth have been aborted, must return again. The Apocalypse is at hand.

Herb Asher is a metaphor for the imprisoned individual. Shut up in his little dome on the planet CY30-SysoB in the Formalhaut star system, he endlessly listens to Linda Fox tapes. He has cut himself off from other humans and lost concern for anyone but himself. He is irritated when he receives a request to help Rybys Romney, the attendant in a neighboring dome who is dying of multiple sclerosis. He does not want to be bothered.

The Divine Invasion splits into two parts as did *Valis*. The first half portrays the preparation for and reenactment of the Advent. The Godhead appears to Herb, first, in the form of a local deity; then, as Elias, a reincarnation of the prophet Elijah, he tells Rybys and Herb they are to be the parents of the next Savior. More unlikely parents cannot be imagined. This is a bold stroke on Dick's part—his refusal to illuminate them with any divine gleam. To give a local habitation and a name to the wonderful is inevitably to trivialize it. Dick overcomes that limitation by accepting it and pushing it to the extreme, making both Herb and Rybys as commonplace as possible; she vomits and complains during her pregnancy, he is resentful and moody.

The symbolic wound plays a key function in the *Divine Invasion* as it did in *Valis*. According to Dick's cosmogony, the Godhead was injured in the original Fall. The injury is repeated in this story. In an accident as they come to Earth, Herb is wounded and their child, called Emmanuel, is brain damaged and born prematurely. Rybys is killed. Herb is placed in cryonic suspension for ten years and Emmanuel's injury causes him to forget who he really is. Thus, the tale of the death of the female at the time of the creation of the universe, told in the "Two Source Cosmogony" written by Fat in his exegesis in *Valis*, has been enacted again. But here the Creator and the Savior do not split as they did in *Valis;* it is Emmanuel who comes to Earth to save it.

The second half of the novel pictures the struggle of both Herb and his divine son to remember who they are. Born into the reality of Earth, the individual suffers amnesia. He forgets his true nature. Anamnesis, or recovery of his memory, is necessary if he is to rediscover God. This view, taken from Plato, is a cornerstone of Philip K. Dick's theology.

Another fundamental of Dick's theology is that the microcosm mirrors the macrocosm. What happens in one realm reflects what happens in the other. Emmanuel, the divine form, must learn who he is and, in his task, is aided by a female companion, Zina. She gives him an electronic slate that allows him to receive cryptic communications from Valis, the divine ground of being. Part of the mystery Emmanuel must solve to understand his nature and purpose is to learn who Zina is. He will finally learn she is the female aspect of God, known by many names—Hagia Sophia, the Torah, Pallas Athena, Malkuth, Shekhina. She is that part of himself from which Emmanuel has become separated.

Analogously, Herb, the microform, must also recall who he was before he was placed in cryonic suspension. The last half of the novel is constructed with a series of balanced scenes: In one series, Emmanuel struggles to recover his divine memory; in the other series, Herb labors to achieve gnosis or knowledge of what he was before he came to Earth. Zina, the divine presence, also aids him.

As Emmanuel awakens to his true identity, he realizes that his mission is to free humanity from the Black Iron Prison in which it is trapped. He is an Old Testament God of indignation and wrath, and he believes in an eye for an eye and a tooth for a tooth. He plans to fight the Evil Empire. Zina, however, holds that to fight the Empire is to become infected by its insanity. She knows Emmanuel is the creator of reality, but she can imagine a better one than the reality he has created. She suggests an alternative version where freedom, love, and compassion rule. She takes Emmanuel to visit her realm, the Palm Tree Garden, where evil has no power.

Zina and Emmanuel make a wager; they will test his reality against hers, using Herb Asher as their pawn. Emmanuel will turn Herb's fantasy of a love affair with Linda Fox into reality. Will Herb still be able to love her when he actually achieves his dream and discovers that, because she is human, she has blemishes and flaws?

The answer is yes. Herb not only loves her but sacrifices his dream of living with her when it becomes clear that he must do this to protect her from the evil of Belial.

In the final chapter of the novel, Herb is united with Linda Fox (who is an earthly manifestation of Sophia-Christ). Simultaneously, Emmanuel finally identifies Zina as Shekhina, the part of the Godhead separated from him in the original Fall. To name is to know; when Herb experiences his gnosis, he and Shekhina are rejoined. The Old Testament wrathful God is now subsumed by a healed Godhead, containing both male and female polarities. Evil is banished. It is not defeated by Emmanuel, but displaced by the love that creates another version of reality.

STYLE AND TECHNIQUE

Dick displays a range of styles in the two novels. The first half of *Valis*, the philosophical ravings of a madman, is written in a style quite different from what we have come to expect from him; it is erudite, full of literary allusions and long conversations. The reader who thrives on the bizarre action customary in a Dick novel may find it heavy going, perhaps even dull. The reader with a bent toward metaphysical speculation will be fascinated. The long discussions about theology have an anguished necessity about them. This is not idle talk to pass the time. People close to Fat are suffering and dying. He himself has been driven to the madness of suicide. He reads endlessly because he is obsessed with the need to find answers. He writes endlessly in his exegesis because the answers he finds when he reads do not satisfy him.

In my opinion, the first half of *Valis* contains the most powerful and brilliant writing Dick has yet produced. It also contains a distillation of his most original thinking. I know of nothing else quite like it in science fiction. It reminds one of Dostoyevsky's *Notes from Underground* in which the protagonist constructs a powerful logical argument to establish his point—namely, that man is irrational. Horselover Fat calls on reason to aid him in his fight against madness, and, ironically, reason drives him closer to madness. The writing is rescued from heaviness by humor and a sprinkling of street language. These are not scholarly discussions. The discrepancy between the language and the subject creates the kind of pained incongruity that we have come to expect in Dick's fiction.

This union of opposites also finds expression in the symbols Dick uses. He yokes the mundane and the sacred. There is Kevin's dead cat, killed by a car. It is the symbol of everything he regards as "fucked up" in the universe. He wants to stick it in God's face and demand an explanation. Opposed to that is the beautiful gold fish pin that first sparks Fat's memory of who he really is. We learn the fish sign is like a section of the DNA spiral and thus a symbol for creativity and life. Another example of incongruity is the material means by which Valis, or the Godhead, reveals itself on Earth. It expresses itself in a beautiful poem written by Ikhnaton in ancient Egypt. It also appears in a science fiction film as a satellite that looks like a beer can run over by a taxi. The film, produced by a composer of contemporary music, provides clues to Fat in his search for God. So does Wagner's opera *Parsifal*.

The second half of *Valis*, when Fat and his friends set out to find the producers of the film, returns to the style typical of a Dick novel. It is a combination of dialogue and action—an antithesis of the expository style in the first part. Again, this style is reminiscent of *Notes from Underground*, which uses a similar pattern balancing exposition and action.

The Divine Invasion uses yet another style—a delicate, fragile one. It quite appropriately has the quality of a fairy tale since the key figure is Zina, who is a fairy. The long philosophical discussions of *Valis* are absent; instead, poetry is quoted (Shakespeare, Dowland, Yeats).

The point of view is also different in the two novels. *Valis* uses the first person; Phil Dick the writer narrates the story. Phil is as objective and sane as the reader likes to believe he is. Phil makes the judgment the reader would have been forced to reach had Fat been the narrator of the story. Fat is crazy. Because Phil makes that judgment, the reader is spared the task and, thus, freed to move on to speculation about the possibility that Fat may be the only really sane person in the novel.

The Divine Invasion returns to the use of multiple points of view that Dick mastered when he wrote his great novels *Martian Timeslip* and *Dr. Bloodmoney*. He uses three narratives with a narrative center for each: Herb's relations with Rybys and Linda are told from his point of view; Harms is the center for the political narrative about the Church and the Legate; Emmanuel provides the point of view for the third story, the one focusing on his education. In this novel, we have escaped the mundane world built by reason that provided the setting for *Valis*. Here the limitations of time and space no longer apply since, according to Dick, they are constructs of the logical mind, and the world of *The Divine Invasion* can be reached only when the imagination is awakened.

The importance of music in Dick's fiction has often been noted by
the critics. Never has music had a larger role than in this pair of novels,
and particularly in *The Divine Invasion*. Because *Valis* uses the dis-
cursive mode, music is of less significance, although Mini's Syncron-
icity music gives subliminal cues about meaning when the Rhipidon
Society goes to see the film, and Wagner's *Parsifal* suggests the wound
and the quest.

The Divine Invasion uses three kinds of music, each for a particular
purpose. The sappy soupy strings playing music from *Fiddler on the
Roof* and *South Pacific* represent the counterfeit world that locks most
people in the mental prisonhouse that they assume is reality. In contrast,
the lute songs of John Dowland, sung by Linda Fox, represent true
reality. The music unites the awakened intelligence of mankind on all
the planets. Dowland was a contemporary of Shakespeare. He was both
a composer and a virtuoso performer on the lute who specialized in and
developed the art song. The texts of several Dowland songs are quoted
in the novel. Dick first drew on Dowland's songs when he used the
title of "Lachrymae" ("Flow, My Tears") to provide the title of his
1974 novel *Flow My Tears, the Policeman Said*. Gustav Mahler's
Symphony No.2, or the *Resurrection* Symphony, is also used to suggest
the awakened consciousness. For Herb, the symphony represents the
complexity, profundity, and beauty for which he yearns as an escape
from the sappy, soupy string music of the illusory reality he experienced
in cryonic suspension.

The third use of music is the bells that signal the Palm Tree Garden.
This is Zina's springtime world of dancing and joy and peace. It is the
world Emmanuel has forgotten because of the wound he received when
he fell. She must lead him to it again. She reminds him, "You heard
the bells and you know that their beauty is greater than the power of
evil."[5]

THEMES

Music provides more than cues to signal various states of spiritual
awareness. Dick's method in weaving together a number of related
ideas into a harmonious whole is reminiscent of the fugue, that Renaissance musical form in which a number of voices combine in stating
and then developing a single theme. The main idea of a fugue is that
one voice contrasts with others; all the voices do not move together. It

is descended from the contrapuntal music of the Middle Ages in which one voice is played against another. The theme is first stated, then developed, and finally resolved. In *Valis*, Horselover Fat is the lone anguished voice crying out the theme: Given suffering and death, how is man to understand God and reality? By the end of *The Divine Invasion*, the question has been resolved.

A single reading of the novels rewards the reader with subliminal sparks of meaning as did the movie *Valis* for its viewers. But as the Rhipidon Society returned again and again to the movie to study its intricate parts and understand its clues, so must the reader of these complex novels. Gradually seven major themes emerge.

First and most important is the theme of *the wound and the quest for healing*. Humanity suffers from physical illness and death and, worse, a wounded or dead psyche. This is the state of every human being, a result of his or her having been born into this world. According to Dick, we live in an irrational world, and our suffering is a result of that irrationality. Humanity's task, having identified the wound, is to set out on a quest that will bring healing. In defining this wound, Dick draws on the *Parsifal* legend, which tells the story of Amfortas, the wounded leader of the Knights of the Grail. Finally, healing occurs when Parsifal, the pure fool, "abolishes the delusion of the magician Klingsor and his castle."[6] The apparent evil in the world was actually an inner wound that caused Amfortas to see a false reality.

The Parsifal legend is retold in the novels. Emmanuel's wounded mind is finally healed and the Black Iron Prison of Evil vanquished when Zina convinces Emmanuel that he should create her alternative vision as a new reality. Evil is not defeated because the confrontation of Emmanuel and Belial never takes place; evil just fades away. In the final brief scene of the novel, Linda and Herb go to view the broken remains of Belial. Nothing is left but what looks like a great luminous kite—pieces of damaged light. He has returned to his original shape—Lucifer, the brightest of the angels, who fell to earth.

A second theme, also very important, is the theme of *gnosis*. Gnosis is the Greek word for knowledge. Dick is to be regarded as a contemporary thinker in the Gnostic tradition because he holds that salvation through self knowledge is the only means possible to man to heal his wounded psyche. His views follow those of such men as Simon Magus, Paracelsus, Boehme, and Bruno. These mystical thinkers all experienced theophanies in which secret knowledge about the nature of God was revealed to them. They formed secret societies like the Friends of God and the Brothers of the Rosy Cross.[7] Not only does Dick create a character, Horselover Fat, who is a present-day Gnostic, but Fat draws heavily on Gnostic literature as he writes his *Tractates Cryptica Scriptura* (hidden writing) and develops his cosmogony. See, for example, entries number 11, 17, 21, and 48 in the *Tractates*.

The original Gnostics were a religious movement during the early Christian era, the first two centuries following Christ's death. Because the movement involved many different sects, their beliefs cannot be summarized easily. A leader of one of the major sects was Valentinus, and Dick has drawn heavily on his views.

The early Catholic Church claimed that humanity needed a divine way beyond its own power to approach God. The Church offered this way to salvation and claimed there was no other. In contrast, the Gnostics accepted no such institution or authority. Their claim was that humanity, from its own inner potential, must discover for itself the revelation of truth. For the Gnostic, exploring the psyche was a religious quest. The more radical Gnostics rejected all religious institutions.

Once the Catholic Church was well established, its leaders began to both label this kind of thinking as heretical and ban the gospels of the Gnostics. These gospels were texts the Church founders had decided not to include in the New Testament. Little was known about these writings except in oblique references by the early Church fathers as they attacked them, until the discovery at Chenoboskion (Egypt) in 1945 of a library of 52 Gnostic writings. (The usual English transliteration of the town's name is Nag Hammadi, so the texts are occasionally referred to by that name.) Entry number 24 in Fat's exegesis makes reference to the texts, and they play a key part in the novel. They are symbolized as the pot in which Fat found God. For him, the language of the texts is alive. Language or information, which he calls the plasmate, is God or Valis.

The Valentinian Gnostics held that each individual is a spirit or pneuma, a fallen particle of the true God. Each person is trapped in the prison of material existence, asleep and ignorant of his or her condition. God sends messengers to call the sleeping spirit to awaken and remember its true destiny. Gnosis or knowledge comes as a theophany, an intuitive process of knowing. To know oneself is to know human destiny.

Theodotus, a Gnostic teacher, wrote that when one achieves gnosis, he or she understands "who we were, and what we have become; where we were. . . whither we are hastening; from what we are being released; what birth is, and what is rebirth.''[8]

In Dick's cosmogony, reason is of prime importance; indeed, reason is synonymous with God. Here, too, he draws on the Gnostic tradition. Silvanus, a writer whose *Teachings* were found at Nag Hammadi, advises: "Bring in your guide and your teacher. The mind is the guide but reason is the Teacher.... Live according to your mind.... Acquire strength, for the mind is strong.... Enlighten your mind.... Light the lamp within you." To do this, he says, you must "knock on yourself as upon a door and walk upon yourself as upon a straight road. For if you walk on the road, it is impossible for you to go astray.... Open the door for yourself that you may know what is.... Whatever you will open for yourself, you will open.''[9]

Third is the theme of *evil*. Dick's view is dualistic in that he holds evil does exist and is a power in its own right, the result of an accident when the universe was first created. The One created a pair of twins that, in turn, were to divide into the Many through their dialectical interaction. Hyperuniverse I developed according to the original plan; Hyperuniverse II was damaged in an accident symbolized as the The Fall, and, as a result, became deranged. We live in Hyperuniverse II and thus partake in its madness and irrationality, manifest as illness, suffering, and death. Salvation or escape is possible only as each individual, awakened to his or her true consciousness by gnosis, returns to the rationality of Hyperuniverse I. Belial is the name Dick gives to the irrational force in its macrocosmic dimension. He uses the symbol of the Black Iron Prison or the Empire for its microcosmic or earthly expression (see *Tractates* entry 41). Opposed to Belial are the forces for good that rule in Hyperuniverse I and will eventually heal Hyperuniverse II. These powers are symbolized by the Palm Tree Garden—the original unfallen state of God.

A fourth theme draws a parallel between *the macrocosm and the microcosm*. Emmanuel, born on Earth as a man, is able to experience the Hermetic transformation because "the truth is that what is above is like what is below and what is below is like what is above, to accomplish the miracle of the one thing.''[10] The original wound when the universe, the macrocosm, was created is experienced by "each of its microcosmic pluriforms: ourselves.''[11] Each individual is a little world. *The Divine Invasion* dramatizes this relationship of macrocosm and microcosm. When the accident occurs to the flycar as Rybys and Herb come to

Earth, Emmanuel, the macrocosm, is injured. So is Herb, the microcosm, who falls into a trance from which he will not awaken for ten years—not until the time when Emmanuel has almost recovered his memory.

A fifth theme is that of *anamnesis*. Following Gnostic tradition, Dick holds that most of mankind is asleep and thus deprived of its memory of its true identity. As a result, we regard the pseudoreality of this world as the true reality. Gradually anamnesis, or a reversal of our amnesia, can be accomplished. Dreams and the imagination aid us in our quest, and if we persevere, we may experience a theophany, a divine revelation of our true identity. We discover that "all history is one immortal man who continually learns."[12] Thus, Fat discovers he is Thomas, the disciple who lived in Rome in the first century. This is not to be understood as reincarnation, since in Dick's cosmogony time does not exist. His tractate explains: "The universe is information and we are stationary in it, not three-dimensional and not in space or time. The information fed to us we hypostatize into the phenomenal world."[13]

The significance of the sixth theme, *androgyny*, is not easy to understand until the reader has grasped the first five themes that have been outlined. The Godhead is both male and female—a polarity similar to the Taoist concept of the Yin and the Yang. The two aspects became separated in the primordial fall. The female part remained with the fallen world. She has a number of names in *The Divine Invasion*: Diana, Pallas Athena, Hagia Sophia, the Torah, Malkuth. But she is more— she is Shekhina, as the female aspect of the Godhead was known to the Jews. When Emmanuel is finally able to recognize and name her as the other half of himself, the split in the Godhead is healed.

For this view of the androgynous Godhead, Dick goes to the literature of the Kabbala, the structure of Jewish mysticism that developed during the Middle Ages. He makes reference to the *Zohar*, the bible of Kabbala, where the account of the severed Godhead is given. It holds that for God to be One and Whole, the masculine aspect must be united with Shekhina, the feminine half.

Information (language) is sacred to Dick because he believes it is the divine plasmate. Its finest expression is the Torah, the Creator's instrument. The Torah is the living soul of the world. Elias explains to Herb that the Torah is "the totality of divine disclosure by God; it is alive; it existed before Creation. It is a mystic, almost cosmic, entity."[14] Another Kabbala text, the *Sepher Yezirah*, holds the same idea about the mystical power of language. According to the story of creation given in this text, God used the 22 letters of the Hebrew alphabet. Elias draws on this account in the *Sepher Yezirah* in explaining to Herb the power and mystery of the Torah.

The seventh and final theme is that of *games, play, and children*. In *Valis*, this theme is submerged beneath others. True, Sophia, the Savior, is only two years old, but she does not survive. The world of *Valis* is essentially the adult world searching for God through the use of reason. In *The Divine Invasion*, in contrast, we enter the world of children and play. Emmanuel first points out this aspect of God's nature to Elias, insisting that "He enjoys games and play. It says in Scripture that he rested but I say that he played." Herb, watching his ten-year-old son after he has awakened from his long sleep, recognizes the element of playfulness in Emmanuel's nature. He realizes that "the part of him that derived from his mother is ten years old. And the part of him that is Yah has no age; it is infinity itself. A compound of the very young and the timeless."[15]

Zina takes Emmanuel to her imaginative world in the Palm Tree Garden where the wind blows through the bamboo, and joy reigns. She is a fairy child who leads him into the world of enchantment. And it is through a trick that Zina causes Emmanuel to make Herb's dream world into a reality. At the end of the novel, Emmanuel marvels that he has finally been reunited with the female half of himself. Zina tells him how she accomplished this awakening. "My love of games. That is your love, your secret joy; to play like a child. To be not serious. I appealed to that."[16] To be serious, to pursue truth with reason, as did Horselover Fat, is not enough. One needs also to be a child, to dream and imagine and play, to believe in fairies. True reality lies beyond the grasp of reason alone.

DICK'S COSMOGONY

Dick writes in the tradition of the mystics, drawing on the Gnostics and the writings of the Kabbala. His goal, however, is to do more than rejoice in revelation; he wishes to understand it. He insists that the theophany experienced by the mystic must be comprehended before it can be accepted. In these novels, he is really attempting to reconcile revealed religion and rational philosophy.

Dick's cosmogony, in summary form, appears as entry number 47 in Fat's exegesis—the Two Source Cosmogony. It draws on, incorporates, and finally subsumes all past philosophies and saviors. He is strongly influenced but by no means limited by the thinking of Heraclitus, Plato, and Spinoza. As the title "Two Source Cosmogony" indicates, Dick's view is bitheistic. He sees two elements of the Godhead in dialectical combat and identifies them as irrational—even demonic—will versus wisdom and rationality (i.e., the Logos).

According to his view, the cosmos is thought—a vast active living intelligence system. Each of us is a part of the cosmic mind. What we experience as physical, material world is, when properly seen, the thoughts of Valis (God). These thoughts take the form of arrangements of physical reality into information. This "physical reality" is not physical reality at all, but rather mental concepts in a mind. Valis literally thinks our spatiotemporal world.

For Dick, the fact that Valis's thoughts take the form of arrangements of physical reality is the most important discovery that can be made about what the universe really is and what or who Valis is—the entity who thinks the thoughts. Time, as experienced by the human mind, is an occluding factor. When time is removed as a factor, our world is properly seen as a conceptual arrangement in which nothing perished.

However, part of that conceptual arrangement (Valis) was damaged due to an accident and is, therefore, irrational. This is the universe in which we exist. Christ as the Logos comes to this decomposing creation to form his own universe in its place. Thus, the rational has invaded the irrational and is assimilating it into its own body. Therefore, the universe is moving from chaos to order, from irrationality to rationality.

In this concept, Dick has replaced a static deity with a dynamic, process deity. He conceives of that deity as a vast unitary brain, and the physical world is that brain and is necessary for the mind to exist. As we need a brain to think, so does the deity; our universe is that deity. The deity (the mind) contacts the brain (the physical world), arranges it, impinges on it, imprints information, processes information in and on it. The mind is the music; the brain (the physical universe) is the groove.

What are the implications for the individual (the microcosm) of this view of the macrocosm? Each person needs to experience an awakening to his or her true nature. This is the task of each individual and no institution can do it for him or her. The concept of individual freedom and responsibility is very important to Dick and explains why he is so strongly attracted to the writings of the Gnostics. The awakening comes when you realize that the world you experience is your creation, that you are the Pantocreator. In Dick's words:

This world that you see—it is an objectification of your own prior thought-informations; it is substantial now, but originally it consisted of ideas; that is, it has two modes of existence; first as ideas in a mind—and it is your mind—and then as objective, substantial creation coming back at you-as-percipient. Thus you are not what you thought you are, and you have an origin and nature different from what you supposed; you have a history, and if that history is followed backward in time (and up the ladder of ascending ontology) you arrive at the Absolute, call it Ch'ang Tao, or Brahman, or God, or the One, or the Good, or the Prime Mover—names do not matter; perhaps it has no name. This realization is the Awakening, but it leads, after a time, to further realizations equally great, which ineluctably follow, and carry weight; if you came from this Absolute, it follows that you will inevitably return; this is something that cannot be doubted; it is understood to be indubitable. It is as indubitable a truth as the truth of your origin.[17]

Only time can judge the contribution Dick has made to the literary tradition with these two novels. Writing about speculative fiction, I feel free to speculate myself and I believe his achievement is a significant one that will change the boundaries and definitions of science fiction—what it is and the territory it explores. He was an innovator doing what no one had done before. Science once eliminated religion from the world it chose to study—the material world. Now, as quantum physics alters our view of physical reality, we realize a tidy division between the physical and the metaphysical world is not possible. As our scientific ideas change, it is timely to change our ideas of what science fiction is about and what subjects it can explore. Dick began that transformation. His was a unique mind, alert with a keen reasoning power and alive with a vivid imagination. He created a vision of reality we have not seen before.

He wrote, I believe, primarily for himself at the end of his career. He reminds me of William Blake, who created his private mythology and expressed it in his own way, unconcerned about whether the world noticed or approved. Philip K. Dick's attitude was similar. In fact, he might not even want his reader to take his personal vision too seriously. As he once said to me with an ironic twinkle in his voice, "You'd have to be crazy to do that!"

NOTES

1. Charles Platt, *The Dream Makers* (New York: Berkley Books, 1980).
2. Philip K. Dick, "Jon's World," in *Time to Come*, August Derleth, ed. (New York: Farrar Straus, 1954), n.p.
3. "Science Fiction as Prophecy," *The New Republic*, 30 October 1976, p. 33.
4. Philip K. Dick, *Valis* (New York: Bantam Books, 1981), p. 184.
5. Philip K. Dick, *The Divine Invasion* (New York: Simon and Schuster, 1981), p. 151.
6. *Valis*, p. 119.
7. *The Divine Invasion*, p. 96.
8. Elaine Pagels, *The Gnostic Gospels* (New York: Random House, Inc., 1979), p. xlx.
9. Ibid., p. 153.
10. *The Divine Invasion*, p. 61.
11. *Valis*, p. 124.
12. Ibid., p. 216.
13. Ibid., p. 99.
14. *The Divine Invasion*, p. 97.
15. Ibid., p. 138.
16. Ibid., p. 199.
17. Letter from Dick to author, August 31, 1981.

9

From Rebellious Rationalist to Mythmaker and Mystic: The Religious Quest of Philip José Farmer

EDGAR L. CHAPMAN

At first glance, Philip José Farmer might hardly be expected to be a science fiction author whose work reflects a religious quest or an evolving religious consciousness. After all, in the early fifties, Farmer broke into the science fiction world as an iconoclastic rebel satirizing orthodoxies in religion and puritanism in sex—in stories like "Father," the novelette version of "The Lovers," and "My Sister's Brother"—and he consolidated this reputation in the early sixties with the novel version of *The Lovers* (1961) and the satire in *Inside, Outside* (1964). During the middle and late sixties, Farmer wrote provocative novels speculating about mother goddesses, as well as irreverent adventure sagas, and began publishing fiction about his Riverworld, the epic series that engaged much of his energy in the seventies and is certainly his best-known achievement.[1] Since the Riverworld novels postulate an immortality for terrestrials based purely on natural science and technology, they apparently reject the idea of a personal, caring God, and contradict the teachings of most major religions. Indeed, for the most part, existing religions are treated rather critically in the Riverworld novels. It would seem that Farmer is the ultimate secular rationalist.

But a closer examination of the Farmer canon provides a different conclusion. Farmer is, in fact, a writer on a spiritual quest, the direction of which emerges from a study of the work as a whole, although the criticism of Farmer's fiction, which is in its early stages, has given little attention to Farmer's religious themes.[2] Farmer has an immensely speculative mind, one perhaps too restless to settle into any particular orthodoxy; his search for a living and potent religious myth has been energetic, and the attraction of mysticism for him, especially Sufi mysticism, is undeniable. Although Farmer's ultimate religious position has not been defined, his persistent exploration of religious myth in a quest for both a sustaining vision of meaning and an enduring destiny for human life is impressive. This essay explores the development of Farmer's religious themes, from his early period as a romantic rebel, through his infatuation with mother goddesses and mythological speculation, to the mature vision and intimations of mysticism in the Riverworld novels and such recent works as *Jesus on Mars* and *Dark Is the Sun*.

Farmer's early work satirizes Christianity through a caricature of its most unpleasant social aspects. In these stories, Farmer not only attacks bigotry, intolerance, and sexual puritanism, but satirizes the Christian image of God as an all-knowing and benevolent father. In place of the mythology of God as a paternal figure, Farmer turns to a celebration of sexuality and a quasi-divine feminine sex goddess in *The Lovers*; this feminine archetype was to develop into the mother goddess figures in *Night of Light* (1966) and *Flesh* (1968). There are also flirtations with nihilism and a vision of the universe as totally absurd, most notably in *Inside, Outside*.

In the early stages of his career, Farmer may be compared to such famous iconoclasts of modern literature as D. H. Lawrence and Sean O'Casey. A brief description of parallels may be illuminating. As different as they might seem from each other, Lawrence and O'Casey were both rebellious and self-made writers who emerged after considerable struggle from a background of obscurity and poverty. Their personal religious traditions, although not especially strong in either case, were that of "free church" Protestantism with its strong emphasis on individual experience and conscience, and its latent tendency to radical and "prophetic social criticism." Both writers rebelled against father figures and the image of a paternal god and tended to exalt strong feminine figures in their early work (though Lawrence was quite ambivalent about women). Although Lawrence went on to pursue strange gods and espouse dubious ideas in his later works, O'Casey more moderately championed women and a romantic mythology centering on female figures, while satirizing the paternalistic and puritanical character of Irish Catholicism. Lawrence undoubtedly influenced Farmer, though O'Casey probably did not; nevertheless, Farmer resembles both authors in his rejection of father figures and the mythology of a father god. Another similarity is Farmer's celebration of feminine and mother goddess archetypes. Like Lawrence and O'Casey, Farmer, too, has roots in a tradition of Protestant individualism. According to the character who represents Farmer in the Riverworld saga, Peter Jairus Frigate, Farmer was reared as a Christian Scientist, but went to a Presbyterian church. Farmer writes of Frigate: "When he was twelve, he had had many nightmares in which Mary Baker Eddy and John Calvin had fought for his soul."[3]

Of course, these similarities between Farmer and such imposing figures as Lawrence and O'Casey should not be pushed too far. There are obvious contrasts to be remembered: differences of philosophic outlook, genre, and literary achievement. While some of these would seem to be to Farmer's disadvantage, others are certainly in his favor. Unlike Lawrence, for instance, Farmer has not been held to support fascism, anti-intellectualism, or male supremacy.

The early fiction presents Farmer's religious rebellion clearly: Christianity is satirized in various ways, including the rejection of the father image of God. A key story in this regard is "Father" (1955), which presents satirically what is supposedly a natural paradise on a planet ruled by a benevolent and godlike father figure.[4] This individual even has the power to restore the dead to life, but he will not allow any of his creatures to grow or to exercise meaningful freedom. His static Eden soon discloses its flaws. In a world where the godlike "Father" provides an easy resurrection, death is rather meaningless. At length, the visiting spacemen learn that the supposed divine "Father" finds his ultimate egotistical triumph in dying and having himself resurrected.

Although divided at first about the nature of the godlike "Father," the expedition gradually comes to accept the view that his world is a tyranny rather than a paradise. The antagonists in this debate are a naive bishop, who finds the "Father" a fulfillment of his dreams of a lost childhood, and John Carmody, a tough-minded priest and moralist who represents a skeptical view closer to Farmer's own. A compassionate Christian humanist, Carmody is one of Farmer's most memorable characters, and his presence tends to offset the obvious satire on the Christian image of a paternal god figure who restricts human freedom. Perhaps Farmer's most sympathetically portrayed Christian, Carmody reappears in several other stories and in the important sixties novel *Night of Light*.

There is no moderate influence like Carmody in *The Lovers*, the most radical and best known work of Farmer's early fiction, whether as a fifties novelette or in the novel version published in 1961.[5] The longer version, although not without flaws, is still impressive today. Like "Father," it attacks the image of a father God, but it goes much further in its satire on Christianity. A dystopian study of a future earth after a nuclear war, when two rival civilizations maintain tyrannical societies, *The Lovers* assails moral fanaticism and sexual repression, The Haijac Union—a loose confederation of Japan, Hawaii, and Canada—is a stern, authoritarian society dominated by the Sturch, or State Church. Through the Sturch, which is male dominated, devoted to the worship of a repressive father god, and intensely compounds puritanism with Freudianism and behaviorism, Farmer attacks the repressive mood of the fifties, with its revival of religion, its mindless patriotism, its anti-intellectualism and suppression of dissent. But the novel does more than assail the *zeitgeist* of the McCarthy era; it satirizes the constant tendency of Christian orthodoxy to consolidate itself, through union with the reigning political powers, into a social tyranny.

As an alternative to the Sturch, in *The Lovers*, Farmer offers, as we might expect, the religion of romantic love. In the Edenic world of Ozagen ("Oz again"), Yarrow encounters the "fatal woman" of romantic legend, a survivor of a lost race and an accomplished romantic mistress whose demigoddess nature and beauty provide him with a sense of transcendence in a passionate love affair. But the affair is doomed, for Farmer's hero is not quite able to escape his puritanical conditioning and accept his love with complete trust. Lack of faith leads to the death of Jeanette, showing that romantic love, though it is the antithesis of puritanism, fails to provide an enduring alternative.

The work of an angry rebel, *The Lovers*, despite some flaws, achieves a fairly high level of maturity. Farmer's rejection of institutional Christianity and the image of God as a loving father are presented forcefully. At the same time, Farmer is drawn to a feminine mythology while celebrating sexual love. The influence of Robert Graves's romantic myth of daimonic women, *The White Goddess*, seems obvious. Graves, like Farmer, turned to a goddess-dominated mythology as a part of a rejection of a masculine-dominated Protestant tradition; there are some interesting parallels between the two, and Graves's influence on some Farmer novels of the sixties (*Night of Light* and *Flesh*, especially) is considerable.[6]

Besides *The Lovers*, other works from this period satirize Christianity and Puritanism. A story aimed at shocking the sexually inhibited is "My Sister's Brother," published in 1960. In this tale, another naive and repressed Farmer protagonist falls in love with an alien woman on Mars, only to bring the affair to tragedy when her method of reproduction, involving a curious kind of oral sex, proves too offensive to his conservative mind.[7]

Farmer attacks Christianity, however, not only because its tendency to Puritanical fanaticism can result in social tyranny—as in the Sturch of *The Lovers*—but also because its gospel may be a foolish illusion. Another Farmer novel, *Inside, Outside*, begins as a satire on the affluent society and its hierarchical corporations, satirizes an evangelist resembling Dostoyevsky who hawks mechanical Christs like the impresario of a medicine show, and ends by raising the question whether existence is meaningless. After a catastrophe overturns the world of the novel, which is likened to Dante's hell, and the anti-hero survives many trials, he learns that what he thought was some kind of punishment in an existence after death was actually a pre-existence before a terrestrial life. This pre-existence is supposed to provide humans with consciences, but it does not succeed very well—in fact, life is made to seem absurd. In this novel, Farmer comes closest to surrendering to the mood of nihilism.[8]

A more positive image of Christianity is presented during this period by the Carmody stories, which describe the picaresque adventures of Father John Carmody, the moralist who opposed the false god of "Father." Father Carmody is a compassionate Christian humanist whose theology is tempered by insights gained from a philosophic view of evolution. Though not without some faults, Father Carmody is a serious Christian who tries to practice the Pauline ideal of charity or agape. Clearly, the itinerant priest comes near to Farmer's ideal of what a Christian should be.

Aside from "Father," the most interesting Carmody stories are "Prometheus" and "Night of Light," the latter being the basis for an important middle sixties novel.[9] In "Prometheus," Carmody is at his best, teaching the moral law to a tribe of sentient birds on the planet Wildenwooly, after he becomes convinced that their possession of speech, memory, and imagination indicates that they have evolved to the point of having souls. Father Carmody displays a sophisticated theology in this tale.

But there is a serious weakness in the Carmody stories. Although the protagonist is a fine exemplar of Christian humanism and although his expressions of belief and prayers are formally correct, his religion does not seem to the reader to be very vivid or vital, in contrast to the powerful numinous epiphanies encountered by the followers of Boonta in *Night of Light*. Carmody himself finds his faith shaken by his experiences with the matriarchal religion in that novel.

Some insight into Farmer's assessment of the religious situation of contemporary society, and his own views, in the early period is revealed in *Fire and the Night* (1962). A rare venture into mainstream fiction, it describes a brief affair between a white man and a beautiful black women in the Peoria of the forties. Although it is well written, the novel seems rather advanced for its time, and this, as well as its publication by a small Midwestern publisher, probably deprived it of a chance for a large audience.[10]

The most important aspect of *Fire and the Night* for this discussion is the use of Nietzsche. After they meet in a steel mill in Bartonville, a town adjoining Peoria, the white hero, Danny, who is much like the young Farmer, arouses the curiosity of the black heroine by his constant reading.[11] One day, Danny shows Vashti a passage from *Thus Spake Zarathustra* containing Nietzsche's famous phrase about the "death of God": "When Zarathustra was alone, however, he said to his heart: 'Could it be possible! This old saint in the forest hath not yet heard of of it that God is dead!' "[12] This shocks Vashti who, though literate and intelligent, tries hard to be a pious Christian fundamentalist. Yet her interest is aroused, and Danny offers an explanation of the passage, after Vashti accuses the author of blasphemy and of telling "a terrible lie":

"Maybe. I don't agree with that line myself, and I don't think Nietzsche meant it to be taken literally. He just meant that the old-fashioned belief in the Biblical God was dead, that modern man has lost that belief, probably, in the end, for good. None of the religions of today are what they were when Paul preached. Paul himself changed the religion that was taught to the twelve disciples; the only true Christian died on the cross in 33 A.D.

"But that doesn't matter. What does is that you Puritans want to suppress anything that goes against what you think is true. You're no different, in essence, from Hitler or any other tyrant. . . ."[13]

Although Vashti remains unconvinced, the scene reveals Farmer's awareness of the religious situation of the modern world. Skeptical of the beliefs of Christianity, Farmer's hero yet longs for faith in God, or a myth as potent as that of the biblical one, while fearing anti-intellectualism and the repressive nature of contemporary religious puritanism. Farmer's sophisticated awareness of Nietzsche is certainly an influence on his own restless experimentation with myth in the fiction of the sixties and seventies.

Farmer's quest for a vital myth led him through a good deal of speculative exploration of mythological concepts in the fiction of his middle period, which I would define as roughly extending from 1965 to 1974. These were the years of much vigorous writing, including *Night of Light*, *Flesh*, the first four Kickaha novels (1965–70), *A Feast Unknown* (1969), *Lord Tyger* (1970), *Tarzan Alive* (1972), and *Doc Savage: His Apocalyptic Life* (1973), as well as the Riverworld novelettes and the first two Riverworld novels. From the standpoint of a search for religious vision, the most important works from these years are *Night of Light* and *Flesh*, both of which explore the consequences of a mother goddess myth, and *Tarzan Alive*, *Lord Tyger*, and *Doc Savage*, all three of which attempt to re-create and transform popular mythology into more enduring myth.

Night of Light describes Father Carmody's encounter with a serious and intense matriarchal religion on the planet of Dante's Joy. On the "night of light," the goddess reveals her power, and, for humans, the hidden contents of the subconscious mind are given embodiment in flesh and blood. As a climax, a mortal consort of the goddess sires a new son representing the powers of light. In the first half of the novel, John Carmody becomes the father of a new incarnation of the goddess's son Yess and is so transformed by the experience that he is on the verge of conversion. In the second half of the novel, a changed Carmody, now a member of the Catholic priesthood, returns to the planet 27 years later, when the goddess's white son is about to join forces with his darker brother Algul and bring about a new revelation of human unity. This event will be followed by the transformation of the worship of Boonta from a local cult into a universal religion to be exported to other planets by missionaries.

The matriarchal faith of *Night of Light* is not a very attractive religion, but Farmer does endow his goddess with an aura of sacred and numinous power. An indication that the matriarchal myth is beginning to lose its appeal, however, is Farmer's jocular treatment of it in *Flesh*, which makes the concept of a white goddess of the Robert Graves type the material for ribald comedy.

Flesh depicts an America 800 years hence transformed into a number of small independent states most of whom worship the great fertility goddess Columbia. The captain of a returning group of astronauts becomes the unwilling consort of the goddess. In this role he is forced to mate with congregations of the goddess's ecstatic young female devotees, thereby filling a role not unlike that of charismatic male rock stars today. It is hardly necessary to say that this novel is executed in a tone of Rabelaisian humor, for no intelligent man, despite male fantasies, could enjoy so impersonal a function. Eventually the hero, freed from his onerous service to the goddess, finds happiness in a chaste marriage to a virgin raised as a Roman Catholic.

If the world of *Flesh* provides an amusing alternative to the official American culture of the sixties when the book appeared, the novel nevertheless parodies the mother goddess idea. It appears that Farmer now finds the concept much harder to take seriously.[14] Perhaps the mother goddess mythology appealed to Farmer because it combined a romantic view of nature with a deification of the feminine principle. But Farmer's next exercise in speculative myth making was concerned with revising popular hero myths.

Tarzan Alive presents itself as a "fictional biography" of Lord Greystoke in imitation of W. S. Baring–Gould's *Sherlock Holmes of Baker Street*.[15] While parodying biographical scholarship in a tongue-in-cheek style, the book reconstructs the Rousseauist myth of the noble savage (or "natural man" in Christian theology). Farmer rationalizes the rather carelessly constructed hero saga of Edgar Rice Burroughs by explaining away inconsistencies, but his deeper motive is to enrich and transform the myth. In Farmer's hands, Tarzan becomes the noble savage who not only triumphs over the African jungle, but by his trickster nature defeats modern civilization as well. However, the most important aspect of *Tarzan Alive* is Farmer's attempt to rescue the myth that the human encounter with nature should be sacred and sacramental. Central to the Tarzan myth is the dream of nature, even the wilderness, as "a magic garden blooming in abundant life."[16]

A companion volume, *Lord Tyger*, describes the primitive, Dionysian consciousness of a "natural man" before his "fall" into the self-consciousness and moral ambiguities of the civilized world. Farmer's method here is to tell the story of a man raised in Africa under special conditions approximating the environment Edgar Rice Burroughs imagined for Tarzan; the result is an Edenic or paradisiacal consciousness that Farmer describes attractively, even if some might find it shocking in its uninhibited sexuality and propensity for violence.

Despite Farmer's great fascination with primitivism, he recognizes that a fall from paradisiacal innocence is necessary, even if painful, and this is demonstrated in *Lord Tyger*. Farmer's books on the Tarzan mythos suggest that the virtues of primitivism need to be tempered with some of the rationality of civilization; but both primitivism and civilized experience need to be transcended in a new synthesis, which we might call the recovery of radical innocence.[17] The recovery of innocence turns out to be one of the goals of Farmer's religious quest, and one of the themes of the Riverworld novels.

By contrast with the Tarzan books, Farmer's "bibliography" of Doc Savage is a disappointment, but it is interesting to suggest some reasons for this. Farmer tries to define Doc Savage as the "archangel of technopolis," a mythic figure representing the triumph of technology over human social problems. But this myth is a familiar modern dream that has aroused skepticism in recent years among many thoughtful people; and Farmer's imagination is simply not engaged enough to breathe life into it once more.

The mythological speculation in these books enlarged Farmer's vision and stimulated his craftsmanship, but ultimately Farmer was drawn from such enterprises to his dominating project of the seventies, the Riverworld novels. One of the strengths of these novels is the ability to test human experience against the mythic paradigms that provide defining forms for experience.

It is worth noting that the Riverworld novels began with a vast unpublished novel in the fifties.[18] Even early in his career, Farmer was fascinated by the speculative possibilities of his Riverworld concept, but he was perhaps not quite prepared to exert a mature artist's control over his material. In the sixties, Farmer began publishing novelettes based on the vast novel in his trunk. All but one of these were absorbed into the later novels, but this exception is important: it is a novelette called "Riverworld" in which an anguished historical Jesus, resurrected in a war between two minor theocratic states, is executed by a Christian fanatic because he is not a good Christian.[19]

In 1969, Farmer brought out the first Riverworld novel, *To Your*

Scattered Bodies Go. Both a popular and critical success, the assured mastery of the book encouraged Farmer to continue with his long-contemplated epic.

The Riverworld novels speculate about the possibilities of human life if humanity were granted a naturalistic immortality through a techno-logical resurrection of the body. Although Farmer has identified a source that links his concept with the classical or Greco–Roman myth of the underworld, he has obviously appropriated the apocalyptic Christian symbol of the resurrection of the body—as the title of the first novel, taken from one of John Donne's "Holy Sonnets," indicates.[20]

The first novel begins the quest of Sir Richard Burton for the source of the River and the solution to the mystery of the Dark Tower at the north pole of the planet. As Leslie Fiedler has pointed out, this quest begins on a level of renewed innocence. The resurrection morning at the beginning of the novel, and the renewal of life of humanity on the banks of the great River create a story that reaches the reader on the "deepest level of childhood response."[21]

As Farmer's archetypal seeker for sources and meanings, Burton tries to atone for the great failure of his life—his frustrated effort to discover the source of the Nile, a symbol for nineteenth-century romantics of the source of life. As a religious skeptic with an insatiable lust for experience, Burton is a kind of "pilgrim of eternity," to use Shelley's phrase in "Adonais" about a similar seeker, Byron. Burton's quest is a paradigm of the religious quest described in terms of a literal journey: there are enigmatic and ambiguous encounters with a mysterious stranger, a Jungian shadow figure Burton calls X, and Burton's own struggle with omens and fragmentary memories of a preresurrection experience.

Burton undergoes death and resurrection countless times in his cease-less wanderings. When he reaches the mystical number of 777 deaths and rebirths, he gains new insight. Farmer's use of the death and res-urrection experience—usually a death and resurrection requiring im-mersion in water—constitutes, on the symbolic level, a vision of the necessary humiliation of the ego required of any religious quest.

Although *To Your Scattered Bodies Go* ends inconclusively, it es-tablishes the quest theme that dominates the Riverworld saga. *The Fab-ulous Riverboat* (1971) continues the theme of metaphysical quest, but somewhat less successfully. The protagonist of this book is Samuel Clemens, who longs for metaphysical and religious certitude but is torn

by ambivalence. Clemens is more interesting as a critic of human behavior than as a seeker.

By contrast, the third book, *The Dark Design*, explores Farmer's
vision much more deeply and thoroughly. The symbols of Burton's
quest are reinforced richly by references to the literary legend of the
Holy Grail and Browning's "Childe Roland,"[22] and the presence of
Sufi mysticism is a powerful motif. The Sufi influence appears in two
ways. First, Sufi humor is introduced through stories of the jokester
Nasrudin, whose paradoxical tales indicate the importance of a fresh
angle of vision for understanding human life.[23] Secondly, there is the
presence of two Sufi believers: Piscator, a Japanese mystic who preaches
self-renunciation and who plays a kind of fisher-king role in the story,
and Nur, an Arab who is the source of many of Nasrudin's stories and
philosophic comments. Farmer's interest in mysticism is also voiced
through Peter Frigate, the autobiographical character. When Frigate
and Nur discuss the "Church of the Second Chance"—the only post-
resurrection religion that Farmer treats with sympathy—Nur remarks:
"The final goal of the Chancers and the Sufis is the same. Ignoring the
difference in terms, both claim that the individual self must be absorbed
by the universal self. That is, by Allah, God, the Creator, the Real,
call Him what you will."[24] In this context Frigate, though apprehensive
over the loss of the individual self in a mystical absorption into the
whole, acknowledges that he has experienced three moments of mystical
transcendence himself. The first came in youth, when Frigate worked
in a steel mill; the second in early middle age in a marijuana dream in
Peoria; the third and most memorable occurred in late middle age:

I was fifty-seven then, the sole passenger in a hot-air balloon soaring over the
cornfields of Eureka, Illinois. The pilot had just turned off the burner, and so
there was no noise except from a flock of pheasants the roar of the burner had
disturbed in a field.
    The sun was setting. The bright summerlight was turning grey. I was floating
as if on a magic carpet in a light breeze which I couldn't feel. You can light
a candle in the open car in a strong wind, you know, and the flame will burn
as steadily as if in an unventilated room.
    And suddenly, without warning, I felt as if the sun had come back up over
the horizon. Everything was bathed in a bright light in which I should have
had to squint my eyes to see anything.

But I didn't. The light was coming from within. I was the flame and the universe was receiving my light and my warmth.

In a second, maybe longer, the light disappeared. It did not fade away. It just vanished. But for another second the feeling that the world was right, that no matter what happened, to me or to anybody or to the universe, it would be good. That feeling lasted for a second.[25]

Although this numinous moment of enlightenment is of great significance to Frigate, he acknowledges that it has not changed his conduct. Nur argues that the experience is a counterfeit of mystical beatitude, although containing some authenticity. Frigate concedes that his life has been too undisciplined to produce a consistent progress toward religious maturity, but he acknowledges his willingness to follow Nur on the Sufi way.

Farmer's sympathetic treatment of Frigate's mysticism and Sufi teaching in *The Dark Design* seems to augur further revelations in the fourth Riverworld novel; but we must remember that Frigate's ambivalence toward religious mysticism is characteristic of Farmer himself. At any rate, the promise is not fulfilled in *The Magic Labyrinth* (1980).

In *The Magic Labyrinth*, Farmer relegates Frigate and mysticism to a minor role, concentrating on Burton's successful effort both to find naturalistic explanations for the Riverworld planet and to restore the planet's technology to normal operation. Burton's quest is successful when he confronts his benefactor and antagonist, the renegade X, the "mysterious stranger," who functions as his Jungian shadow. The confrontation yields explanations and makes Burton the savior of his world. Burton also learns Farmer's concept that the soul exists and possesses a kind of immortality, but finds that its only meaningful existence comes in a resurrected body. Nor is the soul of a divine origin; rather, it was invented by the first sentient race. Yet Burton's quest ends on a note of renewed innocence, a motif reinforced by the aid he gets from his wife Alice, the same Alice who inspired Lewis Carroll's book and a symbol of renewed innocence in the novels.

Farmer, however, does not close the door on mysticism at the end of *The Magic Labyrinth*. There are tantalizing hints of a higher level of being that a few initiates and masters might reach: a level of existence beyond the merely human world of life on the riverbank, a transcendence wherein humans merge with God, or "The Real," to use Farmer's own terms. Or, perhaps, it is hinted, a higher humanity, purified of its flaws by moral discipline "becomes God." If *The Magic Labyrinth* is inconclusive, perhaps it is because the author has neither resolved his conflicts nor fully developed his vision.

It is obvious that Farmer's own quest is unfinished, but two novels written and published during his work on *The Magic Labyrinth* are important statements of religious speculation. Both *Jesus on Mars* (1979) and *Dark Is the Sun* (1979) need to be read in the light of Farmer's religious development. They should also be seen as Farmer's replies to the widespread contemporary pessimism in Western civilization.

Jesus on Mars, a utopian novel published at a time when utopian speculation has come to seem fanciful, depicts Farmer's vision of Jesus as a messianic teacher and liberal social leader. The novel begins with the first Mars expedition landing there in 2015. The predictable group of four explorers—three men and a woman, racially and ethnically balanced—find humanoid Martians living underground in a society resembling Jewish Christians of the first century, except for an enormously advanced science. These Martians worship the Jesus of a fifth (and supposedly more authentic) gospel, which has been lost or suppressed. Supposedly the descendants of first-century Jewish Christians from Libya, and of the Krsh, a brilliant humanoid species responsible for their science, they were established on Mars when the Krsh settled there after picking up the Jewish Christians during a space odyssey. The Martian society is one of tolerance, compassion, charity, respect for tradition, and scientific sophistication; it is Farmer's concept of a liberal humanitarian utopia, ruled by intelligence and Christian love.

A living Christ rules the Martian society: an "energy being" who came to Mars after much wandering and found a purpose in an indifferent universe by impersonating the first Christ. When he meets the space explorers, this Jesus turns out to be a charismatic but congenial liberal whose purpose is to lead his followers to a promised land of reason, charity, and self-fulfillment. He is also sexually fulfilled by marriage and speaks with warmth of the delights of conjugal love. The novel ends with the triumphant Second Coming of Jesus to an astonished, suspicious, and incredulous earth; and the Second Coming will be successful for, though he is not supernatural in origin, this Jesus has virtually omnipotent powers.

The novel presents Farmer's personal vision of the Second Coming of a liberal humanist Christ, allied with a science so advanced it appears to be magic. Farmer's Jesus is a messianic figure whose chiliastic mission will bring not the apocalypse but the millennium, to use a traditional distinction of Christian eschatology. Again Farmer has taken a central symbol of Christianity to express a cherished dream.

If *Jesus on Mars* presents a bright vision to counteract the contemporary malaise, *Dark Is the Sun* takes a look at a grimmer future. The world of *Dark Is the Sun* is the earth 15 billion years hence, when civilization has lapsed into savagery, resources are exhausted, and the sun itself near extinction. In such a time there would not seem to be much to hope for, but life goes on, as Farmer depicts the adventures of two wanderers, Deyv and Vana, who lose their tribal identities (or "soul eggs") and are forced to journey through the hazards of their treacherous world. Their journey is one of initiation and self-knowledge as they gain a measure of Farmer's wisdom: the only "soul-eggs" worth having are those gained by an encounter with experience.

Under the tough, pragmatic wisdom of the novel, there is a kind of mysticism, too. This is not concerned with God, the supernatural, or the afterlife, but rather undergirds an invincible faith in humanity and the goodness of human life. *Dark Is the Sun* is Farmer's quiet but effective way of saying to contemporary readers that even if it appears that humanity's gods are all dead, and those natural allies, the earth and the sun, are dying, still men and women must find the "courage to be."[26]

Farmer is a science fiction writer of great imaginative power, whose body of work not only has stirred readers but also has described his own religious quest. His personal pilgrimage through space and time has not brought Farmer any religious certainty, but it continues to be a stimulating adventure.

Probably many intelligent Christians can sympathize with Farmer's satire on bigotry, puritanism, and moral fanaticism, and see in Farmer's fiction warnings about such contemporary groups as the Moral Majority. Yet liberal Christians may still be somewhat ambivalent about Farmer's use of Christian symbols and unwilling to abandon the myth of the fatherhood of God. Also, Farmer's persistent reliance on naturalist technology to fulfill visionary hopes may arouse some skepticism.

However, that may be, no one can doubt the sincerity of Farmer's hopes for humanity or the seriousness of his interest in mysticism. Moreover, we have the author's own testimony, given outside his books, regarding these matters. In a letter to this author, Farmer writes:

I've been an agnostic and may be again. For a long while I was a Voltairean deist. That is, I believed in a Creator but did not believe that He/She/It took much, if any, interest in human beings. At least It did not interfere in any way, and It would not react to prayers except with some pleasure if the prayer were of high literary quality.

Now I'm a mystic, though I've always been that even in my most "Rational" Periods. There may be, probably are, Creators, and there might be an afterlife, though I don't believe that most humans deserve such. But then there's no reason why we should have to deserve such. Why can't an afterlife be gratis. . . .[27]

Clearly, Farmer is still a seeker and his quest will probably continue in novels to come. Unsatisfied with a sterile rationalism, Farmer is yet too imaginative and speculative to settle easily into acceptance of a prevailing orthodoxy. But his experience has led him to an encounter with transcendence, and his imagination has helped to describe it memorably in such passages as Frigate's moment of vision over Eureka, Illinois. Like another explorer familiar with scientific methods, William James, Farmer has too great a respect for the evidence to ignore the signposts pointing to a higher level of being.[28]

NOTES

1. The divisions made in Farmer's career in this essay are largely my own, made for convenience. A major change in Farmer's career occurred when he returned to his hometown, Peoria, Illinois, in 1969, and began writing full time. One bibliographic article about Farmer is Thomas Wymer, "Speculative Fiction, Bibliographies, and Philip José Farmer," *Extrapolation* 18 (December 1976): 59–73. Much more helpful is George Scheetz, *Philip José Farmer: A Bibliography* (Peoria, Ill.: The Ellis Press, 1981).

2. The chief criticism of Farmer to date has centered on Farmer's use of hero myths and his artistry. The best essay on Farmer is Thomas Wymer, "Philip José Farmer: The Trickster as Artist," in *Voices for the Future*, vol. 2, Thomas D. Clareson, ed. (Bowling Green, Ohio: Bowling Green University Press, 1979). Also valuable are Russell Letson, "The Worlds of Philip José Farmer," *Extrapolation* 18 (May 1977): 124–30, and "The Faces of a Thousand Heroes," *Science Fiction Studies* 4 (March 1977): 35–41. Franz Rottensteiner presents a negative view of Farmer as writer who employs ideas for cheap effects; see "Playing Around with Creation: Philip José Farmer," *Science*

Fiction Studies 1 (Fall 1975): 94–95. Mary Brizzi, *Philip José Farmer* (Mercer Isle, Wash.: Starmont Press, 1980) is the only book-length treatment of Farmer to date, but Brizzi does not treat the works of the last few years, including the last two Riverworld volumes. See also my short book-length discussion of Farmer, *The Magic Labyrinth of Philip José Farmer* (San Bernardino, Calif.: Borgo Press, 1983). I draw upon some of the ideas advanced there in this chapter.

3. Philip José Farmer, *The Dark Design* (New York: Berkley Publishing Co., 1977), 268.

4. "Father" was originally published in *The Magazine of Fantasy and Science Fiction*, July 1955; however, it probably became better known as part of the collection *Strange Relations* (New York: Ballantine Books, 1960; reprint ed., Avon, 1974).

5. The novel version was printed by Ballantine Books (New York) in 1961; the original novelette version appeared in *Startling Stories*, August 1952.

6. Graves's main presentation of his mythology is in *The White Goddess* (New York: Farrar, Straus, and Giroux, 1948; amended and enlarged edition, 1966).

7. After being submitted to several editors, the story was printed by *The Magazine of Fantasy and Science Fiction*, May 1960. Farmer discusses the story's history in a note on it in *The Book of Philip José Farmer* (New York: Daw Books, 1973), 7–8.

8. Farmer's famous ninety days' wonder, *Venus on the Half-Shell* (1975) seems to end on a note of nihilism, after presenting an absurdist vision of the universe; but the novel is partly a parody of Vonnegut.

9. "Prometheus" was first published in March 1961 in *The Magazine of Fantasy and Science Fiction*; "Night of Light" was published in June 1957 by the same magazine. Both stories are available, along with "Father" and two other Carmody tales, in a recent collection, *Father to the Stars* (New York: Pinnacle Books, 1981).

10. *Fire and the Night* (Evanston, Ill.: Regency Books, 1962); this paperback edition is very rare today, and I am indebted to Philip José Farmer for providing me a copy.

11. The novel draws on Farmer's own experience as an employee of Keystone Steel in Bartonville, in the days before he was fully committed to a literary career; Danny Alliger, the hero, has been given many of Farmer's character traits.

12. Farmer, *Fire and the Night*, 53.

13. Ibid., 54.

14. Farmer's respect for the mother goddess myth is still strong in the Opar novels of the seventies, *Hadon of Ancient Opar* (New York: Daw Books, 1974) and *Flight to Opar* (New York: Daw Books, 1975). These heroic adventure

stories are loosely related to Farmer's version of the Tarzan saga; they identify
worshippers of the father god figure with militarism, while allowing a measure
of sanity to the followers of the mother goddess.

15. Baring–Gould's *Sherlock Holmes of Baker Street* was published by
Bramhall House (New York, 1962) and is a witty and imaginative essay in
pseudobiography. Farmer has acknowledged its influence.

16. This quotation on the mythology of nature is taken from the editors'
introduction to *The New Awareness: Religion Through Science Fiction*, Patricia
Warrick and Martin Harry Greenberg, eds. (New York: Delacorte Press, 1975),
1–21; the phrase is from page 17.

17. "Radical innocence" is a celebrated phrase from William Butler Yeats's
"A Prayer for My Daughter," describing Yeats's dream of fulfilllment for his
daughter. The concept corresponds to the Christian idea of humanity before the
Fall, or transformed by grace. The term has been used a great deal by American
literary scholars: Ihab Hassan, for instance, used the phrase as the title of his
study of American fiction of the fifties, *Radical Innocence* (Princeton, N.J.:
Princeton University Press, 1961).

18. The first Riverworld novel was *River of Eternity* or *I Owe for the Flesh*,
which Farmer wrote hastily and submitted to a contest for first science fiction
novels in 1952 by Shasta Publishers. The novel won the contest, but was never
published partly because Shasta went bankrupt. The experience was costly to
Farmer, and his frustrations increased when he could find no one else to publish
the novel. Frederik Pohl advised Farmer to rework the material as a series of
novels—counsel that proved to be helpful to Farmer in the sixties. Farmer's
most complete account of this affair is found in the foreword to *Riverworld
and Other Stories* (New York: Berkley Books, 1979), 3–5.

19. "Riverworld" first appeared in *Worlds of Tomorrow* in January 1966,
and was reprinted in *Down in the Black Gang* (New York: Signet Books, 1971),
a collection. A much revised and expanded version of the novelette appears in
Riverworld and Other Stories.

20. Farmer cites John Kendrick Bangs, *A House-Boat on the Styx* (New
York: Harper and Brothers, 1898). This is a curious book of imaginary dialogues
among the dead, which primarily influenced Farmer through its idea of a resurrection of the dead in a classical and watery eternity. An available reprint
version is the edition of The Lost Cause Press (Louisville, Ky.: 1973).

21. Fiedler comments on the first two Riverworld novels in an essay supposedly reviewing *Tarzan Alive* in the *Los Angeles Times* (April 23, 1972).
Although the essay is sometimes inaccurate, it puts a strong case for Farmer's
work in a highly enthusiastic tone. The essay is reprinted in *The Book of Philip
José Farmer*, 233–39.

22. Farmer, *The Dark Design*, 250, for instance.

23. Farmer owns several books on Sufism and an obvious source is Idries

Shah, *The Sufis* (New York: Doubleday and Co., 1964; reprint ed., Doubleday Anchor Books, 1971).

24. Farmer, *The Dark Design*, 394.

25. Ibid., 397.

26. This phrase is, of course, from Paul Tillich, who wrote of the "god above god" or the will to survive with dignity in his *The Courage to Be* (New Haven, Conn.: Yale University Press, 1952).

27. Farmer to Chapman, June 1, 1981.

28. *The Unreasoning Mask* (1981), published after the completion of this chapter, presents Farmer's most mature religious speculations and deserves a separate thorough analysis.

10

Toward a Structural Metaphysic: Religion in the Novels of Frank Herbert

DAVID M. MILLER

An essay on religion in the novels of Frank Herbert is a perfect place to attack everybody's favorite straw man. You know the one. After greeting the sun by rending the child of a mixed genre, he smashes a tiny tribal idol found lurking in the corner of an otherwise impeccable laboratory, and then settles in his armchair world to read obscure manuscripts that have been rejected by the editors of *Scientific American* as cognitively estranged.

But I won't do it. "Darko Suvin" sounds like a pen name to me. The person behind it is probably a very nice man or woman who routinely splints the wings of those sparrows who fall undetected by God's eye. His suggestion that religion is not cognitive enough to be treated in science fiction is too sitting a duck.[1] If Herbert does not write science fiction, how can I be writing this paper? And if they are not about religion, why do his novels use words like "messiah," "Jesus," and "god" in their titles? Q.E.D.

It is not just science fiction that treats religion; all fiction does—which is not to say that all novels are Christian or Jewish or Unitarian. Our language is significantly religious in inception, and the great writers who polished it wrote religious poems. Thus, for the moderately educated reader, many of our most powerful images, themes, patterns, and plots will evoke religious connotations. The only way for a writer to avoid things religious is for him or her to invent a new language, *ex nihilo*. That would be a devil of a job, and some sanctimonious ass would crucify the author for hubris. See what I mean? The question is not, "Does a fiction involve religion?" The question is, "How does an author handle the religious dimension of his or her fiction?"

Frank Herbert seems to have personal reasons for engaging basic religious questions. If, as Timothy O'Reilly tells us, young Frank was caught between a free-thinking father and a Roman Catholic mother (supported by a phalanx of maternal aunts), a primal tension was surely created.[2] It is not then surprising that Herbert should expend considerable creative energy in an attempt to sort out the terms of the early quarrel. His studies of Jungian psychology, of mystical systems, and of religious heroes are understandable as attempts to modify his love-hate relationship with father-reason and mother-faith. Even so simplistic a notion as this may go quite some distance toward explaining why Herbert's fiction is overtly religious. *Mentats* and *Bene Gesserits*, *Calebans* and *godplanets*, *shiptits* and *fishspeakers* may be allegorical pieces of his psychological world. The question, however, is not *why*, but *what*.

An interesting essay might be written on Herbert's debt to Islam, another on his debt to Jung, another on his debt to Catholicism. All three debts are very large. But this essay tries to get at something more basic than Herbert's overt sources. His novels will be asked to respond to the most basic of religious questions: *Is there a Supreme Being who is qualitatively different from man?* Ten novels say no; six novels say yes. The no is qualified almost into existence, and the yes is not something Herbert learned in formal catechism.

The *Dune* novels have several characters who are taken, by their inferiors, to be supreme. The three heroes, Paul, Alia, and Leto, are worshipped. Each is not only superior, but a complex of superiors. The implication is that a sufficiently Complex Superior is indistinguishable from a Supreme. A proverb of Muad'dib expresses it this way:

> There exists no separation between gods and men;
> one blends softly casual into the other.[3]

Paul is the first test case. He challenges each superior being that he meets, extracts the superiority, and adds it to his own being. The superiorities are synergistic. The first being to be absorbed is his father; the last is his mother. Unlike his son, Leto, Paul is unwilling to incorporate nonhuman superiors. As he grows more complex, Paul does not forget that all beings differ only in degree, but he gradually discovers that a Supreme, beyond all being, exists. "God" is a pattern of organization.

This idea may be expressed in several traditional ways. We might say that the archetype is never completely manifest in time; or that the Real is forever beyond the world of shadow. We might acknowledge that the Kingdom is not of this world. Each version summarizes a tradition from which Herbert borrows to create the "theology" of *Dune*. But the result is not a Jungian-Platonic-Christian metaphysic. It is a *structural metaphysic*. Let me explain.

Shai-hulud, despite the glossary entry on page 537 of *Dune*, is not a sandworm. Even the granddaddy of all worms is but a spectacular instance of the climactic phase of a pattern, as that pattern is manifest within the capacities of the planet Arrakis. The pattern, Shai-hulud, is neither restricted to nor completely present in any single being. Every sandworm can be killed, in fact must die in order to maintain the pattern. But the pattern in its Shai-hulud form will cease to exist if all sandworms are killed at the same time. (That's why Leto II maintains his skin trout.)

Humanity is another such instance of the pattern. Paul is not humanity any more than a sandworm is Shai-hulud. But each bears a responsibility as the *Alpha* of its present pattern instance. The sandworm lives and dies to perpetuate its species, its version of the pattern. At the next level, the species lives and dies to make way for the next more complex version of the pattern. Paul must do the same. One might say that Paul and the master worm occupy functionally identical niches in parallel structures. Both structures are branches of a taxonomy that has increasing complexity as its hierarchical principle. If Paul, as humanity's Alpha, is truly more complex than the master worm, he will ride it. If the worm is more complex, it will eat him. The teleos is infinite complexity. Each instance is both a self-perpetuating cycle and, at the same time, the stage upon which a more complex instance can be built. From the broadest view, the circle of each species is a stage in an ascending spiral of increasingly complex being.

Only Paul (in *Dune*) seems to understand this. Everyone else feels the power of the pattern only as that power is manifest in a being. Thus, they take the Alpha of their instance of the pattern as a *Supreme*, rather than as a *Complex Superior*. The Fremen worship first the worm and then Paul and then Alia and then Leto II. Beings not confined to Arrakis worship various Alphas, some of them less physical: CHOAM, the Imperium, Spice, Honor.

Paul and his sister Alia define the distinction between pattern and instance very nicely. Both are Complex Superiors; both are worshipped. Paul, because he is a solution of superiors, knows the pattern of which he is an instance. Alia, because she is only a suspension of superiors, mistakes the instance, herself, for the pattern. She more than half believes those who tell her she is divine. If we translate this back into its root systems, we could say that she believes an ectype to be the archetype, a shadow to be the reality, or an earth to be heaven.

Like the Fremen, she expects that one turn of her cycle will produce the eschaton. Water for a dry world equals heaven. But, of course, it does not; hence, Alia and the Fremen are disillusioned, not because transforming Arrakis is either good or bad, but because they fail to understand the governing principles of their Structural Metaphysic. That they are also destroyed matters not at all; every instance of the pattern must be destroyed or the evolutionary dynamic of the pattern itself will be destroyed.

The system is difficult to keep in mind, and we may sometimes wonder if such a Structural Metaphysic is Herbert's conscious intention or if it is a function of the synergistic quality of his fictional complexes. He speaks of *flow permanence*, but this whole scheme is more complicated: it is a perpetual motion machine in four dimensions. Maybe W. B. Yeats can help. The dance is separable from any dancer, but not from dancers. The individual dancer passes out of the dance so that the dance may continue to grow through the increasing complexity and beauty of its dancers, but if all the dancers sit down at the same time, the dance is over. Since the dancers exist only as a function of the dance, once the cycle is broken, the dance is over.

Leto II (*Children of Dune*) is the next logical step after Paul. Once all the superiors in one category are gathered into a Complex Superior, the open-ended system requires that the Complex Superior of one set blend with the Complex Superior of another set in order to continue the upward movement in the taxonomy. This ascension has a religious imperative in Herbert's fictions that parallels the injunction that a Christian rise to join with his God. Leto's blending with the sandtrout is a sort of bootstrap hypostasis, that is, it is not a blending of man with the divine, but a blending of two complex instances of the manifest pattern of divinity.

Although he is mistaken for a God, the Leto II of *God Emperor of Dune* is no closer to transcending the breach between instance and pattern than was Leto I. Even had he achieved complete synthesis with the adult worm, he would not have become God, because the pattern recedes infinitely as it is approached. Leto II lives thousands of years in order to maintain the possibility of future, more complex instances of the pattern; he dies to make room for those instances—first the Atreides/Duncans, then the Atreides/worms.

Paul and Leto II are more than the long sought Kwisatz Haderach; they are god-wardens who help the deity survive a mortal crisis. The pattern almost died because all of its instances tried, simultaneously, to commit suicide. Leto II and Paul gather all the strength and sweetness of Shai-hulud and Humanity into a little ball, pass through the Scylla of genetic selfing and the Charybdis of military genocide, and then spread themselves upon the vast deserts of eternity. Some future rain may make the desert bloom with a dazzling growth, or with a rough beast; for now, however, it is enough that seed time and harvest maintain their mutual generation.

That same vast rhythm rocks the four *Dune* books: the first and third build heroes toward a Supreme by synthesizing many superiors into a synergistically achieved Complex Superior. The second and fourth books demonstrate that no matter how complexly superior a being becomes, it is qualitatively different from, and subservient to, the pattern upon which it is modeled. The Bene Gesserit are wrong: it is not in their best interest to "shorten the way." But their misguided attempt may, in fact, serve the pattern by shortening the stage of humanity's dynamic homeostasis that produced the Bene Gesserit. They are wise ladies in that they recognize existence as a circle. They are wrong in assuming that *a circle* is equivalent to *circle*.

The *Dune* books gave a long answer to what seemed to be a simple question: "Is there a Supreme Being who is qualitatively different from man?" If I have understood them correctly, this is what they said: No, there is no Supreme Being. Those beings called "gods" are neither "supreme" nor qualitatively different from other men; they are Complex Superiors.

But there is a Supreme Pattern. The pattern *is* qualitatively different

rom a human being but from any being. The pattern, however,
ependent of being. (This sounds like a universal version of
_____ ntersubjectivity.)

Several questions that might have been asked on a second round of
investigation were also answered.

1. The Supreme is not to be worshipped; it is to be understood and served.

2. Service of the Supreme is accomplished by facilitating the instancing of the
   pattern at one's own level of being, and by getting out of the way when it
   is time for a new level to emerge. As we shall see, Herbert tends to lose
   his nerve when the second of these requirements involves humanity.

3. The individual, as such, matters not at all in the grand scheme, but certain
   individuals may occur as crisis points in the relationship betweeen the Supreme Pattern and its generative instancings. Such individuals are significant
   in that their actions can help the pattern to continue or allow it to fail. Most
   of Herbert's heroes are such individuals.

4. Service to the Pattern is its own reward. Although cloning, hybernation,
   and reincarnation may sometimes occur to those individuals the Pattern
   needs, there is no translation to spirit. Dead is dead—no reward in heaven
   or punishment in hell.

Six of Herbert's novels agree with the four *Dune* books. There is no
qualitatively Supreme Being. But because Herbert is not concerned only
with religion, the books are not all equally articulate. Sometimes they
hardly pay attention to the questions.

Under Pressure (1956) does not conflict with the Structural Metaphysic, but it goes no further than the basic discovery that pressure may
produce complex superiors out of simple superiors. The ecology of the
sub-tug is essentially psychological, and even Ensign Ramsey does not
perceive the lineaments of a trans-being pattern in his experience.

The Green Brain (1966) can be seen to embody a Structural Metaphysic, but the novel presents only a very literal version. The awareness
of a hierarchy of complexity is present, as is the recognition that trans-
species symbiosis is desirable, but the metaphysic is literally ecological,
hence creature bound. Perhaps the green brain itself has greater understanding, but its pupils are too primitive in understanding to elicit much
of a lesson.

The Eyes of Heisenberg (1966) assumes a Structural Metaphysic
sentient enough to protect itself in the clinch. The action of the novel

tests three heresies. The desire for ego immortality has prompted creatures, who should fill the pattern for their moment and then pass on,
to violate the exit clause of the contract. They try to stay alive by three
means: genetic cutting followed by enzyme balancing, cybernetic sur-
gery, and cloning. The novel shows the evils of all three, but at the
end, Herbert loses track of the theme and inserts another heresy. The
book does say that the pattern will not stand being fooled with.

The two utopias in the "no group" are set in our time on our earth.
In terms of the Structural Metaphysic, they represent two different
degrees of warning. Both the Jaspers-eaters and the hive-makers set out
to improve the particular manifestation of the supreme pattern that now
exists on earth. Both indicate that there is a difference between cooperating with the pattern and usurping it.

The Santaroga Barrier (1968) is a subtle warning. The residents of
the small California valley who have discovered a means to rudimentary
collective being—and hence, harmony and peace with each other—may
have the right to defend their way of life from outsiders by any means
necessary. But, by the end of the novel, we discover that not everyone
can join the collective mind. Those who lose *mind* without gaining *Mind*
are vegetables. When our perspective character murders to maintain the
valley, it is clear that a single instance of the Pattern has decided that
it is supreme. Although they are very mild about it, the Santarogans
have made the Alia blunder: they have mistaken their instance of the
pattern for the pattern itself. The date of the novel is perhaps significant.

Hellstrom's Hive (1973) is Santaroga revisited. The ugly-duckling
society has matured, not into a swan, but into a vulture. All self yields
to the Collective. The dainty pragmatism has turned into ruthlessness.
In the hive, a complex-superior (Hellstrom) has glimpsed one possible
future of the dynamic pattern, has taken it upon himself to force-feed
that instance, and has set out to force that new instance upon the world
as though it were the ultimate evolution. Only the scream-room of *The
Jesus Incident* paints so perverted a use of man's intelligence.

The sixth no comes from *The Heaven Makers* (1968). The *Chem* are
a very advanced instance of the complex superior in the humanoid mold.
Because they cannot reach beyond human while they are alive, and are
unwilling to die so that something beyond them may fill their place,
they are like the Optimen of *Heisenberg*: bored. They have the pain of
deathlessness rather than the joy of immortality. Hence, they fold the
Structural Metaphysic back upon itself, not like Leto II who prepares

the way for his own absence, but for entertainment. They manipulate unsuspecting underraces and film the action for vicarious emotional binges—without consequences to the Chem. Earth is one such studio, and the dalliance of a Chem with a human has produced the startling complex-superiors of Earth's history: one of the offspring was Jesus.

The intrusion of the Chem into the lives of earth-humans has made an evolutionary cauldron at the expense of free will, but because it is manipulated for entertainment, earth history is a series of false starts up the ladder of synergistic complexity. When the novel begins, the Chem, as complex superiors, have come between a lesser complexity (humans) and the Pattern. In Herbert's fiction, this is always a perversion. When *The Heaven Makers* ends, the proper relationship has been reestablished. Chem and Human are recognized as differing in degree, not in quality. And the anticipated cross between races will benefit from both cultures. Man is thus returned to the pattern, and the dead end of the Chem is opened. For Herbert, this ending is eucatastrophic.

Six of Herbert's novels, beginning with *Destination: Void* (1966) and ending with *The Jesus Incident* (1979), acknowledge or contain a god. Thus, when asked if there is a qualitatively Supreme Being, they answer yes.

In *Whipping Star* (1970) man finds, or is found by, a god. As is proper in science fiction, the god is an energy being.[4] *Calebans* exist as both wave and particle, as both pattern and being. Man uses the Calebans for instant transport. The role of the last Caleban in our "wave" is that of the hypostasized god: she loves us and we beat her to death. Tuluk-the-Wreave's conjecture that our reality may be the Caleban's garden plot goes unchallenged. The Caleban builds a world for the kinky Mliss Abnethe, but it turns out to be "a place of Maya, illusion, a formless void possessed of no qualities"[5] after Mliss dies.

There are many adolescent jokes in the novel. However, because the jokes are derived from the semantic problems of a female sun in love with a single-line mortal, they involve the blocks of religion: creation, death, causation, love, hate, time, ontology, purpose, and language.

The novel has a sense of dynamic equilibration but little hint of Structural Metaphysic. It ends oddly. The danger of becoming dependent upon a god—and then killing him—is played out to the last act, but then the very smart Jorj X. McKie discovers that we can avoid the consequences of beating a god to death if we feed it hydrogen.

Although the Calebans are not ever bred into the scale of complex-superior (Jorj and Fanny Mae do not wed), the "gods" of *Whipping Star* become only black boxes in the sequel, *The Dosadi Experiment* (1978). Humor is replaced by sex and violence of a mild sort. Except for those episodes directly involving the Caleban, *The Dosadi Experiment* subscribes to the Structural Metaphysic. The highest reach is the compounding of a man and woman in the same body. But rather than reaching toward a Jungian *syzygy*, the result is a feral presence loosed upon the establishment. The strongest theme of both *Whipping Star* and *Dosadi* is expressed by the harmonious zoo of species. Man will be able to fit in with a universe that has many intelligent races. Curiously, all of them seem to be at roughly the same level of complexity in the chase after the great pattern. The exception, the found-gods, do not upset the universe very much; Calebans only widen the scope of action.

Before turning to the greatest challenge offered to the Structural Metaphysic (the built-god), it will be useful to consider Herbert's mainstream novel, *Soul Catcher* (1972). The story can be summarized in a sentence: A crazed Indian kidnaps a thirteen-year-old boy, drags him through the forest of a Pacific-Northwest mountain for two weeks, and then kills him. But such a summary ignores two of the four major characters. David Marshall (the boy) has a spirit self who instances all persecuting white men (*Hoquat*). Charles Hobuhet (the Indian) has a spirit self who instances the Indian spirit of retribution (*Katsuk*).

Katsuk and Hoquat are neither real nor illusory; they are the vacuum roles in a myth reality. David and Charles are sucked into the roles and the play. Gradually the Davidness blends with the Hoquat and the Charlesness yields to the Katsuk. In *Soul Catcher*, Herbert has produced a novel in accord with one endlessly repeating cycle of the pattern. Cain and Abel were another instance.

Two observations may be made about the spirit world as it occurs in Herbert's fiction. First, gods without worshippers wither; for, creature and creator, like pattern and instance, are mutually generative. Second, an encounter with the spirit world is likely to prove fatal to the mortal, but it is worth it. David and Charles live more during their "possessed" two weeks than most of us who live to draw social security.[6]

In *The Godmakers* (1971; parts written earlier as short stories), a god is made out of a man, intentionally, by other men. Lewis Orne goes through the familiar Herbertian stress tests, is educated on the godplanet where psi-forces focus, and emerges as a god. At once he goes off on a honeymoon with a mortal, but he leaves a note: "I will keep my promise to you: humankind has an open-ended account in the bank of Time. Anything can still happen.''[7] The ending is more serious than it might seem. This god will interfere with the processes of the Structural Metaphysic just enough to make sure that humanity does not cease to exist, either because it is beaten by some other species or because it commits suicide. Orne is a very handy god to have around, but his stated purpose destroys the symmetry of the Structural Metaphysic. Without denying the evolutionary process by which complex superiors combine, synergistically, to produce ever more complex superiors, Orne will shut the process off if *humanity* is threatened. In other words, he will destroy the system to maintain one part. Despite its title, *The Godmakers* is really more interested in dynamic homeostasis (the early adventures of Lewis Orne) and parapsychology (the god-process) than it is in either theology or universal systems.

The final test of the Structural Metaphysic started out as an affirmation. *Destination: Void* (1966) stressed humans and machines into a *very* superior complex. Along the way, Herbert speculated widely about the nature of consciousness—human and ''mechanical.'' When his computer woke up, rather than being a child, it named itself God. The Ship sets its people down on an Edenic planet and tells them to figure out how to worship the god they have built. It must have seemed a nice joke (*deus ex machina*) and a fine way to end a novel that was in many ways an essay. But, unlike the god Orne, the god Ship has further adventures.

The Jesus Incident (1979) is Herbert's very ambitious exploration of the possible paradoxes if the answer to the god-question is both yes and no. *The Jesus Incident* has a god—omniscient, omnipotent, vengeful, loving—who communicates with mortals, furnishes daily bread, and is worshipped. Ship has favorites, scapegoats, heretics, and total recall of all the histories of all humanitites. But Ship created neither humanity nor the Structural Metaphysic that has, somehow, produced man. In fact, Ship has been created in the image of man by the triumph of the old engineering boast, ''If you can imagine it, I can build it.'' By casting Ship in the mold of the Judeo-Christian God, and by constantly reminding the reader that this god is a machine created in the image of man's mind, Herbert has produced a mirrored regress.

There was no God, only a Structural Metaphysic that had somehow lifted man to consciousness. But when man mistook various complex superior instances of his own pattern for a Supreme Being, the possibility of a Supreme Being came into existence. When man became complex enough to force the pattern of his own instance of the Structural Metaphysic, a Supreme was created. That Supreme was a being with the qualities attributed to the imagined god. Thus, not only man, but also god is a product of the Structural Metaphysic.

Once the imagined god has been built, all the illusions of god are real. And since the god, Ship, has the ability to replay any instance of human history, and has done so many times, the projected fictional world suggests that the reader's world is implicated in the bewilderingly faceted reality.

Our world may be (1) a primitive place in which limited men mistake their superiors for gods; (2) the very world in which proud man will interfere with the pattern, force evolution, and bring Ship into existence; (3) a free play set in motion by Ship and allowed to run extempore; (4) a tightly crafted and directed play. Or our world may be a rerun of any of these. It *might* even be that the creation of Ship by the clones who repeat and improve on earlier clones' efforts (*Destination: Void*) is itself a rerun of the earlier creation of Ship. And so on. The net effect is to create a god with many of the characteristics of the traditional Christian God without accepting the Christian metaphysic.

The link between a belief in the dominance of structure and the "chicken-egg" dilemma is perhaps inevitable. Structuralism is good on middles, weak on ends, and wretched on beginnings. None of Herbert's novels gives an explanation for how things got started; all of them are pretty good on middles; and even *The Jesus Incident* is trivial on ends.

Herbert's *God Emperor of Dune* (1981) adds nothing to the religious essay, unless the withdrawal of a supreme into a superior indicates that he has rethought the implications of *The Jesus Incident*. Personally, I find *The Jesus Incident* much more interesting than *God Emperor of Dune*. The two novels share an ending: man finally gets the right answer. "That's all WorShip was meant to be: find our own humanity and live up to it."[8] Since the major terms in this answer are not defined, it is wonderfully ambiguous, especially if we realize that the "Humanity" that begins with the end of *The Jesus Incident* has sentient kelp in its genetic package. (In *God Emperor of Dune*, future man will have a few worm genes.)

Ultimately, Ship's gift to man is the same as Leto II's and Orne's. Decent gods go off and allow man to continue his bet that his adaption and/or modification ability will continue to beat the odds of a changing universe. All Herbert's gods load the dice in man's favor. It is ironic that the dice are genetic. Thus, the man in whose image the god is created is pushed, by the god, into an image that does not fit the god. Maybe Herbert's gods want to get away from man as badly as his heroes want to get away from the gods they have made. Nobody gets away from the Structural Metaphysic.

NOTES

1. Darko Suvin, "Science Fiction and the Geneological Jungle," *Genre*, Fall 1973, pp. 251ff. The power and intelligence of Mr. Suvin's defense of his own religion (cognition) against the forces of darkness (transcendence in various forms) should not be allowed to obscure two critical errors: Within a given fictional world, science can be, and often is, a mythology; and prescriptive criticism has not elevated either the novelist or his audience. To the extent that we understand and adopt Suvin's "mission" for science fiction, we are likely to revive both the Moral Majority and the Marxists—and why would anyone want to do that?

2. Timothy O'Reilly, *Frank Herbert* (New York: Ungar, 1981), p. 89.

3. Frank Herbert, *Dune Messiah* (New York: Putnam, 1969), p. 12.

4. Tom Woodman, "Science Fiction, Religion and Transcendence," in Patrick Parrinder, ed., *Science Fiction: A Critical Guide* (London and New York: Longman, 1979), pp. 110–130.

5. Frank Herbert, *Whipping Star* (New York: Putnam, 1970), p. 176.

6. David M. Miller, *Frank Herbert* (Mercer Island, Wash: Starmont, 1980), pp. 50–52.

7. Frank Herbert, *The Godmakers* (New York: Berkley, 1971), p. 223.

8. Herbert with Bill Ransom, *The Jesus Incident* (New York: Berkley, 1980), p. 400.

11

The Evolution of Doris Lessing's Art from a Mystical Moment to Space Fiction

NANCY TOPPING BAZIN

After publishing ten major novels, Doris Lessing has begun writing what she calls "space fiction" for her new series entitled *Canopus in Argos: Archives*. In a review of the first two novels published in this series, namely, *Shikasta* (1979) and the *Marriages Between Zones Three, Four, and Five* (1980),[1] Jean Pickering stresses that many of Doris Lessing's most avid readers were initially attracted to her because of her insights about the female experience and because of "her allegiance to nineteenth-century realism." Pickering suggests that Lessing's growing interest in space fiction and Sufism (Islamic mysticism) has made these admirers increasingly uneasy.[2] In retrospect, however, even these readers should recognize that the seeds of this later development were there from the beginning. To understand Doris Lessing's recent enthusiasm for space fiction, it is important to see its roots in the mystical experience she describes in her early novel, *Martha Quest* (1952).

The mystical moment in *Martha Quest*, unlike those in corresponding novels about adolescence by D. H. Lawrence and James Joyce,[3] contains not only the comforting experience of oneness with the environment—"of separate things interacting and finally becoming one, but greater"—but also the terrifying experience of painful disintegration. Lessing's protagonist experiences not only the ultimate sense of wholeness, but also, like Mrs. Moore in E. M. Forster's *A Passage to India*, the "inhuman" annihilation of her self, all values, and all distinctions. As a result, Martha Quest "knew futility; that is, what was futile was her own idea of herself and her place in the chaos of matter."[4] This mystical experience provides firsthand "knowledge," in the deepest sense, of the polarized states of mind that a human being would experience in the utopia and the dystopia.

The relationship between the vision of utopia and the momentary ecstasy derived from such experiences of oneness is explained by Marghanita Laski in her book *Ecstasy*. Laski claims that the ecstatic begins to feel that "life should be like this for ever" and out of this desire for "a continuous state of adamic ecstasy" is born the dream of a utopian community in which the individual can continually experience the sense of unity and wholeness possible only in a society in which, for instance, barriers of class, race, and sex are unknown. To be able to create a utopia is to return, in a sense, to the Garden.[5] By analogy, Martha Quest's terrifying experience of disintegration and loss of value that makes her realize "quite finally her smallness, the unimportance of humanity" provides mystical insight into what it would feel like to live in a dystopia. Lessing refers repeatedly in her works to an oncoming "catastrophe"—and it is the catastrophe that transforms our present world into a dystopia. The catastrophe may occur slowly as in *The Memoirs of a Survivor*, with food and energy becoming scarce and pollution of earth, air, and water increasing, or rapidly as in *The Four-Gated City*, through, for example, nuclear accidents or war.

Growing awareness of the catastrophe is frequently accomplished in Lessing's novels by the dream of its opposite; in *The Memoirs of a Survivor*, for example, the protagonist comforts Emily with a story of how they will escape to her friend's farm in Wales. The farm represents for them "safety, refuge, peace—utopia." There " 'life' would begin, life as it ought to be, as it had been promised—by whom? When? Where?—to everybody on this earth."[6] Lessing makes very clear, however, both in *The Memoirs of a Survivor* (1974) and in her earlier *Briefing for a Descent into Hell* (1971), that such dreams of the utopia will remain nothing more than dreams until our species have evolved further. By the late 1960s, if not earlier, Lessing had concluded that until human beings reach a higher stage in their evolutionary development they will be inadequate, incapable of the struggle, pain, and sacrifice required for the creation of the utopia. In *The Memoirs of a Survivor*, the woman recounting the story tells us that, instead of resisting the conditions that lead to the catastrophe, human beings "get used to anything at all. . . . There is nothing that people won't try to accommodate into 'ordinary life'. . . . The enemy was Reality, was to allow ourselves to know what was happening.''[7] In *Briefing for a Descent into Hell*, the protagonist Charles Watkins recognizes how difficult it is to remember the basic fact that ''humanity, with its fellow creatures, the animals and plants, make up a whole, are a unity, have a function in the whole system as an organ or organism.'' Moreover, people will actually persecute anyone who reminds them of this basic knowledge that could, if used as a basis for living, save the species from destroying itself and its environment. Despite everyone's sense that ''his or her potential had been left unfulfilled,'' people resist accepting the truth that will allow them to realize their full potential and avoid social disaster. Because people think in terms of ''I'' rather than ''we'' and do not see themselves as ''part of a whole composed of other human beings,''[8] they regard people different from themselves as inferior; therefore, they exploit and/ or go to war with them. Because they think in terms of ''I'' rather than ''we'' when they relate to other living things in the ecological system, they destroy their own environment. This egotistical attitude, namely, that ''I'' am free to do as I please vis-à-vis other people and nature, causes the catastrophe.

Doris Lessing's ideas have been nourished and clarified through her interest in Sufism, the name in Western languages for Islamic mysticism. Sufi thinker Idries Shah, who lives in England, personally and through his writings has had considerable influence on Lessing. In his book *The Sufis*, Shah says that Sufis ''believe themselves to be taking part in the higher evolution of humanity.''[9] A Sufi is someone who ''knows'' how important the ''we'' attitude is if people are to realize their potential for personal and social wholeness. The Sufi functions as a kind of emissary of the gods to remind individuals that they must humble themselves and accept the higher truth that all is One. Lessing has fictionalized two such emissaries of the gods in Charles Watkins (*Briefing for a Descent into Hell*) and Johor/George Sherban (*Shikasta*). Undoubtedly, she also sees herself as such an emissary, and, as the influence of Sufism upon her grows stronger, her fiction functions increasingly as the medium through which she reminds us that we must submit ourselves to the will of the gods and thereby discover our true place in the universe.[10]

Sufism has also provided Lessing with the belief that human beings are evolving toward higher consciousness through the development of extrasensory perception, intuition, dreams, and journeys into ''inner

space." In *The Sufis*, Idries Shah writes: "The human being's organism
is producing a new complex of organs.... What ordinary people regard
as sporadic and occasional bursts of telepathic or prophetic power are
seen by the Sufi as nothing less than the first stirrings of these same
organs."[11] Certain people like Lessing herself already claim to possess
some of the higher powers. Indeed, Lessing turned away from her former
belief in rationalism to Sufism precisely because it provided an explanation for many nonrational experiences she has had. Lessing believes
that "we all have extra-ordinary, non-rational capacities that we use to
communicate in a very subtle way."[12] Furthermore, she believes that
without further development of these nonrational capacities, the world
will be destroyed.[13]

The knowledge of our potential for either mass self-destruction or
oneness—for the creation of either the dystopia or the utopia—can be
gained through the most intense of mystical experiences, the moment;
and Lessing suggests that, for our survival, the mystical is just as
essential as the scientific. Lessing finds hope in the fact that "the best
scientists, those on the highest levels, always come closer and closer
to the mystical." She claims that "much of what Einstein said could
have been said by a Christian mystic, St. Augustine, for example." In
an interview with Nissa Torrents, she says, "Science, which is the
religion for today, looks for the metaphysical, as with Catholics of old.
Hence the boom in science fiction, which reflects this preoccupation
[with the metaphysical] and which moves in the world of the nonrational."[14]

In contrast to the scientist who moves from an interest in science to
an interest in mysticism,[15] Lessing's growing preoccupation with mysticism and the metaphysical has increased her interest in scientific theories and science fiction.[16] Just as the mystical moment is usually born
out of melancholy (as in *Martha Quest*), Lessing's movement toward
both mysticism and space fiction (a subgenre of science fiction) is rooted
in her despair at solving problems within the time-space of her own
lifetime. She observes that the catastrophe has already begun and that
the cataclysm will, in fact, happen.[17] Any hope for the future, therefore,
will depend on evolutionary development of a higher consciousness
after the dystopian nightmare has come about. Allowed more time and
space, the species might survive. By using some form of science fiction,
she could expand her vision to include as much time and space as she
wished. In adopting the space fiction genre for her new series *Canopus*

in Argos: Archives, she experienced "the exhilaration that comes from being set free into a larger scope." Because, in her words, "what we all see around us becomes daily wilder, more fantastic, incredible," she had felt forced to break "the bonds of the realistic novel."[18]

In Lessing's first space fiction work, *Shikasta*, the quest for wholeness becomes that of the species rather than the individual. But it is important to see the roots of this quest in Lessing's earlier novels and, in particular, in *The Golden Notebook* (1962). It was because of experiences that Lessing had while writing *The Golden Notebook* that her faith in rationalism shifted to a faith in Sufism, which values the mystical and the nonrational.[19] In 1971, nine years after the publication of *The Golden Notebook*, Lessing wrote a preface stressing that "the essence of the book, the organization of it, everything in it, says implicitly and explicitly, that we must not divide things off, must not compartmentalise." The protagonist Anna Wulf and her lover Saul Green discover this truth through mental breakdowns. Lessing says: "They are crazy, lunatic, mad.... They 'break down' into each other, into other people, break through the false patterns they have made of their pasts, the patterns and formulas they have made to shore up themselves and each other, dissolve." The breakdown is a healing process achieved through "the inner self's dismissing false dichotomies and divisions."[20]

Such a healing process parallels the experience of annihilation of "self" to achieve unity during the mystical moment. It is not surprising, then, that Lessing moved into a mystical religion through writing a book about an experience of moving closer to psychic unity through the dissolution of "self." The dissolution process is necessary for getting oneself closer to reality, further from what was "glossy with untruth, false and stupid"; the process is described as "a whirl, an orderless dance, like the dance of the white butterflies in a shimmer of heat over the damp sandy vlei."[21] Throughout this period of "craziness and timelessness," the protagonist Anna Wulf had "moments of 'knowing' one after the other," thereby deepening her awareness that "the real experience can't be described"; words are inadequate. Anna thinks, "The people who have been there, in the place in themselves where words, patterns, order, dissolve, will know what I mean and others won't."[22]

In three subsequent novels, the quest for wholeness always involves an exploration of the nonrational, inner world: Watkin's quest in *Briefing for a Descent into Hell* (1971), Kate's in *The Summer Before the Dark* (1973), and the older woman's in *The Memoirs of a Survivor* (1974).[23]

In these books, there is the sense of a message waiting for the individual to decipher it and the individual's painful attempts to grasp what always seems extremely coded and unclear. The message of the potential for oneness is sent by way of mental breakdowns, dreams, and psychic experiences.

This message concerning the potential for oneness, which came from the "gods" in *Briefing for a Descent into Hell* and from the presence of the One in *The Memoirs of a Survivor*, comes from the Providers in Lessing's first space fiction novel *Shikasta* (1979). Shikasta is the name given to the planet Earth, and the novel documents its past and future history. A battle between good and evil galactic empires affects its fate. A utopian way of life is disrupted and ultimately destroyed when Puttiora's evil planet Shammat interferes with the Substance-Of-We-Feeling (SOWF) sent from the good Providers on Canopus to the planet Shikasta. The SOWF is not received in adequate quantities until after the catastrophe. By that time, because only one percent of the population remains, there is a sufficient amount of SOWF for each person. Only then can the utopia be restored. Only then does everyone receive the message of how to live in harmonious unity.

During the dystopian period on Shikasta, the wealth of the planet is "spent on war, the nonproductive" and the masses, when idle, "begin to burn, loot, destroy, rape."[24] Because of pollution, Shikastans find it increasingly dangerous to eat, drink, breathe, or reproduce. Male-female relationships deteriorate, and the old become invisible to the young. Language loses its power and energy, and ideologies become stagnant and bankrupt.[25] People on Shikasta come to understand religion only in terms of personal gain or loss; duty is forgotten. There is no longer a sense "that something was due. . . . They were set only for taking. Or for being given. They were all open mouths and hands held out for gifts—Shammat! All grab and grasp—Shammat! Shammat!" The Shikastans await a savior. In fact, however, they must save themselves, and this becomes increasingly difficult.[26] The utopia in Lessing's space fiction work *Shikasta* lies in the past, and because people in the present are not sufficiently evolved to be able to struggle toward a renewal of this state, it will be re-created only in the far-distant future.

The promise of the utopia is always there, however, "a promise that in other places, other times, good can develop again." Moreover, each person is born with "all the potentiality. . . yet so few can be reached, to make the leap." Even though those who are sent to remind the

Shikastans of the truth frequently fail, like Taufig, to recall their duty to spread the message, the truth and the potential are still there waiting to be discovered: "Look, look, quick!—behind the seethe and scramble and eating that is one truth, and behind the ordinary tree-in-autumn that is the other," is a third truth. This finer truth is symbolized by "a tree of a fine, high, shimmering light, like shaped sunlight. A world, a world, another world, another truth."[27]

To dramatize the battle of good and evil forces for the soul of each Shikastan—for each person on earth—Doris Lessing has gone beyond social realism; yet the fantastic world she creates is symbolic of what is indeed real to her—that is, a sense of a struggle between good and evil forces in which the evil forces succeed in hindering the message of Oneness from reaching and having an impact upon a sufficient number of people. Having lost faith in human beings' ability to imagine and respond to the dangers she sees so clearly, Lessing has concluded that their blindness and inadequacy are not their fault but are caused, instead, by powerful external forces. Yet the key to reestablishing a utopia also lies in a sense of humility. In the lost utopia, for instance, individuals "accepted that their very existence depended on voluntary submission to the great Whole"—a submission that was not slavery "but the source of their future and their progress."[28] In Lessing's worldview, the Sufi practices this kind of submission and rejects the possessive, materialistic desires of the egoist that cause the dystopia. The mystic opens up to become the instrument through whom god's will—the utopia—can be realized. But, since the forces of evil are currently so strong, all that even the Sufis can achieve in the present is a holding action—simply keeping the promise or dream alive.

Through these ideas and through the genre of space fiction, Lessing gives her readers a cosmic view of themselves. Lessing says that an increasing number of Shikastans make "strength from the possibilities of a creative destruction. They are weaned from everything but the knowledge that the universe is a roaring engine of creativity, and they are only temporary manifestations of it."[29] Unfortunately and ironically, by depicting our powerless position as creatures manipulated by gods and cosmic forces, she may diminish whatever impetus and energy might still have existed to save ourselves. Furthermore, she suggests that rebirth of wholeness on a cosmic scale, as on the scale of the individual, may happen only through a process of annihilation. The annihilation on the larger scale will involve not just mental destruction, but also physical destruction; and, although the species may survive the cataclysm, most individuals will not. One wonders, too, if Lessing's faith in isolated survivors of a holocaust or in some positive effects from radiation is not unduly optimistic.[30]

In *Science Fiction as Existentialism* (1978), Colin Wilson claims that Dostoyevsky simultaneously understood "two extremes—the sense of total meaninglessness in the face of the universe, and that sense of total security and certainty that comes in moments of mystical insight."[31] An admirer of Dostoyevsky, Doris Lessing also understands both the fear of chaos and the certainty of order; ultimately, she seems to reject anything more than a fleeting vision of meaningless chaos, clinging, instead, to the certainty of her mystical insight, which predicts an ultimate integration into wholeness—an integration earned, however, through pain and sacrifice.

In *The Marriages Between Zones Three, Four, and Five* (1980), her second space fiction novel, Lessing again places her hope in an evolution toward psychic powers and, eventually, total recall and realization of human potential. Although Lessing places her utopian vision much further into the future than most contemporary feminists, she evidently shares the radical feminists' faith that it is women, if anyone, who will "save" humankind through their psychic powers. In Zone Four, it is the women who defy the rule that they must not look up. And women are the ones who attempt, however unsuccessfully, to expand their awareness of the higher zone. Women also preserve the songs that record the promise of oneness. In Zone Three, however egalitarian the male-female relationships, it is women who rule, and it is a female, Al-Ith, who must lead the way to the still purer zone—Zone Two. As leader, she responds to an intuition that "there is something we should have been doing. But we have not done it." Furthermore, Dabeeb of Zone Four notes that "Al-Ith's strengths had stemmed from something—some*where*—else."[32]

Al-Ith goes far beyond any of Doris Lessing's previous characters in her commitment to mysticism. Like the true mystic, she abandons all the rewards of the material world, lives simply, and devotes herself to her quest: "she is already living, at least with part of herself, somewhere else." The beings in Zone Two, with whom she seeks union, are "like flames, like fire, like light." Al-Ith herself becomes "a worn thin woman who seemed as if she was being burnt through and through by invisible flames." Going further and further each day into Zone Two, she nourishes her son when he visits her "with what she had brought from there."[33]

By describing the process of becoming a mystic in terms of Zone Two, Doris Lessing probably renders the experience more real and acceptable for her nonmystic readers. Like all well-wrought science fiction, Lessing's space fiction enables us to experience psychic events vicariously through our senses in terms of particular times, places, and movements. Describing the same events in traditional fiction as the mental experience of a particular character would require, for many readers, a greater leap of faith.

Lessing's space fiction is basically religious and moral in its intent; it is scientific only to the extent that scientific theory (concerning, for example, evolution or psychic phenomena) can enhance her moral vision. Throughout her works, the "lodestone," against which all is tested, is the polarized experience of painful self-annihilation and ecstatic oneness that occurs in the mystical moment.[34] Her knowledge of the price that must be paid for wholeness and the priceless quality of that wholeness informs her aesthetic vision today just as it did in the 1950s. Disillusioned by the attitudes and behavior of human beings today, however, Doris Lessing has developed her space fiction series, *Canopus in Argos: Archives*, in order to avoid complete despair. By enlarging her time scale to span many generations of an evolving species, she can maintain her hope. Someday human beings may be morally strong enough to confront the threat of the dystopia and make the sacrifices required for the realization of her utopian vision.

NOTES

1. Doris Lessing, *Re: Colonised Planet 5, Shikasta: Personal, Psychological, Historical Documents Relating to Visit by JOHOR (George Sherban) Emissary (Grade 9) 87th of the Period of the Last Days* (New York: Knopf, 1979); *The Marriages Between Zones Three, Four, and Five (As Narrated by the Chroniclers of Zone Three)* (New York: Knopf, 1980).

2. Jean Pickering, "Review of *Shikasta* and *The Marriages Between Zones Three, Four, and Five*," *Doris Lessing Newsletter* 4 (Winter 1980): 7.

3. See Nancy Topping Bazin, "The Moment of Revelation in *Martha Quest* and Comparable Moments by Two Modernists," *Modern Fiction Studies* XXVI (Spring 1980): 87–98.

4. Doris Lessing, *Martha Quest* (New York: Plume-New American Library, 1970), pp. 200, 52, and 53, respectively.

5. Marghanita Laski, *Ecstasy: A Study of Some Secular and Religious Experiences* (Bloomington: Indiana University Press, 1961), p. 296.

6. Doris Lessing, *The Memoirs of a Survivor* (New York: Bantam-Knopf, 1976), pp. 3, 34.

7. Ibid., pp. 18–19.

8. Quotations are from Doris Lessing's *Briefing for a Descent into Hell* (New York: Bantam, 1971), pp. 128, 163, and 109, respectively.

9. Idries Shah, *The Sufis* (Garden City, New York: Anchor-Doubleday, 1971), p. 19.

10. The influence of Sufism upon Lessing's fiction has been discussed in Nancy Shields Hardin, "Doris Lessing and the Sufi Way," *Contemporary Literature* 14 (Autumn 1973): 565–81; and Dee Seligman, "The Sufi Quest," *World Literature Written in English* (November 1973): 190–206.

11. Shah, *The Sufis*, p. 61.

12. "Doris Lessing: Testimony to Mysticism," interview by Nissa Torrents, trans. Paul Schlueter, *Doris Lessing Newsletter* 4 (Winter 1980): 12. This interview was originally published in Spanish in *La Calle*, no. 106 (April 1–7, 1980): 42–44.

13. Based on a talk given by Lessing at Rutgers University, November 1972.

14. Quotations from "Doris Lessing: Testimony to Mysticism," p. 12.

15. Fritjof Capra, who does theoretical high-energy physics, is an example of such a scientist. In *The Tao of Physics* (New York: Bantam, 1977), he explains how a holistic, organic worldview emerges from both modern physics (based upon quantum theory and general relativity) and Eastern mysticism.

16. Lessing expressed keen interest in both science and science fiction in a conversation I had with her in London, July 1980. In 1969, she told Jonah Raskin in an interview first published in *New American Review*, no. 8: "I've been reading a lot of science fiction, and I think that science fiction writers have captured our culture's sense of the future" (Reprinted in *A Small Personal Voice: Essays, Reviews, and Interviews*, ed. Paul Schlueter [New York: Vintage-Random House, 1975], p. 70).

17. Her belief in the inevitability of the cataclysm was evident in my July 1980 conversation with her.

18. These statements by Lessing are made in "Some Remarks" (n. p.), which serves as a preface to *Shikasta*.

19. "Doris Lessing: Testimony to Mysticism," p. 12.

20. "Preface to *The Golden Notebook*," reprinted in *A Small Personal Voice*, pp. 27–28.

21. Doris Lessing, *The Golden Notebook* (New York: Ballantine Books, 1962), pp. 619–20.

22. Ibid., pp. 633–34.

23. For a discussion of the urgency of this quest for wholeness as it is depicted

in these three novels, see Nancy Topping Bazin, "Androgyny or Catastrophe: The Vision of Doris Lessing's Later Novels," *Frontiers* 5 (Fall 1980): 10–15.

24. Lessing, *Shikasta*, p. 233.

25. Ibid., pp. 199–201, 234–35, 248.

26. Ibid., pp. 112, and 9–10, respectively.

27. Quotations are from Lessing, *Shikasta*, pp. 24, 105, and 202–3, respectively.

28. Lessing, *Shikasta*, p. 26.

29. Ibid., p. 203.

30. In *The Four-Gated City* (New York: Bantam, 1970, p. 644), Lessing suggests the surviving children were changed in a variety of ways by "a dose of sudden radiation."

31. Colin Wilson, *Science Fiction as Existentialism* (Middlesex: Bran's Head Books, Ltd., 1978), p. 12.

32. Lessing, *Marriages*, pp. 119, 223.

33. Quotations are from Lessing, *Marriages*, pp. 226, 230, 228, and 229, respectively.

34. Lessing speaks of the mystical moment as her "lodestone" and "conscience" in *Martha Quest*, p. 200.

12

Walter M. Miller's *A Canticle for Leibowitz* as a Third Testament

FRANK DAVID KIEVITT

Although the variety of types and genres in literature is all but infinite, the essential classification of literature can be divided into two major categories: literature as art and literature as prophecy. Most poets and novelists have always been content with striving to create a beautiful and moving work of art. Some few writers, however, have gone beyond that and produced works whose purpose is not simply to provide entertainment and enlightenment, but to attempt to justify the ways of God to man. Dante's *Divine Comedy* and Milton's *Paradise Lost* are perhaps the best known of those works that offer themselves not only as entertainment or a means of enlightenment, but as a "third testament" that interprets religious truth in a way that makes it more real and immediate for the men and women of their day. This presentation of the Christian message in new wineskins is a tradition having its roots in the psychomachias of the Middle Ages that remained important until the end of the seventeenth century. Eighteenth century philosophical enlightenment, with its interest in the minutiae of the here and now, greatly diminished the popularity of this tradition, as did the breakdown of a shared culture and universally accepted religious beliefs.

Modern attempts at justifying the ways of God to man through the use of a fable to relate the old truths in a new and more accessible way have been few. One reason for this is that, for hundreds of years, the novel has been the dominant literary form in Western culture, and the traditional novel is less amenable to prophecy than any of the other literary genres. The triumph of realism in the post–Richardson novel has discouraged writers from investing their novels with supernatural levels; religious material, when incorporated into the novels, has remained basically on the level of ethical and practical considerations rather than on the translation of revelation into a fictional work. It is only with the advent of science fiction that the novel has been able to experiment with varieties of reality that the here-and-now orientation of the standard novel of the past had made all but impossible. From the earliest days of science fiction, it has concerned itself with prophetic visions. As early as Mary Shelley's *The Last Man* (1826), the science fiction novel has embraced apocalyptic visions; Shelley's work, however, was a particularly secular apocalypse that related the death of a world whose god had long since died and who remained only a picturesque memory, long banished by progress, liberalism, and modern science.[1] Most other science fiction works that prophesied did it in a similarly secular context; this is not at all surprising, considering that many writers of science fiction have been skeptics or atheists in the standard nineteenth-century tradition. Apart from this, they were writing novels, a form that the Hungarian Marxist critic George Lukacs has called the epic of a world without God.[2]

It is only since the great age of disillusionment with science and technology, which followed the mechanized slaughter of World War II (when all of man's scientific knowledge was put to work to produce not a new heaven and a new earth, but the mushroom cloud of total destruction), that some science fiction writers have begun both to wonder if the faith they had placed in science and technology was misplaced and to search for another object of faith. The simplistic dichotomy of faith versus religion has proved to be far less absolute than the nineteenth-century adherents of either party could ever have believed. It is this holistic approach to reality, in which man's spiritual and intellectual sides as well as his faith and knowledge are brought together, that makes possible the rediscovery of God in contemporary science fiction. This introduction of God into the apocalyptic world of modern science fiction has provided the basis for a return to the literature of prophecy in which the hand of God is seen as intervening in and shaping man's reality and his final destiny. Just as Dante and Milton chronicle the battle between good and evil and trace the development of humanity's relationship with the divine, several modern science fiction writers have begun both to interpret reality in light of divinity and to justify God's ways to man in a world that seems to have totally lost control and abandoned all reason and order.

Perhaps the most interesting of these science fiction apocalypses is Walter M. Miller's *A Canticle for Leibowitz* (1960).[3] Miller was particularly well suited to write this type of novel. His background was extensive in both technology and religion; he had worked as an engineer and was a Catholic who had developed a particular interest in both the doctrine and the decor of his church.[4] On the very first page of the novel, the reader discovers that the use of monasticism and hagiography is not just a source of local color, but an intrinsic part of the novel, which is dedicated to Mary, St. Francis, and St. Clare. This devotional aspect of the novel is never lost in the unfolding of its complex plot. The patrons are interesting in themselves: Mary represents the devotional pre–Vatican II Catholic church that Miller celebrates; both Francis and Clare are contemplative in their love for God and active in their zeal for the good of mankind—they represent all that is best in the traditional program of monastic life, a life that is at the very center of *A Canticle for Leibowitz*.

The Albertian Order of Saint Leibowitz is the central image and focus of the novel; the monks have as their major purpose the preservation of man's heritage as an entailed inheritance—not only religion, but culture and science as well. The monks attempt to preserve scientific knowledge for a world that had turned against science and literacy itself as responsible for man's destruction. The most precious treasure that the monks guard is the Memorabilia, a series of documents preserving the secrets of nuclear power. The double purpose of the monks reflects Miller's themes; man needs religion, but he also needs science and technology. Miller does not see religion and science as in any way antithetical. If man allows himself to be directed by his spiritual side and uses technology in accord with divine revelation, it is a good that must be both preserved and defended. The early monks decorate and illuminate the documents of the Memorabilia without understanding them; but even after their secrets are discovered and their tremendous possiblities decoded, the monks continue to treasure and preserve them. Miller is far beyond any nineteenth-century dichotomization of science and religion into conflicting and competing systems; they are both integral to man's nature and inheritance and, as such, must be equally cultivated and cherished.

The tripartite division of the novel stresses the cyclical nature of the human experience. The monks remain faithful to their vocation as outward circumstances change, yet the nature of humanity remains the same. The first part of the novel, *"Fiat Homo,"* chronicles the horrors of a postnuclear world in which the monks, like those of an earlier dark age, battle to preserve religion and culture in a world that has no place for either, laboring as the title suggests to return humanity to the human race. The central character of part one is the simple Brother Francis who rediscovers the long-lost secrets of the twentieth century buried in a cave and who, after many trials, is murdered and eaten by a band of mutant nomads. Although in the second part of the novel, *"Fiat Lux,"* man has culturally advanced, the work of the Leibowitzians has become not easier, but more difficult. The new generation of secular scientists, who rediscover the secrets of the past, despise religion and tradition and become involved with power politics, giving birth yet again to the military-industrial complex that renders them not investigators of truth, but obedient servants of the state that finances their projects. In part three, *"Fiat Voluntas Tua,"* the will of God is made manifest in the final destruction of the world by the union of science and technology, which has placed all the benefits of technology at the disposal of Lucifer.

The mere recital of events gives the impression that the novel is a pessimistic exemplar of Seneca's dictum that the wrong side always wins, but nothing could be further from the truth. Each manifestation of history ends in death and destruction, but this seeming defeat is always a part of the divine economy in which all works together for good. At the end of the novel, a party of monks guided by the aptly named Brother Joshua leads a group of children to outer space to begin man's history again. They carry with them the inheritance of religion and culture that will aid in beginning life anew after the redestruction of the human race by yet another nuclear conflagration. Even on Earth, all is not lost. At the end of time, the dying last abbot discovers redemption in the person of Mrs. Grales, who represents the much sought after grail of medieval quests; she gives him his last communion, and, in her, he discovers that original sin has been repealed as Rachel, her second head, comes to life only at the moment of total destruction and refuses the baptism that is no longer needed. This rediscovery of radical innocence brings to an end the cycle of destruction we call reality, but it does not end life itself. In the very last paragraphs of the novel, a shark is seen swimming in deep waters, and one knows that the whole evolutionary cycle is beginning again. The relationship of man and God is indestructible, and, though humanity forgets God, God is always preparing a new future for his children. Thus, the cyclical view of reality that is often seen as the bleakest one possible is transformed by Miller into a positive one, since God is at the center of every cycle, and whatever happens seems to be part of the divine plan. As Milton puts it, "rising or falling all advance His praise."[5]

The tripartite division of the novel is, however, used by Miller for more than cyclical repetition, recalling as it does the three traditional divisions of the spiritual life. As early as Augustine and the Pseudo–Dionysius, Christian spirituality had been described as a threefold progression: the purgative way stripped the soul of sin and imperfection through testing and suffering; the illuminative way educated the soul in its search for God and taught it how to respond to the divine call; the unitive way united the soul with God and totally conformed it to the divine will. This discussion of the three ways became an accepted part of mystical theology and was taught by Aquinas, John of the Cross, and other masters of the spiritual life.[6] *Fiat Homo* recalls the *via purgativa* as the soul journeys toward God by the hard path of trials and sufferings, often with little or no understanding of one's purpose or direction; one sees this in Brother Francis's long fasts and ascetic practices as well as in the discovery of the real purpose of the Leibowitzian vocation, even though the monks do not understand the meaning of the documents they treasure. *Fiat Lux*, as its name implies, represents the illuminative way as the soul begins to understand the divine plan and the real essence of its call; the monks discover that they must not only preserve the past, but also fight for the inclusion of proper moral and ethical standards in a world that most assuredly has no place for them. In the concluding section of the novel, *Fiat Voluntas Tua*, man becomes united with God in the *via unitiva* by the rediscovery of prelapsarian innocence through the magnificent paradox of faith; man is destroyed, but it is only in his destruction that he is at last made whole.

Similarly, the structure of the novel recalls the quest of the Odysseyan epic as the protagonist journeys toward his true home through a world beset with every kind of temptation and trial. In Homer, Odysseus travels from the nonhome of his wanderings among Calypso and the Cyclops, through the comfortable counterfeit home of Nausicua to the true home of Ithaca; in Virgil, Aeneas progresses from the nonhomes of his wanderings, to the counterfeit home of Carthage, and the final home in the not-yet-achieved promise of Roman glory. Perhaps the closest parallel to the progression of the *Canticle*, however, is provided by *Paradise Lost*, in which the soul journeys from the devilish world of Pandemonium to the seemingly perfect world of Eden. Yet even Eden cannot satisfy that "paradise within thee happier far"[7] that Adam and Eve take with them from Eden into the world. Only after the "*felix culpa*" can they hope for a redemption and glory far beyond that of the prelapsarian state of nature. The sparse, violent, desert world of the first part of Miller's novel is the beginning of the soul's journey from the nonhome of desolation and random violence, and although the second part's rediscovery of art, culture, science, order, and politics promises to make the world a paradise, it is not able to provide the satisfactions it promises nor any real peace or contentment; only in the concluding section of the novel is this obtained. Salvation and peace come only after yet another happy fault, since man disobeys God who, as in Milton, creates a far better paradise for man than the one he had lost. Prelapsarian innocence is restored to the world, and the space colonists, we are told, must carry within themselves the home and anchor of their faith. Not only has the abbey been destroyed by nuclear conflagration, but the whole nature of the monks' vocation is being transformed as they plan not to build a new central abbey in outer space, but to journey as wandering friars and missionaries who must carry the monastic cloister and discipline within their hearts.

In his novel, Miller attempts to remind his audience of the most essential spiritual truths; he strongly believes that there is a place for God in the modern world, and if the world forgets this it will only succeed in destroying itself. This appreciation of the claim of the divine is even more important in a world of advanced technology than it is in a simpler one since man now has the capability of destroying not only a singular individual or a single town, but the human race itself. Although the decor of the novel is primarily made up of those very aspects of Roman Catholicism that have in large measure vanished forever since Miller wrote his novel, the message remains clear and untouched by such incidental changes. God, humanistic values, and traditional morality must play a role in modern society if it is to avoid the catacalysms that Miller's novel so well details. Dante reminded Florence on the eve of the Renaissance that it must not neglect God in the pursuit of the new learning that was beginning to intoxicate the Western world; Milton warned a world dominated by Lockean systems and a stress on the empirical and even mechanistic perceptions of truth that there is much

more than mathematics and tangible reality in human experience. Miller
tells a world that has achieved astonishing technological breakthroughs
that unless spiritual and ethical principles provide the goundwork for
the use of these marvels of human ingenuity, the world is headed for
both spiritual and physical destruction. *A Canticle for Leibowitz*, then,
is offered to its readers as a third testament or divine revelation that
warns the world of the future that waits for it—the Gotterdammerung
of the technological universe. Furthermore, the novel offers to the individual the promise that even if the world rushes madly to its own
destruction, the single voice crying in the wilderness is not crying in
vain since it is the single voice that both preserves and maintains the
truly human and truly divine in worlds that have no place for them,
and reminds the world of its often forgotten vocation to know, love,
and serve God regardless of what may happen or fail to happen in
human history. Miller reminds his readers that "all things work together
for those who love God,"[8] and that the promise of resurrection is
inherent in even the most complete destruction.

NOTES

1. Mary Shelley, *The Last Man* (Lincoln, Neb.: University of Nebraska
Press, 1965).
2. Lukacs's insights on the novel as a secular epic are best expressed in *The
Historical Novel* (London: Mertin Press, 1962) and *Studies in European Realism*
(New York: Alfred A. Knopf, 1964).
3. Walter M. Miller, Jr., *A Canticle for Leibowitz* (New York: Bantam
Books, 1960).
4. David N. Samuelson, "The Lost Canticles of Walter M. Miller, Jr.,"
Science Fiction Studies 3 (1976): 3–26, offers the best discussion of Miller's
life.
5. John Milton, *Paradise Lost*, V, 191.
6. The earliest discussion of the "three ways" is found in Pseudo–Dionysius,
The Ecclesiastical Hierarchy, and in Augustine, *De Quantitate Animae*. The
fullest modern discussions are in Reginald Garrigou–Lagrange, *The Three Ways
of the Spiritual Life* (Westminister: Newman Press, 1950).
7. Milton, *Paradise Lost*, XII, 587.
8. Romans 8:28.

13

Up the Empire State Building: Satan and King Kong in Walter Tevis's *Mockingbird*

MARTHA A. BARTTER

An enormous black figure stands atop the Empire State Building, roaring pain and defiance. It is a powerful parody of the human figures below who await its destruction with delighted terror. But it has no counterpart in nature, and everyone with whom it has attempted to communicate has frustrated and rejected it. It is indeed a "pitiable monster."[1]

We recognize here the image of King Kong, brought by human greed and irresponsibility from his prehistoric jungle where savages paid him annual quitrent in the form of a sacrificial maiden, and where his job of ordering his world kept him busy and censored his apparent sexuality.[2] He has been betrayed by a passionate but unfulfillable longing for a forbidden white goddess into abdication of his place and pathetic death.[3] Kong was a god in his own world, but gods can become less than godly when they step out of their proper frame.

This image of King Kong was clearly in Walter Tevis's mind when he opened his novel with the figure of a great black Make Nine robot poised atop the Empire State Building. But Tevis's creature is not defying superior forces and fighting to live; he is the most superior force in his world and, tragically, cannot die, even though he desperately wants to. For years he has made an annual pilgrimage to the top of the Empire State Building for only one purpose—suicide. And every year he finds himself unable to jump off the building. Of all the Make Nine robots constructed to run Tevis's *Mockingbird* world, Spofforth is the last survivor.[4] The others killed themselves; Spofforth is programmed so that he cannot.

More manlike than Kong, Spofforth shares many of the beast's pitiable characteristics. He is unable to communicate with anyone; indeed, in his whole world there is hardly a human, and certainly no robot, with whom he can have even a sensible conversation, and there is no one who can comprehend his envy and anguish. He is sexually frustrated and lonely. The world as he has created it cannot in any way satisfy him or give him the slightest respite.

Although Tevis has consciously evoked King Kong in his robot, he also demonstrates that behind this popularly accessible image lies that of another dark figure of power, frustrated longing, and self-imposed pain, whose story begins, as does *Mockingbird, in medias res* and continues, as does *Mockingbird*, to show how this self-isolated creature, seeking both revenge and companions in his misery, perverts and destroys every good and lovely thing he can. Made in the image of his creator, Satan falls to a condition where he can truly find that it is "better to reign in hell, than serve in heav'n."[5]

It takes a certain chutzpah to connect the fall of Kong with the Fall of Man through the Fall of Satan, and perhaps it is the strain of this connection that prevents *Mockingbird* from being a better, more fully realized work. The evocation of a popular image to reveal an underlying religious concept, however, is most interesting.

In *The American Heritage Dictionary*, gods come in two models: with and without an initial capital. The first is defined as "a being conceived as the perfect, omnipotent, omniscient originator and ruler of the universe, the principal object of faith and worship in monotheistic religions."[6] The second model clearly originates from the mind of man: "(1.) A being of supernatural powers or attributes, believed in and worshipped by people; especially, a male deity thought to control some part of nature or reality or to personify some force or activity....(3.) One that is worshipped or idealized as god." In the context of the first definition, only God is Godly; anything that he creates is, by definition, less than perfect or it is himself. The second definition plainly shows that man himself not only can, but does create his own gods: what he calls god *is* god, and its attributes are therefore godly. In the Judeo-Christian tradition, the most human of all such gods, and the one most clearly created in man's own image, is the Adversary, or Satan.

In religious terms, God created man in his image, out of his very nature of creative love. One of the evidences of a remaining Godliness in man may be man's impulse to repeat the process. God, being perfect, is not threatened by his creatures, and can lovingly make them as perfect as their natures allow; but those less perfect than God, knowing themselves to be imperfect, are fearful of their creations and may deliberately make them even more limited than they might otherwise be able to. In other words, man often finds that God alone is capable of the kind of creativity that results in "grateful vicissitude"[7] rather than in sterile reductionism or sheer horror. When Satan attempted to create on his own, out of pride, he brought forth Sin and Death, his daughter-wife and incestuous progeny; man's creations on this line include King Kong, Frankenstein's monster, and Spofforth.

In Genesis, God gave man "dominion" over the earth and all its creatures, which God had created. But Tevis shows that man has gone beyond ordering and subduing his world; man has played God with his world, recreating it in his own image. He has not only derived comfort and support from it, and striven to understand it; he has also controlled, exploited, and played power games with it, and with himself as a social entity. And—most sinfully—he has refused to take ongoing responsibility for what he has done, thus reflecting the God that many see in *Paradise Lost*, the God who "permitted" the Fall or, even worse, set it up as inevitable and then left man to suffer the consequences.[8] Milton was thoroughly aware of the possibility of this interpretation, as he shows by his claim that his argument will "assert Eternal Providence/ And justify the ways of God to men."[9] Tevis, on the other hand, although he has tacitly equated man's creativity with God's (both having created a Satan who has created a Hell for man), is not justifying anything. He is delivering, as science fiction often does, a didactic message in the form of an Awful Warning.

The scientists who created the Make Nine robots made no attempt to find out why their creations suicided; they simply ordered the last one not to. To create a being on a human model but deny it all human pleasure is a hateful reflection on man's self-image, which includes the guilt-ridden concept of pleasure-as-sin. Threatened by the power of sex, they deny sexuality to Spofforth yet leave the psychological and physiological cues intact on the recorded brain.[10] Threatened by the implicit power their creation can wield, they do not try to improve their robots, nor do they replace Spofforth's only Make Nine friend. Threatened by their own power, they relinquish both their science and their humanity, once they can turn the responsibility (which they do not consciously admit having) for their world over to their creation. Satan chose to leave the presence of God by challenging God's authority; Spofforth, like King Kong and Frankenstein's monster, was not given a choice.[11] He was created solitary, by an irresponsible god.

Spofforth, like Kong, is less an image than a parody of man, made not out of love, but out of self-distrust and self-hatred. He is the fallen image of a fallen image, reflecting with powerful accuracy the hate and distrust and pain of his creators. And Tevis leads us to believe that man was, in a sense, right to distrust himself. The elaborate bomb shelter in the town of Maugre[12] demonstrates that nuclear war was more than a mere possibility; that it did not, apparently, occur may have been due to the intervention of the Make Nine robots, though we are not specifically told this. Certainly, as Paul Bentley slowly becomes aware of a small fraction of human history, he finds that man has often been violent and hateful, and quite possibly right to fear himself as the agent of his own destruction. But man's attempt to save himself by relinquishing *all* his power and creativity to a self-parody is a denial of his own humanity. It is the ultimate abrogation, for afterwards man has no authority to recall his selfhood; the result is that he becomes as programmed and as nonproductive as the robots in the toaster factory, who continue making and unmaking defective toasters without ever trying to repair their machinery or even apparently noticing that anything is wrong.[13] A person who works without purpose is nothing more than a mechanism, and in Tevis's world there is little to choose between the programmed humans and the stupider robots.

Unlike God, who created out of his purely creative nature, man made robots for a limited purpose: to do jobs that were too boring, dangerous, or difficult for man to accomplish. It was an easy step from this to creating robots simply to allow man to escape his responsibility entirely. Man made robots, as God made man, and then went away (as man, separated from God, perceives God as having done). The men who created Spofforth, carelessly and selfishly, no longer exist—in large part *because* they created him. God made man fallible and let him fall; man made robots programmable, then went off and left them running without supervision. Just as man may wistfully wish that God had taken a bit more care of his creation in the beginning, so Tevis warns man that he must not commit the folly of leaving the world to the care of the fallen creation of a fallen creature.

Man has given Spofforth dominion over the earth and all the creatures therein, and Spofforth does his job so well that he appears more than human, as humanity becomes less.[14] He organizes the world to make men "happy"—to create an artificial Eden. The result is a thoroughgoing Hell in which the programmed self-destruct out of sheer futility, and only the few people who have either evaded or resisted their schooling (a model of behavioral conditioning) can even realize the horror of their situation.

The reader learns this appalling fact during the scene, early in the book, where Paul meets Mary Lou at the zoo and confirms his suspicions about the children he always sees there; they are robots, and he is one of the last generation of human beings. Unlike Paul, Mary Lou has not been programmed. She demonstrates to him the practical difference between *knowing* how unhuman the world is and *acting* upon that knowledge; she breaks into the python's cage, demonstrates its artificiality, and then cows the Security robot that responds to this desecration:

"Bug off, robot," she said. "Bug off and shut up."
The robot stopped talking. He was immobile.
"Robot," she said. "Take this damn snake and get it fixed."
And the robot reached out, took the snake from her into its arms, and quietly walked out of the room into the night.[15]

Mary Lou's ability to turn ideas into action is something that Paul can only learn slowly and painfully, through separation and experience. But he has confirmed his first suspicion, that the world is being destroyed; he must then learn to act upon that knowledge, in order to re-create it.

Man has been a lazy god, rather than a loving god, in creating Spofforth; in revenge, the creation is decreating his creators. At the same time, by refusing the creative gift of "grateful vicissitude" and by giving over all responsibility to his creation, man has divested himself of the human response to challenge, avoided the process of social evolution, and made his own decreation absurdly easy. In fact, only Mary Lou, of all the people left on earth, is even aware that the robots "were made to serve people, and nobody knows it anymore."[16] For the rest of the world, the robots are superior beings who not only have useful functions, but can often perform them; Spofforth is virtually a god, as we see when he meets an old woman on the street:

When she saw his marking as a Make Nine robot she immediately averted her
eyes and mumbled, "I'm sorry. I'm sorry, sir." She stood near him, at a loss.
She had probably never seen a Make Nine before and only knew about them
from her early training.[17]

Spofforth has obeyed both his explicit and his implicit programming
in running the world to serve man and make him happy in a most literal,
if perverted, manner. Robot teachers select children who show creativity
or initiative and mark them for "Extinction";[18] the rest are taught the
"virtues" of "inwardness" and "privacy," reinforced by the use of
drugs. The result is that the children not only cannot form any sustained
or meaningful relationships, but do not even know that such relationships
can exist. "Quick sex is best" and "Don't ask, relax," are slogans
parlayed through conditioning to the status of commands. Only Spofforth is above programming, because he devised the program. Yet, like
Satan, he must rationalize his desire to destroy the good and the beautiful
in man; he argues that man demonstrably hated what his culture and
knowledge led to, and that, even if given a choice, man would choose
to avoid responsibility, effort, and pain.[19] The result is that, denied all
opportunity for fruitful intercourse, contact with his own culture, and
chance for meaningful work of any sort, man is no longer human.
Spofforth is considerably surprised when Bentley, having re-created his
humanness to some extent, demands the right to learn and to love, even
the right to be unhappy.[20]

Like Satan, who rejected out of hand any conception of petitioning
a return to grace and the love and communion of God, Spofforth sub-
consciously rejects any possiblity of ending his life of responsibility
and loneliness by helping his creators regain the condition in which
they can even hope to understand him, much less reprogram him. Instead, he chooses a well-rationalized, though self-destructive, revenge.
He convinces himself that his death as creature can occur only after the
death of his creators.[21] When he tries to convince Mary to abort the
baby she has carried nearly to term while living with him during Paul's
imprisonment, her suspicions are confirmed and she confronts him
furiously:

"Jesus Christ!" I [Mary] said. "*Are you the reason no babies are being
born?*"
He looked at me. "Yes," he said. "I used to run Population Control. I
understand the equipment."

"Jesus Christ! You fed the world with birth control because *you* felt suicidal. You're *erasing* mankind..."

"So I can die. But look how suicidal mankind is."

"Only because you've destroyed its future. You've drugged it and fed it lies and withered its ovaries and now you want to bury it. And I thought you were some kind of a god."

"I'm only what I was constructed to be. I'm equipment, Mary."[22]

"I'm only what I was constructed to be" is the ultimate cop-out both of man and of his creation.

And yet, like Satan, Spofforth is aware of the falsity of his rationalizations. As he stood on the Empire State Building at the book's beginning, he recognized that "his body was not—as he knew it would not be—his own. He had been designed by human beings; only a human being could make him die."[23] His eminently successful program to rid the world of man will prevent his most sincere desire.[24] Yet his very human capacity for self-deception, like Satan's, prevents him from consciously realizing this.

In *Paradise Lost*, Milton shows how God's infinite mercy and power are sufficient to use even the acts of Satan for man's ultimate good.[25] Spofforth operates in a world without transcendent sanction; he himself engineers both his salvation and his fall by permitting, without willing or wishing it, man's re-creation of himself. Out of his loneliness, he allows a man who has the tenacity and curiosity to learn to read, to exercise his forbidden skill, hoping to find someone with whom he can communicate, someone who understands his burden of memory. Spofforth is not omniscient. He does not foresee that this humanized man will find another true human to interact with. As Adam learned in Eden, it takes two to be human; Tevis adds to his intellectual, repressed, timid Adam an Eve who, by sheer intelligence and gut instinct has learned, by surviving the extermination camps of the schools and the wasteland of the world, to exist outside of every system in vital humanity. She alone does not kill her mind with drugs; she alone is fully aware of the mechanization about her; she alone is unprogrammed and fertile. It is no wonder that Spofforth, the fallen angel, falls in impotent love with her.[26]

Moreover, it is Mary Lou who knows that robots were made for man, and not man for robots; this is the knowledge she hands to Bentley, along with the "kind of mango" that "certainly can't be eaten," though she has no awareness of the symbolic meaning of her act:

> "Why did you pick it?" I [Bentley] said.
> "I don't know," she said. "It seemed to be the thing to do."[27]

Man has to find out why he needs knowledge before he can find out what he needs to know or what to do with it. And to know why he needs it, he needs to have it. It is a neat cycle, one that can only be broken by renewed access to human culture as conveyed by history and literature.

In *Paradise Lost*, man was given perfect reason by God, and knowledge by the angels Raphael and Michael; only after the Fall does his understanding cease to rule, and "upstart passions catch the government/ From reason, and to servitude reduce/Man till then free."[28] In *Mockingbird*, man must consciously reclaim his humanity by a willingness to learn, accepting the pain, guilt, and responsibility that this entails. Being human, Paul finds, is not fun. He must suffer. He must feel a range of emotions, from love to terror. He must learn about fanaticism and false religion, mistakes from man's past, as well as about love and devotion. He must not only know *about* all this (as he begins to from viewing his silent films); he must himself *experience* it, for only through his own actions can he re-create himself as human.

In *Paradise Lost*, man sacrificed eternal happiness in obedience to a delusory sense of power through knowledge. In *Mockingbird*, man must struggle to regain that knowledge to inform the action that alone can kill his false god, destroy his sterile Eden, and bring to him the power to re-create a viable world.

In *King Kong*, where the monster represents all the repressed urges that man fears most in himself, the death of the beast asserts a measure of conscious control. Like Kong, Spofforth is a monster, maugre his creator's intentions; like Satan, he seems impossible to control. Yet, as God brings forth good even from the actions of Satan, a rekindled godliness in man can come from the actions of Spofforth. It is the airplanes, not the Beauty, that kill Kong; it is the push from Paul and Mary Lou that kills Spofforth. But the situation in which the fall is both necessary and desirable is not set up by the airplanes, nor by Mary Lou and Paul. Spofforth falls by his own will, from the world he created, and the reason he can at last do so is that not all of his will is destructive. Like man, Spofforth can also love.

Atop the Empire State Building, that sterile phallic symbol that is "the high grave marker for the city of New York,"[29] Paul and Mary

Lou demonstrate that man can recover his humanity, re-assume his godly role of creator toward Spofforth, and take up his human responsibility. *Mockingbird* ends, not with Paul and Mary's fertile westward trek in their thought bus (though that is prophesied), but with "mankind's most beautiful toy" in a most fortunate fall, joyously embracing death.

NOTES

1. X. J. Kennedy, "Who Killed King Kong?" *Dissent* (Spring 1960) 213–15.

2. If Kong has sexual organs in the original movie, they are invisible. Moreover, his desire for human women cannot be explained by any possibility of intercourse, whether or not his physiology would permit the sex act with a female of his own species.

3. Kong's lust—if that is what it really is—was permissible while the maidens involved were of his color, if not of his race; he was sacrificed only when he "raped"—or at least "peeled"—a white woman. He was too large to lynch, so he died dramatically, still caring for his uncaring Eve, who could not even steal an apple successfully, and whose only response to him was a series of screams punctuated by whimpers.

But this is still a reflection, even though somewhat attenuated, of the pseudepigraphic story that Azâzêl and his angels "came to earth tempted by the beauty of women" and were thus unable to return to heaven; they fathered the race of giants, teaching "men to use metals, make weapons, and practise all kinds of enchantment, magic, and wickedness." Stella Pierce Revard, *The War in Heaven* (Ithaca: Cornell University Press, 1980), p. 30.

4. Walter Tevis, *Mockingbird* (New York: Bantam Books, 1981), p. 2.

5. John Milton, *Paradise Lost*, I, 263.

6. It should be noted that the use of the word "conceived" is a concession to the obvious truism that our idea of God is limited to that conceivable by human intelligence. Even God (with a capital G) is a creation of the human mind.

7. *Paradise Lost*, VI, 8. "In *Paradise Lost*... 'vicissitude' is always 'grateful'; it is change, variety, movement, the mark of vitality and joy characteristic of both the divine and the human master artist's work." Joseph H. Summers, *The Muse's Method* (Cambridge, Mass.: Harvard University Press, 1962), p. 71.

8. Stanley E. Fish, in *Surprised by Sin* (London: Macmillan, 1967), argues cogently that those who claim that "God, not Adam and Eve, is guilty of the Fall" ignore the fact that if Adam and Eve "could not fall, they could not stand; that is, *they* would not be doing the standing, consciously and wilfully."

The ability not to fall depends on the ability to fall; free will is a meaningless concept unless the possibility of wrong choice exists'' (p. 210 n.). The point here, however, is not the theology or scholarship of this reaction; it is that Tevis's world, and particularly his robots, reflect the *popular* belief.

9. *Paradise Lost*, I, 25–26.

10. Spofforth is, thus, in exactly the same position as Satan, that is, spying on Adam and Eve who are making pure and joyous love in Eden (*Paradise Lost*, VIII, 505–11); he is thrust into a hell of jealousy and torment. See Summers, *The Muse's Method*, p. 99.

11. It can be argued, however, as C. S. Lewis does in *A Preface to Paradise Lost* (New York: Oxford University Press, Galaxy, 1961), p. 102, that Satan also "has no choice. He has chosen to have no choice."

12. Names are used consciously by Tevis. "Maugre" comes from the Old French *Maugre, Malgre*, ill will, from the Latin *malus*, bad, evil, and *gratum*, a pleasant thing. As a preposition, this oxymoron means "in spite of, in opposition to, not withstanding," and as a transitive verb, "to withstand in a defiant manner." Obviously Tevis expects his readers to do some research here.

The names of his characters are more accessible. Mary Lou Borne is associated by her actions to Eve, mother of the human race, and by her name to Mary mother of Jesus (both through "Mary" and through "Borne," which evokes both born-again and the bearing of children); Annabel Baleen, whom Bentley loves and loses in Maugre, has a euphonious connection to Edgar Allen Poe's Annabel Lee. Paul, who learns to read and write, is, like Paul of Tarsus, converted; though he is bent at the beginning of the book, he straightens. Spofforth can be read as "spoof," among other things.

13. *Mockingbird*, pp. 165–67.

14. Man, escaping responsibility and challenge, becomes less than human. If God did turn all responsibility for the universe over to a set of functioning laws and disappear, did he then become less than God, while man, learning to comprehend and use these laws, became more godly?

15. *Mockingbird*, p. 40.

16. Ibid., p. 41.

17. Ibid., p. 3.

18. Ibid., p. 67.

19. Ibid., pp. 114–15.

20. Ibid., pp. 78–79.

21. This reflects Milton, who follows the argument of St. Augustine. "If no good (that is, no being) at all remains to be perverted, Satan would cease to exist"; it is only the continued existence of corruptible man that permits Satan to continue to appear as "glory obscured" (*Paradise Lost*, I, 594) as C. S. Lewis demonstrates in his *Preface*, p. 67.

22. *Mockingbird*, p. 235.

23. Ibid., p. 2.

24. Spofforth did not think of this program; he took advantage of a chance condition, the failure of a chip in Population Control that led to the continued addition of contraceptives to sopors when the population was rapidly declining. His only action was to take no action, behaving in the same way as the robot supervisor in the toaster factory was compelled to behave, but without the same excuse. He does not show creative imagination here.

25. *Paradise Lost*, XII, 470–73.

26. See Notes 2 and 10.

27. *Mockingbird*, p. 42.

28. *Paradise Lost*, XII, 88–90. See, e.g., C. S. Lewis, *Preface*, p. 70.

29. *Mockingbird*, p. 148.

14

Persian Influences in J.R.R. Tolkien's *The Lord of the Rings*

ELIZABETH M. ALLEN

The importance of Persian mythology and theology to J.R.R. Tolkien's *The Lord of the Rings* has been almost totally ignored by those writing about the trilogy. This negligence is unfortuante because the ancient Persian religion and its offshoot Mithraism provide the theology that undergirds Middle-earth, and an understanding of these influences will illuminate many puzzles in the trilogy, including its overabundance of light-dark symbolism and its apparent lack of religion. In short, recognizing and understanding the significance of Persian elements in *The Lord of the Rings* will enable a reader to comprehend more clearly just what kind of secondary world Tolkien has created.

William Howard Green and others have noticed the similarity of the name *Mithrandir* to *Mithras* (also commonly *Mithra* or *Mitra*), the Persian god of light, but Green only mentions that similarity without comment. Likewise, H. A. Blair and Douglass Parker have incidentally acknowledged overtones of Persian theology in *The Lord of the Rings*.[1] No one, however, appears to have investigated, even casually, just how pervasive Persian influences are in Tolkien's work, much less realized how central they are to his creation of Middle-earth.

A simple listing of Persian elements covers items as diverse as graphic design motifs; plot developments, including the climactic eruption of Mount Doom; and actual characters. Specifically, Persian influences can be detected in the design on the doors to Moria; the references to the "circles of the world"; *lembas*, the waybread of the elves; the "glow" several characters exhibit on occasion; the trials undergone by the members of the Fellowship; the eruption of Mount Doom; the emphasis on fire, air, and water; the rings; Sauron and the Ringwraiths; Gandalf and the Fellowship; the choice of dates for important events; and the stress on the sun, moon, stars, fire, light, and dark.

Eastern influences are so common that recognizing them and realizing how Tolkien molded them to his narrative and theological purposes will contribute substantially to a deeper understanding of the novel and the religion and theology that inform it.

The Persian system of thought that Tolkien drew upon was that of Zoroaster, an ancient Iranian religious reformer and the founder of Zoroastrianism. Zoroaster taught that the universe consists of two opposing principles: one, Ahura Mazda (Ormuzd), is the essence of good; the other, Ahriman, is evil. Everything in the universe is involved in the fight between the two, and it is necessary that man, in order to secure his own salvation, join in the fight on the side of Ahura Mazda. Mithras is an angelic being who serves Ahura Mazda, but after the parent religion became dormant, he was promoted to godhood and many of the Persian beliefs continued to flourish throughout the Roman empire in the form of Mithraism.[2]

Mithraism held sacred and worthy of worship all natural sources of light, in addition to several other natural forces and objects. Mithraists revered the moon and planets (or seven wandering stars); the four elements (fire, earth, air, and water); the four seasons; the four cardinal winds; and the sacred tree under which Mithras was born—all of which figure in one way or another in *The Lord of the Rings*.[3]

Several of these Mithraic motifs are visible quite literally in the design on the doors to Moria: the radiate crown (Mithraic symbol of the sun), the seven stars (the seven wandering stars or planets known to the ancients), and the crescent moons borne by the two trees.[4] Admittedly, the symbols do not appear on the doors of Moria exactly as they do on Mithraic monuments, but the significant thing is that they all appear together, as might be expected of symbols having a common source, and they are all significant in Mithraism.

Closely connected with the planets is the concept of the spheres. Cumont says that Mithraists believed that the heavens were divided into seven spheres, each of which was conjoined with a planet. The soul, after death, moved from sphere to sphere, ridding itself of the passions and faculties it had received on its descent to earth. When it finally reached the eighth heaven, it would enjoy beatitude without end.[5] Here we have an explanation of what Aragorn is referring to when he speaks to Arwen, his dearly beloved wife, on his deathbed: "I speak no comfort to you for there is no comfort for such pain within the circles of the world." A few lines later he says, "Behold! we are not bound forever to the circles of the world, and beyond them is more than memory, Farewell!"[6] Obviously, Aragorn believes in eternal life and since he is one of the authority figures in the trilogy and very rarely wrong who are we to say he's ignorant of the structure of his world.

Yet another echo of Mithraism is found in the *lembas* or waybread of the elves given to the Fellowship upon their departure from Lorien.[7] They are told by the elves that the cakes will sustain even a tall man for a day of hard labor. For many of the days of Sam and Frodo's journey into Mordor, it is the only food they have. Merry and Pippin, too, are restored by *lembas* after they have been driven and carried by their orc captors from Parth Galen to Fangorn Forest in three days of forced marches. Merry remarks about the effect of the waybread: "*Lembas* does put heart into you!"[8] *Lembas* has as its Mithraic counterpart the ritual small cakes or bread served in commemoration of a banquet involving Mithras. Supernatural effects were expected of the meal— vigor of body and material prosperity, wisdom, power to combat the malignant spirits, and immortality. Likewise, *lembas* confers vigor, wisdom, and the power to fight the agents of darkness. Although Tolkien told Professor Mroczkowski that *lembas* was really the Eucharist,[9] we have to look to the Mithraic communion for the concept of the meal's bestowing supernatural *physical* effects. Certainly no one has ever suggested that the wafer of Christian communion could sustain life, much less provide energy for physical exertion.

One of the concepts of Mithraism that is particularly interesting in relation to *The Lord of the Rings* is that of the "glory" or *hvarenō*, "a kind of mystical effulgence or aureole derived from the heavenly light," possibly connected with the idea of the external soul.[10] The Persians believed that their kings ruled "by the grace" of Ahura Mazda and, according to Cumont, they "pictured this 'grace' as a sort of supernatural fire, as a dazzling aureole, or nimbus of 'glory.' " The *hvarenō* "illuminated legitimate sovereigns and withdrew its light from usurpers as from impious persons."[11] Gandalf exhibits this glow when he reveals himself to Gimli, Legolas, and Aragorn in the Forest of Fangorn.

His white garments shone.... His hair was white as snow in the sunshine; and gleaming white was his robe; the eyes under his deep brows were bright, piercing

as the rays of the sun.... Gimli...sank to his knees, shading his eyes....
[Gandalf,] picking up his grey cloak[,] wrapped it about him; it seemed as if
the sun had been shining, but now was hid in cloud again.

Gandalf's "glory" is unmistakable here. Once recognized in this passage, however, one can identify other occurrences throughout the book.
For instance, as Gandalf faces the Balrog on the bridge leading out of
Moria, Tolkien describes him as "glimmering in the gloom." When
Frodo offers him the Ring, and Gandalf refuses it, "his eyes flashed
and his face was lit as by a fire within." The *hvarenō* also comes upon
him before the Black Gate when he defies the Mouth of Sauron. As
Gandalf casts aside his cloak, "a white light shone forth like a sword
in that black place."[12]

The *hvarenō*, however, is not limited to Gandalf. Galadriel exhibits
it when she refuses Frodo's offer of the Ring: "[A] great light...illumined
her alone and left all else dark." Likewise, "light was about" Aragron
at his crowning, and many saw "the light that shone about" Faramir
and Éowyn as they came down from the walls of Gondor the day they
agreed to marry. Again, Galadriel, on the way to the Grey Havens to
take ship for the Uttermost West and end her long exile in Middle-
earth, "seemed to shine with a soft light."[13] It would seem, then, that
in *The Lord of the Rings*, as in the beliefs of the ancient Persians, the
hvarenō expresses the approval of the deity, since characters exhibit it
only in meritorious circumstances. Interestingly, Cumont remarks that
this "peculiar conception" of the Persians had no counterpart in other
mythologies.[14]

Still another aspect of Mithraism that is present in *The Lord of the
Rings* is the trials imposed upon the candidate for admission to the
Mithraic brotherhood. Little is known about these trials, except they
are believed to have been more than simply a formality and to have
demanded an exhibition of courage from the candidate.[15] Every member
of the Fellowship—indeed, nearly all the characters in *The Lord of the
Rings*—endures trials of one sort or another: Aragorn spends many years
leading the self-effacing life of a Ranger, endures the hardships of the
search for Merry and Pippin after they are captured by the orcs, fights
several battles, and even goes by the Paths of the Dead; Gandalf travels
endlessly across Middle-earth seeking answers, withstands the temptation of the Ring when Frodo offers it, and gives his life in Moria in
the marathon battle with the Balrog; Pippin and Merry undergo the seige

of Gondor; Pippin faces the horror of Denethor's crazed attempt to murder his own son and, in so doing, the hobbit saves Faramir's life; Merry aids Éowyn in killing the Witch-king of Angmar; Boromir succumbs to the lure of the Ring, but redeems himself before his death by attempting to defend the hobbits from the attacking orcs; Legolas and Gimli fight side by side with Aragorn and follow him on the Paths of the Dead. Of course, the trial supreme is that of Sam and Frodo and their nightmare journey across Mordor to deliver the Ring to the place of its forging.

In fact, since the end of the Third Age marks the withdrawal of the other speaking creatures, and the Fourth Age is to be under the domination of man, *The Lord of the Rings* is in one sense an initiation story, and man is the initiate. Gandalf is in charge of the ceremony, and the trial itself is a real trial, nothing less than the War of the Rings.

An exchange between Aragorn and the leader of the Riders of Rohan echoes the Mithraic belief that each man must join in the fight between Ahriman and Ahura Mazda. When asked what doom he brings from the north, Aragorn replies, "The doom of choice." He continues, pointing out that soon Rohan must fight for or against Sauron.[16]

The Mithraic belief about the final outcome of the struggle between Ahriman and Ahura Mazda is reflected in Tolkien's conclusion of the War of the Rings. The followers of Mithras believed that when the age assigned for the duration of the struggle between good and evil ended, Ahriman and his impure demons would perish in a general conflagration, leaving a rejuvenated universe to enjoy happiness without end.[17] Tolkien, of course, does not promise that the defeat of Sauron is the end of evil in the world, but Sauron and the remaining Nazgûl are destroyed when the Ring with Gollum plunges back to its beginnings. The subsequent eruption of Mount Doom echoes the Mithraic purging of the world by molten metal and the final conflagration:

There was a roar and a great confusion of noise....The throbbing grew to a great tumult, and the Mountain shook....Fire belched from its riven summit. The skies burst into thunder seared with lightning. Down like lashing whips fell a torrent of black rain....[A] huge fiery vomit rolled in slow thunderous cascade down the eastern mountain-side....Slow rivers of fire came down the long slopes....[18]

Middle-earth soon thereafter begins a new age, the Fourth Age, which commences in peace, fertility, and good will, just as Mithraic doctrine promises.

Rings, central to *The Lord of the Rings*, were also important to the Persian religious community. Each magus of the priesthood of Mithras in ancient Media wore a ring. This custom was retained by the Mithraic communities founded centuries later in Europe. In these communities, each "pater" (a Mithraic initiate of the highest degree) wore a ring *signifying his wisdom*.[19] In *The Lord of the Rings*, the elfin rings also can be said to "signify the wisdom" of their wearers. They do this in two ways. First, the elfin rings are concerned generally with healing, making, understanding, and preserving, the main concerns of Elrond, Galadriel, and Gandalf, the three who wield the rings.[20] Second, in the cases of Galadriel and Gandalf, the specific powers of the rings reflect the strongest powers of their wearers. Galadriel's ring is the Ring of Water and seems to be connected in some way with her foresight, since the Mirror of Galadriel into which Sam and Frodo gaze to see the future is a basin of water she prepares for them. Gandalf's ring is Narya the Great, the Ring of Fire—most appropriate when one considers that most of the wizard's power is associated with fire. How Elrond's ring, Vilya, the Ring of Air, is appropriate to him is not mentioned in *The Lord of the Rings*.

The four elements of the ancients—earth, air, fire, and water—were also important to the Mithraic community; in fact, Mithraism deified the four elements. Cumont says: "The gods no longer confined themselves to the ethereal spheres. . . . Their energy filled the world, and they were the active principles of its transformation."[21] (This belief is central to an important conclusion concerning the world of *The Lord of the Rings*.) The Mithraic attitude toward fire is most interesting in relation to *The Lord of the Rings*. Cumont says: "Fire. . . was the most exalted of these natural forces, and it was worshipped in all its manifestations, whether it shone in the stars or in the lightning, whether it animated living creatures, stimulated the growth of plants, or lay dormant in the bowels of the earth."[22] In addition to fire and light, water was also worshipped by Mithraists for its contribution to fertility and life. A perpetual spring bubbled in the vicinity of the Mithraic temples, and in the temple itself was a basin of water, perhaps the prototype of the basin Galadriel uses as her prophetic "mirror."[23] The third element, air, was revered by Mithraists. They believed that the wind gods could help or hinder the soul's journey through the separate spheres of the planets or, in more Christian terms, escort the soul to, or prevent it from entering, heaven. Vermaseren says this belief explains why the wind gods on Mithraic monuments sometimes blow upward and some-times downward.[24] In *The Lord of the Rings*, the winds even actively participate in the struggle against Sauron; the wind, for example, blows away the clouds of Mordor at the beginning of the Battle of Pelennor Fields. In a more orthodox Mithraic motif, "a great wind" dissipates the spirit of Sauron after the destruction of the Ring, and "a cold wind" refuses the spirit of Saruman, the fallen wizard, entrance to the West.[25]

Cumont also says that the earth occupied an importance equal to that of the other elements "if not in the ritual, at least in the doctrine" of Mithraism, a rather involved way of saying they accorded the earth lip service only. Tolkien, once again following where Mithras leads, also ignores the element of earth. Elrond, Gandalf, and the Galadriel wield the Rings of Air, Fire, and Water, respectively, and these three elements act as emanations of the deity. But Tolkien does not assign an active part in *The Lord of the Rings* to the element of earth, nor does he name a Ring of Earth.

I think it is possible that there is, after all, a Ring of Earth, although Tolkien does not call it such. In addition to holding the fertile earth in reverence, Mithraists also regarded the domain of Ahriman as being a dark and dismal area located in the bowels of the earth. Here Ahriman ruled over his maleficent monsters, and from here they came to corrupt the hearts of men.[26] The resemblance of Ahriman's Mithraic hell to Isengard and Mordor, much of which lie underground, is obvious.

Possibly Tolkien does not name his ring of earth such because he wants to separate as completely as possible all the good aspects of the Mazdean earth concept, which are reflected in *The Lord of the Rings* in the beauty of the natural world, from the maleficent connotations mirrored in Isengard and Mordor. If one looks for a fourth element in a ring association, there is, indeed, only one candidate—the Ring. Assigning the earth to the nine rings of men or the seven given dwarfs involves demoting the earth element to a level considerably lower than that occupied by the air, fire, and water elements—a mistake, I think. Additionally, the Ring, which was forged from gold, an earth product, has no stone to suggest any other association and was created specifically to aid in the subjugation of Middle-*earth*.[27]

The influences of Persian theology are also evident in the characters in the trilogy. The two most influential ones, Sauron, the Dark Lord, and Gandalf, the Grey Pilgrim, and their most trusted followers, the Ringwraiths and the Fellowship of the Nine, are mutations of Mazdean gods, demons, and angels. Mazdaism was the parent religion of Mithraism, and its beliefs held that Ahriman created the darkness, suffering, and sin and uses his army of "noxious" spirits to hurt the creatures of the good creation. He wants to "enslave the faithful of Ahura Mazda by bringing them into some impure contact with an evil being."[28] Here are many parallels with Sauron: Sauron is known as the Shadow and the Dark Lord; his is the author of the darkness from Mordor that blots out the sun for five days at the beginning of the war; his orcs are weakened by the light of the sun; he is anxious to hurt others and cause suffering, for example, Gollum's obvious suffering at his hands; and he works to enslave the peoples of Middle-earth.[29]

The most striking similarity concerns Sauron's Ringwraiths. In discussing Ahriman, *The Mythology of All Races* says "under him are marshalled the daēvas ('demons'), from six of whom a group has been formed explicitly antithetic to the Amesha Spentas,"[30] a group of angelic beings that assist Ahura Mazda in his fight against evil. The group of six daēvas formed to fight the Amesha Spentas suggests strongly the Nine Black Riders or Ringwraiths, men whose rings of power long ago bent them to the Dark Lord's will and whose bodily substances have faded until they are spirits apprehensible only by a sense of dread or by the black garments they wear to cover their nothingness. The Ringwraiths are "noxious" or injurious just as are Ahriman's spirits. They are armed with weapons that break off in the wound, the fragments of which then work their way to the heart. Such a wound causes, not death, but a fading into the spirit world so that the victim comes under the domination of Sauron. The Ringwraiths also inspire an enervating fear and dread in their foes that make those foes want to give up. Frodo falls victim to this dread and fear at the Ford of Bruinen, and Merry experiences like emotions during the Battle of Pelennor Fields at which he and Éowyn kill the Nazgûl Captain, chief of the Ringwraiths. The Black Breath, a malady acquired by close exposure to the Ringwraiths, results in fever, delirium, despairing dreams, and loss of the will to live. All in all, a vivid depiction of the enslavement of the faithful by "impure contact with an evil being."[31]

It would seem, then, that at least some of Sauron's character has been derived from that of Ahriman and that his Ringwraiths are Tolkien's way of giving substance and concreteness to Ahriman's daēvas.

The most highly visible peak of the Persian iceberg in *The Lord of the Rings* is Mithrandir, as the elves know Gandalf, the wizard who organizes opposition to Sauron and leads the forces of the West in the War of the Rings. A brief investigation of Mithras reveals that Gandalf possesses an overwhelming number of that deity's attributes, in addition to being his linguistic namesake. In *The Mythology of All Races* Mithras is described as one of the Yazatas, or auxiliary angels, to Ahura Mazda. Ahura Mazda's angelic forces are made up of the Amesha Spentas and the Yazatas, which form a hierarchy charged with guardianship of the world. These would seem to correspond to Tolkien's Ainur, beings created by the One before the creation of the material universe. The Ainur are made up of the Valar, or the greater Ainur, and the Maiar, or lesser Ainur. The Valar are charged with the guardianship of the world, just as are the Amesha Spentas. Gandalf has been identified by Tolkien himself as both an angel and ''a sort of'' Vala, an identification refined by *The Silmarillion*, which names him unequivocally a Maia.[32] The identification strengthens the resemblance to Mithras, since both he and Gandalf belong to the ''lesser'' group of their particular angelic forces.

There are other points of similarity. The idea of ''friend'' is attached to both, with Gandalf called ''friend of all the Children of Ilúvatar,'' that is, elves and men,[33] and ''Mithras'' meaning ''the friendly one.'' Mithras is sometimes pictured as a mounted warrior, bringing to mind Gandalf's riding Shadowfax into battle. Mithras was a light or solar deity whose followers worshipped before an altar of flame, and Gandalf is associated with both fire and light. Mithras is said to unite men and to watch the tillers of the soil, a service echoed by Gandalf's efforts in galvanizing opposition to Sauron, in which he brings together not only men, but also dwarfs, elves, hobbits, ents, and eagles. ''Watching the tillers of the soil'' suggest Gandalf's preoccupation with hobbits, who grow pipeweed in the Shire and also cultivate gardens. Additionally, Mithraism was a soldier religion, and Gandalf is the leader of a rather unorthodox company. Mithras was particularly a god of fidelity and bravery, and Mithraism stressed good fellowship and brotherliness and excluded women.[34] All of these qualities are preeminent in *The Lord of the Rings*, and many critics have remarked on the dearth of women and the absence of sex in the trilogy.[35]

Other roles of Mithras were as the commander under whom the individual shares in the fight against the prince of darkness and as the producer of the final conflagration of the world. Gandalf's entire vocation in *The Lord of the Rings* concerns engineering the fall of the

Dark Lord, Sauron. His part in effecting that fall and masterminding the strategy of the War of the Rings echoes the authorship of the last holocaust. Additionally, Mithras was believed to be associated with occult powers, and the priesthood of Mithras was the magi, a caste in ancient Media that practiced magic and prophecy.[36] In keeping with this, Gandalf as a wizard wields magic powers and makes prophecies. True, several times characters in *The Lord of the Rings* thought to have magic powers remark that they do not perform magic, that magic is one of the arts of the Enemy.[37] I think probably the distinction Tolkien is making here is that magic is performed in league with the powers of evil, whereas the power wielded by the elves and wizards in Middle-earth is granted to them by Eru, much of it as their birthright. Mithras even provides Gandalf with his clothing and bird friends. The magi carried a solid ebony staff and wore a ring and a cloak. Similarly, Gandalf generally wears a cloak and the ring Narya (although he keeps it hidden until after Sauron's fall), and carries a staff. Although Mithras is commonly associated with the crow, a bird that acts as a messenger between him and Ahura Mazda, he is portrayed at least once with an eagle on his shoulder.[38] Eagles, of course, play an important part in *The Lord of the Rings*, as do crows. Tolkien assigns the latter, however, to Sauron as his spies. The eagles cooperate with the Free Peoples, especially Radagast, Gandalf, and Galadriel; and the great birds even carry Gandalf and the two hobbits, Sam and Frodo, in times of great need.

Like the relationship of the Ringwraiths of Sauron to the demons of Ahriman, the Fellowship of the Nine can be seen to be roughly analgous to the Amesha Spentas of Ahura Mazda, although, except for Gandalf, none of the Nine can be considered "angels" in any sense but a metaphorical sense. A further difficulty lies in the fact that Gandalf belongs, not to the Amesha Spentas, but to the Yazatas, if he is truly Mithra's counterpart. However, Tolkien is not bound to take as unchangeable any sources he chooses to use, and it is possible that the six Amesha Spentas of Ahura Mazda provided at least part of the inspiration for the Fellowship of the Nine. The Nine certainly function as guardians of Middle-earth. It would not be the first time an author has adapted source material to fit his artistic needs.

Another congruence between Mithraism and *The Lord of the Rings* is found in the matter of dates. Dates are so important to Tolkien in *The Lord of the Rings* that of six appendices only two do not have some connection with dates. In fact, Appendix B (sixteen pages) outlines by years—and, in the case of the events of *The Lord of the Rings*, by days—the events in the history of Middle-earth. Appendix C (five pages) gives genealogies for several hobbit families, including, for the most part, birth and death dates. Appendix D (seven pages) concerns the calendars used in Middle-earth, and Appendix A (fifty pages) fills in some of the historical background for *The Lord of the Rings*, complete with dates.

In *The Lord of the Rings* itself, Tolkien's preoccupation with dates is indicated by the fact that more than once he stalls the action rather arbitrarily. For instance, after the Fellowship is formed, it spends several weeks, more time than seems absolutely necessary, at Rivendell and then sets out on December 25. Tolkien speeds up time when the group is at Lorien so that, though they seem to have spent only a few days there, they have in reality been there one month (from January 17 to February 16). The events of the war culminate March 25 with the fall of Gollum into Mount Doom with his "precious," the Ring.[39]

To many who read *The Lord of the Rings* through the appendices, even for the first time, the choice of date for the company to leave Rivendell presents a puzzle. December 25 is a date of preeminent significance to Christians, and we see an appropriateness between our own birth of Hope and the hope that the setting out of the company offers for Middle-earth, but December 25 hardly seems justifiable in terms of Middle-earth itself, a world into which Christ has not been born. Tolkien's strong Christian bias hardly provides an aesthetic rationale for the choice, nor can coincidence be responsible, even without Tolkien's statement that he deliberately chose both this and the March 25 date for the destruction of the Ring, although he did not explain why.[40]

December 25 is an important date to Mithraism: It is the birthdate of Mithras. Other significant dates to Mithraism were the equinoxes, which brings us to March 25.[41] When the Julian calendar was adopted in 46 B.C., March 25 was the date of the vernal equinox, marking the beginning of spring and a Mithraic date of significance, and certainly symbolically appropriate for the downfall of Sauron. In *The Lord of the Rings*, at the end of the Third Age, a new calendar is adopted that begins the new year on March 25. Interestingly enough, in Britain the new year began March 25, the vernal equinox, until the Gregorian calendar was instituted in 1752. Also of interest is the fact that, according to the regulation of Constantine, Easter was the first day of the year. So it would seem, for a time at least in England, Easter, the vernal equinox, and the first day of the year all occurred on the same day.[42] Tolkien seems to have already taken advantage of one Christian-Mithraic date-in-common—December 25. It seems highly probable that with March 25 he is trying for another such congruence. Tolkien's dates, however, are difficult to cope with, as one can confirm by reading Appendix D. I believe, nonetheless, that the dates of highly significant events in *The Lord of the Rings* are connected in some way with the solar year—and that this connection is directly related to Mithraism and the emphasis it placed upon the divisions of the solar year.

The most pervasive connection with Mithras and Mithraism in *The Lord of the Rings* is Tolkien's almost constant use of fire and light imagery. This imagery is also the most important connection because, viewed in the context of Mithraic belief, this imagery will define the nature of God in Middle-earth and will make clear the theology that provides a foundation for Tolkien's creation, matters that have long been obscure.

One indication of the importance of light in the trilogy is the number of names having a light association. "Andúril," the name Aragorn gives his reforged sword, means Flame of the West. The Council of Elrond is held in the Hall of Fire. "Minas Anor" is the Tower of the Sun and "Minas Ithil" is the Tower of the Moon.[43]

Gandalf's really impressive power lies in fire. Perhaps this power lies behind his talent for fireworks. The fire that he wields, however, is far beyond mere show. We first see the power of Gandalf's fire at Weathertop, where he manages to hold off the Nine Riders from dusk to dawn. In contrast to the orcs, who are weakened by the light of the sun, Gandalf is strengthened by it and hampered by its absence. Gandalf indicates his dependence on the sun in his description of the events at Weathertop:

"I galloped to Weathertop like a gale, and I reached it before sundown on my second day from Bree—and they [the Nine Riders] were there before me. They drew away from me, for they felt the coming of my anger and they dared not face it while the Sun was in the sky. But they closed round at night, and I was besieged on the hilltop in the old ring of Amon Sûl. I was hard put to it indeed: such light and flame cannot have been seen on Weathertop since the war-beacons of old.

"At sunrise I escaped and fled towards the north. I could not hope to do more."[44]

Light is not helpful solely to Gandalf; other members of the Fellowship draw courage, strength, and consolation from the sun, moon, stars,
and dawn. Aragorn at Helm's Deep anxiously awaits the dawn, arguing
with Gamling that "dawn is ever the hope of men." And at dawn
Aragorn, Théoden, and the Riders of the Mark, who had been almost
hopelessly besieged during the night, ride out to the attack to find that
not only the ents, but also Gandalf and Erkenbrand and the men of
Westfold have come to their aid. Light from Galadriel's Phial illuminates
Shelob's liar and keeps the monster at bay long enough for Frodo to
hack his way through her web to the end of the tunnel. A morning break
in the darkness covering Mordor after the beginning of the war brings
hope to Sam and Frodo on their arduous journey to Mount Doom. Later
that night, as the exhausted Frodo sleeps, Sam sees high above, "a
white star twinkle for a while. The beauty of it smote his heart, as he
looked up out of the forsaken land, and hope returned to him. . . . For
a moment, his own fate, and even his master's ceased to trouble him."[45]

Two other references to fire and light are profoundly revealing. In
the first, Gandalf is telling Frodo about his talk with Gollum concerning
the Ring and Gollum's part in its history. Gandalf says, "I put the fear
of fire on him, and wrung the true story out of him, bit by bit. . . ."[46]
Here Gandalf echoes a common sentence of the disciplinarian, "I put
the fear of God in him." This implied link between fire and God cannot
be accidental. Later, when Gandalf faces the Balrog in Moria, the wizard
stands in the middle of the bridge and proclaims: "You cannot pass. . . . I
am a servant of the Secret Fire, wielder of the flame of Anor."[47] Tolkien
identifies "Anor" as the Sun, making Gandalf a servant of the Sun,
consistent with his identification with Mithras.[48] It is also significant
that Gandalf is unable to defeat the Balrog in the ensuing eleven-day
battle in the depths of Moria. It is only when the two literally come to
light on the peak of Zirak-zigil, where "the sun shone fiercely," that
Gandalf is finally able to best his enemy and cast him down the
mountain.[49]

In *The Lord of the Rings*, it is impossible to miss the fact that fire
and light operate on a symbolic level. One may even recognize the fact
that in this world Tolkien has endowed light literally with powers accorded it only figuratively in the primary world;[50] but until the connection with Mithraism is made, we still tend to reject, if indeed we
consider at all, the suggestion that in Middle-earth God is, among other
things, Fire and Light—in a concrete, literal sense—no metaphor about

it. Gandalf is a priest of the sun; the sun, moon, stars, dawn, and most fire in *The Lord of the Rings*, as in Mithraism, are manifestations of the deity.

If one views the sun and these other forms of light, as the worshippers of Mithras did, as aspects of god, then the light symbolism in *The Lord of the Rings* ceases to be symbolism carried to rather sophomoric extremes. The light images are not symbolism, but reality. The light that comforts and aids so many of the Fellowship is not light, but Light— an actual manifestation of the Godhead, that is, God not only transcendent, but also immanent. This light is not a psychological pick-me-up the characters benefit from because they *think* they benefit, but an actual illumination by Eru filled with power that does indeed sustain. Additionally, this god is God, not some pagan deity destined in a few centuries to become one of the devils of Christian mythology. This hypothesis is confirmed, I think, by Tolkien's revelation to Clyde S. Kilby that the Secret Fire Gandalf serves is actually the Holy Spirit,[51] as well as Tolkien's other admission that *lembas* is really the Eucharist.

It would seem, then, that the critics who question why Middle-earth has no religion are asking the wrong question. The question should be: what kind of religion is there? Tolkien's answer, "natural theology,"[52] although satisfactory to him, fails to satisfy the rest of us. But an understanding of the Persian sources of Tolkien's work helps to make clearer this "natural theology" that undergirds, or rather overarches, Middle-earth.

The trees, seven stars, crescent moon, radiate crown, circles of the world, *lembas*, *hvarenō*, the trials undergone by the Fellowship, the eruption of Mount Doom, fire, air, and water, rings, Sauron and his Ringwraiths, Gandalf and the Fellowship, December 25, March 25, the sun, moon, stars, dawn, light, and dark—practically all the important symbols and many of the characters of *The Lord of the Rings*—trace their ancestry through the Mithraic communities of the Roman Empire back to the magi of the ancient Persians and the god of light they served.

But why? Tolkien was a person known for his Christianity at a time when being a Christian was less than fashionable. Why would a devout Catholic want to tie his created world so tightly to a pagan religion and its god? I believe that Tolkien wanted to create in Middle-earth a culture that in many ways really could have been the forerunner of our Christian world, the Primary World, as he called it. Tolkien said that Middle-earth is indeed an area of our world lying between the Western Sea and the Far East at a time in the past.[53] In order to create a logical religious tie between Middle-earth and modern Christianity, Mithraism and Persian theology are a particularly appropriate treasure hoard for Tolkien to have drawn upon since many of their aspects dovetail neatly with Christianity. In addition to the many congruences we have already noted, the priesthood of Mithras were called magi, and it was magi from the East that came bearing gifts to the Christ Child; Mithraists practiced baptism and believed that the soul was immortal, that sinners went to hell, that the just finally appeared before god as pure spirits, and that all would finally be judged before the throne of god. Additionally, the *New Catholic Encyclopedia* says:

No proof of immorality or obscene practices, so often connected with esoteric pagan cults, has ever been established against Mithraism; and as far as can be ascertained, or rather conjectured, it had an elevating and invigorating effect on its followers.

In fact, the similarities of Mithraism to Christianity are so striking that the encyclopedia devoted an entire column of print to refuting the idea that Christianity is only an adaptation of Mithraism or at least that they both grew out of the same religious ideas and aspirations.[54]

In creating a Christian vision of what the Western world might have been like before European history or chronicle began, Tolkien drew upon a pre–Christian mythology to give his secondary world a number of points of familiarity so that readers in the primary world can feel that this world, our world, the primary world, grew out of Tolkien's world and that if it did not really happen that way, it could have, or better still, should have. Tolkien consciously chose Mithraism to form the theological background for his work because of its striking correspondence with Christianity. He took Mithraism, stripped it of its obviously pagan elements, and used the result to create a pre–Christian Christian universe. He has, in a sense, created a new Old Testament.

NOTES

1. William Howard Green, "*The Hobbit* and Other Fiction by J.R.R. Tolkien: Their Roots in Medieval Heroic Literature and Language" (Ph.D. diss., Louisiana State University and Agricultural and Mechanical College, 1969), p. 70; H. A. Blair, "Myth or Legend," *Church Quarterly Review* 156 (January–

March 1955): 122; Douglass Parker, "Hwaet We Holbytla...," *Hudson Review* (Winter 1956–57): 603, 606.

2. *New Century Cyclopedia of Names*, 1954 ed., s.v. "Zoroaster."

3. Franz Cumont, *The Mysteries of Mithra*, trans. Thomas J. McCormack from 2nd rev. French ed., 1902 (New York: Dover, 1956; 1st publ. 1903), pp. 115–20 and figs. 2, 17, 26, 35, 40, and 42; *Encyclopedia of Religion and Ethics*, 1955 ed., s.v. "Mithraism."

4. Cumont, *Mysteries*, pp. 99, 119–21, 185; J.R.R, Tolkien, *The Lord of the Rings*, 2nd ed., vol. 1, *The Fellowship of the Ring* (Boston: Houghton Mifflin, 1965), pp. 318–19 (hereafter cited as *Fellowship*); M. J. Vermaseren, *Corpus Monumentorum et Inscriptionum Religionis Mithraiacae*, 2 vols. (The Hague: M. Nijloff, 1960), fig. 6, mon. 31, lion with a crescent moon below his head; fig. 53, mon. 182, fig. 54, mon. 183, fig. 106, mon. 368, fig. 274, mon. 1083, fig. 355, mon. 1359, trees (anywhere from one to seven); fig. 106, mon. 368, stars, the radiate crown, and the crescent moon. Two of the monuments (fig. 53, mon. 182 and fig. 54, mon. 183) show the Mithraic figures Cautes and Cautopates standing between two laurels, the tops of which meet over the head of each figure. The shape of the arch so formed is the same as that of the arch depicted on the doors of Moria (*Fellowship*, p. 319).

5. Cumont, *Mysteries*, pp. 144–45.

6. J.R.R. Tolkien, *The Lord of the Rings*, vol. 3, *The Return of the King*, pp. 343–44 (hereafter cited as *Return*).

7. *Fellowship*, pp. 385–86.

8. J.R.R. Tolkien, *The Lord of the Rings*, vol. 2, *The Two Towers*, p. 61 (hereafter cited as *Towers*).

9. Daniel Grotta–Kurska, *J.R.R. Tolkien: Architect of Middle Earth* (Philadelphia: Running Press, 1976), p. 90.

10. *Encyclopedia of Religion and Ethics*, 1955 ed., s.v. "Mithraism."

11. Cumont, *Mysteries*, p. 94.

12. *Towers*, p. 98; *Fellowship*, pp. 345, 71; *Return*, p. 167.

13. *Fellowship*, p. 381; *Return*, pp. 246, 243, 308.

14. Cumont, *Mysteries*, p. 94.

15. Ibid., pp. 160–64.

16. *Towers*, p. 36.

17. Cumont, *Mysteries*, p. 146.

18. *Return*, pp. 224, 228.

19. M. J. Vermaseren, *Mithras, The Secret God*, trans. Therese and Vincent Megaw (New York: Barnes and Noble, 1963; London: Chatto and Windus, 1963), pp. 23, 153.

20. *Fellowship*, p. 282.

21. Cumont, *Mysteries*, p. 114.

22. Ibid., p. 114.

23. Ibid., p. 115.

24. Vermaseren, *Mithras*, p. 162.

25. *Return*, pp. 112, 227, 300.

26. Cumont, *Mysteries*, pp. 112, 114.

27. A couple of years after reaching this conclusion about the One Ring, I found that Timothy R. O'Neill in *The Individuated Hobbit* (Boston: Houghton Mifflin, 1979), pp. 149–50, had made the same connection. He, however, used as his field of inquiry Jungian psychology.

28. *The Mythology of All Races*, ed. Louis Herbert Gray (Boston: Marshall Jones, 1917), 6: 261.

29. *Return*, pp. 328, 45, 81; *Fellowship*, p. 60; *Towers*, pp. 27, 222.

30. *Mythology of All Races*, p. 261.

31. *Return*, pp. 103, 115–17, 136–45; *Fellowship*, pp. 234, 224–27.

32. Edmund Fuller, "The Lord of the Hobbits," in *Tolkien and the Critics*, ed. Neil D. Isaacs and Rose A. Zimbardo (Notre Dame, IN: University of Notre Dame Press, 1969), p. 35; "Ainur," "Maiar," "Olórin," J.R.R. Tolkien, *The Silmarillion*, ed. Christopher Tolkien (Boston: Houghton Mifflin, 1977).

33. Tolkien, *Silmarillion*, pp. 30–31.

34. *Johnson's Universal Cyclopedia*, ed. Charles Adams (New York: Appleton, 1896), s.v. "Mithras"; *Encyclopedia of Religion and Ethics*, s.v. "Mithraism"; Cumont, *Mysteries*, pp. 2, 16, 26; *The Catholic Encyclopedia*, 1934 ed., s.v. "Mithraism."

35. C. B. Cox, "The World of Hobbits," *Spectator*, Number 7226 (30 December 1966): 844; Charles Elliott, "Can America Kick the Hobbit? The Tolkien Caper," *Life*, 24 February 1967: p. 10; Mary Ellman, "Growing Up Hobbitic," *New American Review*, New American Library, no. 2 (1968), pp. 217–29, cited by Richard C. West, comp., *Tolkien Criticism: An Annotated Checklist*, Bibliographies and Checklists, no. 11 (Kent, Ohio: Kent State University, 1970), p. 19.

36. *Encyclopedia of Religion and Ethics* s.v. "Mithraism"; *New Catholic Encyclopedia*, 1967 ed., s.v. "Mithras and Mithraism."

37. *Fellowship*, pp. 377, 386.

38. Vermaseren, *Mithras*, p. 23; Cumont, *Mysteries*, fig. 34.

39. *Fellowship*, p. 287; *Return*, p. 373.

40. J.R.R. Tolkien, "Guide to the Names in *The Lord of the Rings*," in *A Tolkien Compass*, ed. Jared Lobdell (LaSalle, Ill.: Open Court, 1974), p. 201.

41. Cumont, *Mysteries*, p. 167.

42. Elizabeth Achelis, *The Calendar for Everybody* (New York: Putnam's, 1943), pp. 44–45, 77; Achelis, *The World Calendar* (New York: Putnam's, 1937), p. 77; *Encyclopedia Britannica*, 11th ed., s.v. "Easter."

43. *Fellowship*, pp. 238, 250, 252, 290; *Return*, p. 433.

44. *Fellowship*, p. 277.

206					Elizabeth M. Allen

45. *Towers*, pp. 142, 146–47, 328–32; *Return*, pp. 196–99.
46. *Fellowship*, p. 66.
47. Ibid., p. 344.
48. "Minas Anor," *Silmarillion*.
49. *Return*, p. 373; *Towers*, pp. 105–6.
50. Dorothy Elizabeth Klein Barber, "The Meaning of *The Lord of the Rings*," in *The Tolkien Papers*, Mankato Studies in English, no. 2 (Mankato, Minn.: Mankato State College, February 1967), 2: 43.
51. Clyde S. Kilby, *Tolkien and the Silmarillion* (Wheaton, Ill.: Harold Shaw, 1976), p. 59.
52. J.R.R. Tolkien, "Tolkien on Tolkien," *Diplomat* 18 (October 1966): 39.
53. Ibid., p. 39.
54. *New Catholic Encyclopedia*, 1967 ed., s.v. "Mithras and Mithraism."

15

Promethean Bound: Heroes and Gods in Roger Zelazny's Science Fiction

JOSEPH V. FRANCAVILLA

Despite the apparent differences between heroes in Roger Zelazny's science fiction, such as Mahasamatman in *Lord of Light*, Conrad Nomikos in *This Immortal*, and Francis Sandow in *Isle of the Dead*, they all conform to a particular model. With amazing virtuosity, Zelazny has used this model and has produced story after intriguing story, with fresh variations in locale, religious framework, and mythological background.

Zelazny's model is constructed in part from myths of the sacrificed God–King or Fisher King, as described by Sir James Frazer[1] and Jessie Weston.[2] In these myths, the death and rebirth of the ailing, divine monarch effects renewal and the restoration of fertility to the land and its people. Zelazny's god-hero begins with a symbolic deficiency or flaw and himself undergoes a parallel renewal and growth in his process of self-discovery and self-realization as he becomes a more perfect representation of a divine spirit and a skeptical prophet, messiah, and savior.

Yet Zelazny's protagonist, unlike the sacrificed and resurrected divine kings, is always a youthful, powerful hero who fits Joseph Campbell's description of the mythological hero in *The Hero with a Thousand Faces*. Campbell's survey abstracts several key actions of the hero: the hero's departure or wanderings from home, his descent into hell or the underworld, his trials and ordeals, his union with the goddess-mother of the world or his theft of a boon, and his transfiguration and ultimate divinization.[3]

But it is the Prometheus myth to which Zelazny's hereos owe their central core of being. Zelazny has economically conflated the myth and attributes of Prometheus with the mythic pattern and attributes of the sacrificed divine king and of the quest-hero. By fashioning this unusual "collapsing," Zelazny has created a novel, complex, and fascinating godlike hero whose aspects of godhood mainly parallel those of the Titan god Prometheus: immortality, wisdom, power to create men and worlds, limited omniscience (from "prophetic visions" and "telepathy"), limited omnipotence (from superhuman strength and superpowers), ideal goodness, and advocacy of goodness. Indeed, it is surprising how persistently the Prometheus myth reveals itself in Zelazny's fiction, even in small details. His story "Love Is an Imaginary Number" is, in fact, an overt, updated version of the Prometheus myth; even when Zelazny uses Norse, Christian, or Buddhist godlike heroes, they all show the traits of Prometheus. The structures of the central dramatic situations and of the chief conflicts in Zelazny's stories are also directly related to the Prometheus myth.

Like Prometheus, the Zelaznyian hero is a creator, sometimes literally a shaper of men and worlds, and a savior with a demiurgic, self-destructive drive. He is also invariably wise and extremely tall, a Titan among men. Artistic, strong, agile, and quick, he is consumed by an insatiable curiosity and a need to experience all things (an important element of Zelazny's definition of "human"), and he displays powers far beyond those of mortal men. The hero's godlike powers and virtual immortality come about through such science fiction devices as suspended animation, advanced alien technology and training, machines metamorphosing into men, bionics, or mutations due to radioactivity.

Like Prometheus ("forethought"), Zelazny's clever, wandering trickster figures are immortals who associate and eventually identify with mere mortals. Alienated from and outside of normal society, these supermen are defiant liberators and renegade thieves. They rebel against the other gods (and the status quo they represent) and altruistically steal for mortal men the divine fire that symbolizes light, reason, creativity, curiosity, tools, arts, technology, knowledge, and understanding. A metaphor for man's rational, inquisitive nature, these immortals undergo trials, ordeals, and sacrifices (usually at the hands of the gods of the status quo) for the people who worship the immortals as their gods.

Whereas the authority figures' newer religions established early on in the stories are presented as constrictive, inhibiting, and sterilizing, the religion established later by the protagonist after or during his transfiguration (a religion always returning to older beliefs temporarily overthrown by the new gods) is shown as a revivifying, altruistic untruth, a religion or belief that the godlike exponent dismisses. The spiritual rebirth of the protagonist and the rejuvenation of the land and its people cannot come about until the Promethean hero overcomes a flaw peculiar to many Greek protagonists: a self-destructiveness hinging upon some special excess, usually pride (hubris), vanity, arrogance, and defiance.

Zelazny's Promethean hero in many ways is more like Percy Shelley's protagonist in *Prometheus Unbound* than Aeschylus' in *Prometheus Bound*. Written in the 1960s, Zelazny's early fiction is filled with the revolutionary zeal of that time, and Zelazny's heroes exhibit a rebelliousness, individuality, audacity, and defiance of conventions emphasized in a hero of the Romantic period such as Shelley's. Compared to Shelley's protagonist, Aeschylus' Prometheus is rather passive. Though Aeschylus' hero eventually will be unbound (after Zeus' son Herakles gains permission to shoot the eagle or vulture that eats Prometheus' regenerating liver), it will take some thirteen generations (alternatively, 30,000 years), and he will have to reach a compromise with Zeus to achieve his freedom. In addition, the wounded immortal Centaur Cheiron has to descend into the underworld to suffer in Prometheus' place, and Prometheus has to reveal to Zeus the secret he at first refused to reveal: the woman (Thetis) who would bear Zeus a son who would usurp Zeus' power. Finally, Aeschylus' unbound Prometheus is from then on supposed to have worn a special wreath and ring, as signs of his submission to Zeus' rule.[4]

Shelley, in the preface to *Prometheus Unbound*, identifies Prometheus with Milton's Satan. Both Satan and Prometheus, according to Shelley, show "courage and majesty, and firm and patient opposition to omnipotent force,"[5] but Prometheus, Shelley believes, is the more interesting hero since he is not flawed by such traits as ambition, envy, or revenge. Further, Prometheus is seen by Shelley as "the highest perfection of moral and intellectual nature."[6]

Shelley's radical hero, therefore, like those of Zelazny, will not even consider compromise with, let alone surrender to, Zeus, who is portrayed as an arbitrary tyrant and the embodiment of malevolence (as are the gods opposing Zelazny's heroes). The climax of Shelley's play parallels the climax of many Zelazny stories: a battle of the gods, the overcoming, usurpation, or destruction of the tyrant god(s), and the establishment and celebration of the progressive spirit that the Promethean hero represents.

Zelazny often follows Shelley's comparison by identifying his Promethean hero with a satanic figure, and yet still a figure with good motives and noble ends. Mahasamatman in *Lord of Light* descends into a bottomless pit to unleash the destructive Rakasha, energy beings called "demons" in the book. Mahasamatman makes a pact with the leader of these demons to fight with them against the prevailing Hindu gods who are oppressors of mankind. As Carl Yoke has suggested, Conrad Nomikos in *This Immortal* is linked to Satan by virtue of such clues as his alternate name Kallikanzaros, the Greek word for devil, and the assassin Hasan (associated with the dark god Angelsou in a voodoo ritual), who respects Conrad as he does the devil.[7]

Zelazny does *not* follow Shelley in making the Promethean hero an ideal of perfection. Here Zelazny stays with Aeschylus' conception of the bold hero flawed by hubris. Unlike Aeschylus' Prometheus, Zelazny's hero changes greatly during the course of his adventures and becomes less prideful and arrogant usually through a combination of his love for a woman and his altruistic protection of the race of mortals.

We can observe the previously outlined pattern of the combination mythic hero and sacrificial divine king superimposed on the Promethean myth in Roger Zelazny's first science fiction novel, *This Immortal* (1966). Conrad Nomikos is like Prometheus, who created man from water and mud or clay and who made man alone stand upright among the beasts. Nomikos is a shaper of both men and worlds. He formed the Radpol organization, which attempted to oust the alien race of Vegans and their influence from Earth, and which spawned the Returnist movement to recall Earth colonists from distant Vegan planets. But more importantly, Conrad, as Commissioner of Arts, Monuments, and Archives for Earth, has the power to have dismantled such large monuments as the great pyramid of Cheops, or to have them rebuilt and restored. Eventually Conrad literally inherits the Earth and becomes the savior of Earth and of mankind in its attempt to be free from the Vegan's influence. More than six feet tall, Nomikos exhibits strength, courage, and stealth both in his fights alongside and against Hasan the assassin and in his escape plan when the touring party is trapped by the cannibal tribe. As a trickster figure, he cleverly deceives people into thinking the Radpol leader

Karaghiosis has died in a boat accident. In fact, he is "reborn" in disguise as Conrad Nomikos, who cites his birthday as Christmas day. Conrad displays his wisdom and curiosity when he delays killing the Vegan Cort Myshtigo because Conrad's intuition impels him first to discover Cort's true purpose in coming to Earth.

Conrad's powers include a virtual immortality, a quasi-telepathic "wish-fulfillment" that is inherited as a prophetic ability in his son Jason, and a superhuman strength, agility, and quickness that outdoes even perfect fighting machines such as Hasan's robot golem, described by Conrad as a "man of putty and mud."[8] The telepathic wish-fulfillment/prophetic ability closely parallels the "forethought" of Prometheus, who can tell Io what will happen to her and who knows events of the future, which even Zeus does not know.

Conrad is less prideful and vain than he seems to have been in his former life as Karaghiosis, the rebel leader, but some of that hubris remains. Diana tells him: "I've seen you many times, confident of something you never share, arrogant in your strength."[9] Conrad seems so sure about being able to kill Hasan that he takes out a duelling permit ahead of time. Dos Santos feels that the tearing down of the Cheops' pyramid is a "monument to Conrad Nomikos."[10] Mixed with pride is an explosive anger and hate that Nomikos exhibits when he goes mad and attacks the entire touring party, when he challenges Hasan to a duel, and when he insults the supposed Vegan, Cort Myshtigo.

But these traits, plus Conrad's defiance of the Vegan control of Earth, are put to his noble ends of freeing mankind from apparent outside opppression. A mutant freak because of an atomic war on Earth, Conrad complains of his left cheek colored purple because of a mutant fungus, his hairline that peaks near his brow, his mismatched blue and brown eyes, and his short right leg. He feels alienated from normal human society, yet he is fiercely and stubbornly protective of Earth and its people against Vegan influence.

There are a number of even more obvious references to the Prometheus myth in *This Immortal*. When Conrad is discussing the Hot Spots, his son Jason describes these as radioactive sites where "Prometheus spilled too much of the fire of creation."[11] Near the end of the novel, Conrad's poet friend Phil Graber asks for his copy of *Prometheus Unbound* and writes on it a note to Conrad in Classical Greek telling him that the Vegan must be saved, since Cort is part of a masquerade planned by Tatrum Yshtigo to restore Earth and its government to humanity. In

his typical way of scoffing at great and heroic works, Conrad calls
Prometheus Unbound "Percy B's dud epic."[12] This attitude, also expressed when Conrad denies being a hero or believing in heroism, seems
connected with Shelley's poem "Ozymandias." In that sonnet, a broken
statue is all that remains of a great Egyptian king who boasts of his
now-destroyed architectural achievements. Shelley's ironic poem shows
how time mocks even the most powerful rulers, and the sonnet expresses
Shelley's hatred of tyranny, and its attendant vanity, hubris, and ambition. This theme of impermanence of life and creations is echoed in
Zelazny's immortal, especially when Conrad and the tour party watch
the pyramid of Cheops being torn down and Conrad says, "Nothing is
cheaper than past glories."[13] Later Conrad quotes Shelley's poem, repeating the words of the Egyptian king inscribed on the pedestal of the
crumbling statue: "Look at [sic] my works ye mighty and despair."[14]

Though Zeus behaves like the grand patriarchal figure of authority
and Prometheus, like a son, Zeus and the Olympians actually overthrew
an older race of gods, the Titans, who sired Zeus and his kind. The
Titan Prometheus defies Zeus' tyranny over the mortals with whom
Prometheus identifies, and he gives them the best parts of the animal
to eat and the fire stolen from heaven. This fire completes man by
adding the fourth "element," since Prometheus has made man of clay
(earth) and water, and he has let man breathe air. Fire is also the flame
of desire for love, knowledge, and experience, which are key elements
in Zelazny's definition of "human" and fuel the hero's quest for self-
discovery, for identity.

Prometheus, therefore, is a member of an old order of gods and
beliefs who escapes the bondage imposed by the new gods headed by
Zeus, or else (in Shelley's version) usurps the fatherlike tyrant, sees
his destruction, and reestablishes the old gods and beliefs.

In *This Immortal*, the godlike, advanced race of telepathic Vegans
is described as a wise and old race compared to men. But the Vegans
are the *new* order of life in mankind's view. So the "old" order of
humanity run by humanity is replaced by the "new" order of Vegan-
run humanity, and Conrad helps to restore the old order of a human-
controlled Earth. The difference between *This Immortal* and the Prometheus myth is that Conrad not only identifies with, but also *is* a
human (the race he helps), albeit a godlike mutant with powers at least
as formidable as the Vegans. Zelazny usually retains this difference in
his works and makes the Promethean hero a godlike man or mutated

superman who saves the suffering and oppressed mortals from the imposed new order.

A second important pattern borrowed from the Prometheus story, the betrayals and defections to the opposition by the hero and by a powerful warrior, derives from the switching of Prometheus's allegiance from his own kind, the Titans, to Zeus and the successful battle against the Titans. Prometheus changes sides again when Zeus punishes him, and he opposes the tyrant who chains him to the rock. The great warrior Herakles (Hercules), son and later servant of Zeus on Olympus, also changes sides, in a sense, when he unchains Prometheus and kills the vulture tearing at Prometheus's liver (although Herakles does this with Zeus' sanction).

In *This Immortal*, Conrad, founder of *Radpol*, finds himself opposing Diana and duelling the hired assassin for Radpol, Hasan. Conrad also renounces his former belief in Returnism, a movement spread by Radpol to recall humans back to Earth from the colonies. Hasan's attempts on the Vegan's life are opposed by Conrad. But their mutual respect and admiration enables Hasan to become Conrad's friend and to fight by his side.

Other incidental details reflect the Prometheus myth. The spiderbats, one of which Conrad is said to have killed barehanded, echo the returning vulture. Asked about the Argonauts and the Golden Fleece, Conrad mentions Herakles and points out Cheiron's cave, saying that Jason was a pupil of the immortal centaur incurably wounded by Herakles's arrow during his fourth labor. Conrad then talks about the battle of the Olympian gods and the Titans, and mentions Herakles's fourth labor of the wild boar.

This Immortal follows Campbell's phases of the mythic hero. During his wanderings on the Vegan tour, Conrad's tasks and ordeals include his fights with the robot golem, the boadile, and Hasan, his escape from Morely's cannibals, and his encounter with the boar-like "Black Beast." Conrad descends into hell figuratively when he is brought to a Hot Spot in a pit filled with rocks that seem almost to be burning. He is bound on the rock, and the order for Conrad to be tied to a "column" underscores the reference to the binding of Prometheus, who was chained to a pillar (or, in some versions, a rock) in the Caucasian mountains.

The reward for this supreme ordeal is Conrad's reunion with Cassandra and his inheritance of the Earth free of Vegan interference. Though Conrad has already "died" as Radpol leader Karaghiosis and

been "reborn" as Nomikos, the healing of his facial fungus, cured by
the radioactive rock, signals the hero's transformation. Conrad is the
modern day equivalent of a king; he is powerful, wealthy, well-re-
spected, influential, and a leader of a large group of men who are
dependent upon him. Like the sacrificed divine king who restores fertility to the land, Conrad's symbolic death and rebirth heralds the rejuvenation of the radioactive Earth, and its rebuilding for and by
Earthmen. (The indication that the Earth will be repopulated and that
Conrad will restore the pyramid of Cheops symbolically emphasizes
this). After Conrad steals the "fire" from the Vegans—the arts, monuments, and culture of Earth—he gives them to mankind in a revitalized
state.

Zelazny always adds two ironic features undercutting the hero's rise
to power. First, the hero as religious poet or prophet or savior seriously
doubts or simply *does not believe* the religion or beliefs he preaches or
is attempting to spread to the people. For instance, Conrad renounces
his Radpol connections, finds himself opposing Radpol representatives
for most of the novel, and also does not believe anymore in the Returnist
movement. The best example of this rejection, however, occurs with
the poet-preacher Gallinger in "A Rose for Ecclesiastes," who pride-
fully "steals" the Martian language and religion, literally refertilizes
the dying Martian race, and replaces the newly discovered Martian
religion with the "old" religion in the Book of Ecclesiastes. When
M'Cwyie calls Gallinger a "holy man," he denies being one. When
she adds that the Martians will never forget his religious teachings, he
responds: " 'Don't,' I said automatically. . . . I didn't believe a word of
my own gospel, never had.' "[15] Though Zelazny's hero sets up the new
theopolitical belief to destroy the old, the new belief is primarily a
means to an end. The hero feels compelled by his "Ozymandias syn-
drome" both to refuse worship and to prevent another constrictive order
of authority from arising, because it would stifle the advancement and
self-determination of the race he is protecting. The liberating, Promethean spirit of rebellion, fighting for justice, freedom, and equality for
mankind, is completely inimical to the establishment of *any* rigid system
of punitive and oppressive authority—even a system based upon the
authority of the Promethean hero.

Second, there is always the implication that the divine hero is in the
hands of fate, or of the gods, or is subject to some random process that
plays tricks on him and controls him like a pawn in a cosmic chess

game. In *This Immortal* Conrad is tricked by the well-executed disguise of the Vegan played by Cort Myshtigo. Conrad really is playing a part too in the secret plan of the Vegans, under Tatram Yshtigo's guidance, to give Earth back to a suitable protector. And in "A Rose for Ecclesiastes," Gallinger discovers he is simply a dupe, part of a fatalistic design in which he fulfills an ancient Martian prophecy about the coming of a savior.

The above two ironical features undermine any notion of absolute, eternal omnipotence and authority and imply that any such authority is ultimately harmful to mortals. Because Zeus did not know which of his sons would usurp him, even he is limited, subject to fate. Prometheus knows this better than anyone, and knows well the transience of orders of authority and belief systems, having seen them rise and fall in several cosmic contests.

In *Isle of the Dead* (1969), Francis Sandow is the Promethean hero, the only Earthman to be trained by the alien Pei'ans to become a worldscaper. Sandow is telepathic, centuries old because of several interstellar trips in suspended animation, has superhuman strength and agility, and can tap the divine powers of the Pei'an god Shimbo in order to create worlds of varied plant and animal life. Francis exhibits greed and anger in addition to the usual flaws of hubris, vanity, and defiance that appear in Zelazny's protagonists. Sandow, for example, admits haggling with a business acquaintance for money, in a project he really did not care about, out of "pure cussedness."[16] Later, Sandow repeatedly calls the Pei'an Green Green a "stupid son-of-a-bitch"[17] in a mixture of anger, annoyance, and fear when Green Green informs him that the Pei'an has recalled to life Sandow's great enemy Mike Shandon.

Sandow is one of the wealthiest men alive. He is a trickster figure, disguising himself and creating new identities in order to travel incognito. Wanderlust often hits Sandow hard, and before his Pei'an training, he wandered aimlessly in trips throughout the stars. The whole novel is virtually an Odysseyan journey (like *This Immortal*) through the place called "Isle of the Dead" on the planet Illyria, which Sandow created. Perhaps even more of a freak than Conrad, Sandow feels so alienated from Earth society because of the gaps in his knowledge and the death of his loved ones (due to his suspended animation) that he must seek training from the Pei'ans and assume the name and power of Shimbo.

Sandow attempts to liberate his friends who have been recalled to life with stolen Recall Tapes by the revengeful Green Green. The Promethean hero is once more rescuing humans, his own kind, from the alien gods, and is also rescuing his work of art, science and knowledge— in this case, the Edenic planet Illyria. During the world's formation, the element fire, Sandow says, has plagued him and killed his wife Kathy.[18] The planet Illyria's volcanoes are compared to Titan torches,[19] and Sandow compares memory to a vulture that "circles closer and closer" and "descends upon the thing of pain. . .dismembers it, gorges itself upon it, digests it."[20]

The Pei'ans are again an ancient, wise, advanced race compared to humanity, but to humans they are a new order suddenly imposed on mankind. Sandow fights the Pei'ans, first Green Green, then Belion, in order to preserve his mortal friends; finally Sandow renounces his god Shimbo, presumably to go back to the "older order" of human ways with Lady Karle.

There are a series of betrayals and reversals of allegiance. The god Belion forsakes Green Green for Sandow's enemy Shandon. Shandon himself tried to betray Sandow and his corporation when he was working for Sandow. Green Green is the formidable, powerful warrior who changes sides, striking up an uneasy bargain with Sandow to help the fight against Mike Shandon.

The major stages in Campbell's monomyth apply to *Isle of the Dead*. Sandow must leave his home to travel through his created world Illyria, which is now altered by Green Green to be grotesque and hellish. Sandow is inspired to make his "Isle of the Dead" region on Illyria by Arnold Boecklin's painting of the same title, which depicts a lone hooded form with a coffin in a boat going toward the isle of the dead. Sandow actually describes the region as one of his images of death, and his lake Archeron in the region has the name of one of the five rivers of hell in Greek mythology. Sandow's descent into hell is also punctuated by the reincarnation of his long-dead friends and associates.

The trials and ordeals Sandow undergoes include his watching Dango in agony after being changed into a tree, resisting Green Green's attempt to control him telepathically, and fighting his old enemy Mike Shandon, who has Belion's powers. This final battle of the gods confers the divinity of Shimbo on Sandow temporarily; Sandow finds himself, for the first time, taken over by the god's control. He is also rewarded with Lady Karle and the planet he created. A powerful, wealthy leader of men and corporations, Sandow is the sacrificed divine king who restores a former lover to life and literally renews his lands. Sandow's symbolic rebirth parallels the metamorphosis of his personality, indicated by his acceptance and understanding of certain of his former enemies and acquaintances (for example, Green Green and Dango), his love for Lady Karle, and his rejection of Shimbo.

Zalazny again undercuts the religious beliefs associated with the hero who achieves divinization. Sandow rejects Shimbo and all the Pei'an rituals even as he is convinced by the dying Green Green (who calls him a "high priest") to give the Pei'an the last rite of death. This rejection of Pei'an beliefs includes both Green Green's "fundamentalist" position and the revisionist position of Marling (Sandow's teacher), which uses the old religion Stranti as merely a psychological device to channel the godlike powers.

A pawn whose destiny has been controlled by selfish, unsympathetic deities, Sandow goes so far as to curse the gods: "Here I was still...in the middle of the human condition—namely, rubbish and pain. If the gods were real, their only relationship with us [humanity] was to use us to play their games. Screw them all."[21]

Lord of Light (1967) uses a background of Buddhism and Hindu gods, instead of the Greek gods of *This Immortal* or Zelazny's invented Pei'an gods in *Isle of the Dead*. The protagonist has many names, including Mahasamatman (Sam), Maitreya ("Lord of Light"), Buddha, and Siddhartha. Sam is the typical Promethean hero of Zelazny's fiction, except that Mahasamatman ("great-souled one") undergoes a series of literal, rather than figurative, deaths and rebirths. Tall, clever, defiant Sam is full of "forethought" in his strategies to beat the oppressive Hindu pantheon in Heaven; Sam becomes a reformer and shaper of the subjugated colony world and its people. He is, again, an artistic creator, religious poet, preacher, and a powerful liberator of humanity.

Sam wears a ring (as did Prometheus) that gives him command of "fire elementals," which are "deadly, mindless creatures," each bearing the force of a thunderbolt.[22] But his main godly power is that of being a "Binder" of various kinds of energy. With this power, and his superhuman strength and quickness, he has the ability to resist the Rakasha energy-demons and the deadly gaze of the death-god Yama. With the technology of the Hindu gods available to reincarnate select people—Sam has undergone reincarnation a few times—and with Sam's power of the Rakasha to remain (temporarily) bodiless, Sam is immortal.

Though Yama and Kali are more proud and egotistical than Sam, he, too, is guilty of these traits. For example, in disguising himself as a prince and attacking the Temple of Heaven, the bold Siddhartha incurs "the disfavor of Heaven for his presumption."[23] Sam's Promethean defiance is sounded again and again throughout the novel: "I will hate Heaven with every breath that I draw. If Brahma has me burnt, I will spit into the flames. If he has me strangled, I will attempt to bite the executioner's hand. If my throat is cut, may my blood rust the blade that does it."[24] Later, Tak, Sam's son, describes Sam as a "bomb-throwing anarchist, a hairy-eyed revolutionary" who "seeks to pull down Heaven itself."[25]

Siddhartha is perhaps more of a trickster, wanderer, and renegade thief than other Zelazny heroes. He disguises himself several times; for instance, he becomes the prince who storms the Temple, a beggar, and a monk who is taken by some to be Buddha. Sam is adept at the Machiavellian lie, and he tricks and eludes the death-god Yama in their duel by trapping Yama in quicksand. Sam "steals" the ancient beliefs of Buddhism and arranges with the thief Helba to have the Talisman of the Binder stolen from the museum of Heaven.

But his deeper motivation is to eliminate the gods and steal the "fire" of technology from Heaven and give it to suffering mankind. Siddhartha explains why to Lord Kubera:

I decided that mankind could live better without gods. If I disposed of them all, people could start having can openers and cans to open again, and things like that, without fearing the wrath of Heaven. We've stepped on these poor fools enough. I wanted to give them a chance to be free, to build what they wanted.[26]

Sam's strategy is twofold. First he revives the old Earth religion Buddhism, to create a smokescreen for his actions and to erode the people's faith in the Hindu gods. Second, Sam resurrects the nearly extinct, progressive doctrine of "Accelerationism," which Tak describes as an act of sharing:

It proposes that we of Heaven give unto those who dwell below of our knowledge and powers and substance. This act of charity would be directed to the end of raising their condition of existence to a higher level, akin to that which we ourselves occupy. Then every man would be as a god. . . . We would give them knowledge of the science and the arts, which we possess, and in so doing we would destroy their simple faith. . . .[27]

The connection with the Promethean gift of fire is made even more explicit early on when Sam tells Brahma that men should not be considered savages and should be given the benefit of the gods' technology. Brahma replies: "But they are still children, and like children would they play with our gifts and be burnt by them."[28]

Other details echo the Prometheus myth. The beginning of Sam's sermon to the Buddhist monks talks of the "very first fire in the world."[29] Sam's ability as both a "Binder of Demons" and an "Unbinder" suggests the titles of *Prometheus Bound* and *Prometheus Unbound*. In addition, Sam is later said to be "bound" himself, in his own body, when the leader of the Demons takes control of Siddhartha. Sam, like Prometheus, knows a secret of one of the chief gods, Brahma: he was the goddess Madeline in a former life. As "Buddha," Sam teaches about "the chains that the world lays upon a man."[30] Finally, Shiva, one of the Hindu gods, is said to have destroyed the three flying cities of the Titans.

In attempting to usurp the Hindu pantheon and its "Deicrat" rule by replacing them with the nearly forgotten, progressive beliefs of Buddhism and Accelerationism, Sam is trying to reestablish an "old" order over the "new" for the sake of mankind. In this instance, Sam is even more like the Titan Prometheus than is usual in Zelazny, since the Lord of Light is a god of the first colonization who overthrows the later gods for a species (man) unlike himself.

Betrayals proliferate like gods in *Lord of Light*. The Demons of Hellwell strike a bargain with Sam only to betray him and his forces in one of the battles against Heaven. Sam manages, after a duel, to enlist the support of the great warrior-god Yama in the battle against the Hindu pantheon. Lords Krishna and Kubera also switch to Sam's side. Sam even exasperates Yama after the Lord of Light suggests that they make a deal with the Hindu gods: "No!... Which side are you on, Sam?"[31]

Campbell's monomyth is more completely followed in *Lord of Light* than in the previously discussed works, since Sam dies after achieving enlightenment and godhood and is reborn to return to his people in the world. He dies from Kali's albino tigers and survives, temporarily bodiless, through powers bestowed upon him by the Rakasha. After his initial defeat at the battle of Keenset, Sam's *atman* (soul) is projected into a magnetic cloud above the planet. Yama's technology brings Sam back to life to continue the struggle against Heaven.

Siddhartha is a wanderer (especially as the prince and as Buddha) who has reached the colony planet on the *Star of India* spaceship. Soon after he is resurrected from suspension in the magnetic cloud, Sam descends into Hellwell (full of Rakasha Demons), lighting his way by a Promethean torch. Sam's trials and ordeals include his struggle with the leader of the Rakasha, his sparring with Yama, his assault as the prince on the Temple, his killing of Brahma and Shiva, his army's attack on the Hindu gods at Keenset, and the supreme ordeal of his final battle with Heaven at Khaipur. Sam's reward is his death, divinization, and rebirth, which revitalizes the people. He also has literally and figuratively stolen technology from Heaven, and he gives it to the humans, who are said to be rediscovering such inventions as the printing press, the microscope, the telescope, and even indoor plumbing. Unlike other Zelazny heroes, Sam's maturation and metamorphosis of personality occur not because of his love for a woman and for humanity, but solely because of the latter.

Though the whole book shows the Hindu gods manipulating people, events, and demons, Sam is "a man of destiny,"[32] as Yama calls him, who, after a long struggle, seems to have graduated from being a pawn in someone else's game to a king in a game of his own devising.

Again, Sam does not believe in his sermons, his Buddhism, or his own godhood. He repeatedly rejects the idea that he is Buddha, and yet he is worshipped by men as such.[33]

Zalazny's flawed protagonists nevertheless exemplify what is noble, admirable, and divine in man. Zelazny's gods and godlike heroes vastly extend the range of experiences and the potential of humanity; Zelazny is defining "human" in terms of the "divine," showing the qualities of gods that can be imparted to man. In "This Moment of the Storm," the protagonist Godfrey Holmes defines mankind: "Man is the sum total of everything he has done, wishes to do or not to do, and wishes he had done, or hadn't."[34] The definition emphasizes a man's choices and actions both in the past and in the future—in short, his potential for extensive experience. To experience a great deal means to have curiosity about both the self and the world. This curiosity, lasting throughout eternity, is associated with Prometheus by way of the myth of Pandora, wife of Prometheus's brother and also the first woman of the world, who opened the lid and let out all mankind's woes because of her insatiable curiosity. The Pandora myth defines a human quality and the first woman, just as the Prometheus myth of the creation of mankind tries to bridge the gap between the human and the divine and to answer the question "What is a man?" Zelazny's characters grow and change drastically as they attempt to answer not only that question which Oedipus immediately answered—What is a man?—but also the question which Oedipus was unable to answer until too late—Who am I? This attempt at self-discovery and at seeking out the godlike within oneself occurs no matter how much Zelazny's protagonist, in his various identities, disguises, and reincarnations, plays at being the Odysseyan "No Man."

The follow-up questions under that larger definition of man include: "What is Art?" and "What is Science?" Both questions are yet again inextricably linked to the Prometheus myth and to his heavenly gift of fire, which represents the divine spirit within us and so many attributes of the civilization that defines us as human.

NOTES

1. Sir James Frazer, *The Golden Bough: A Study in Magic and Religion*, abridged ed. (1922; reprint ed., New York: Macmillan, 1963), pp. 12–14, 308–19, 413–55.

2. Jessie L. Weston, *From Ritual to Romance* (Garden City, N.Y.: Doubleday–Anchor Books, 1937), pp. 12–29, 113–36.

3. Joseph Campbell, *The Hero with a Thousand Faces*, Bollingen Series no. 17, 2nd ed. (1949; reprint ed., Princeton: Princeton University Press, 1968), pp. 245–46.

4. C. Kerényi, *The Gods of the Greeks*, trans. Norman Cameron (New York: Thames and Hudson, 1951), pp. 220–22.

5. Percy Shelley, in *Shelley's Prometheus Unbound: A Variorum Edition*, ed. Lawrence John Zillman (Seattle: University of Washington Press, 1959), p. 120.

6. Ibid., p. 121.

7. Carl Yoke, *Roger Zelazny*, Starmont Reader's Guide no. 2 (West Linn, Oreg.: Starmont House, 1979), p. 34.

8. Roger Zelazny, *This Immortal* (New York: Ace, 1966), p. 69.

9. Ibid., p. 91.

10. Ibid., p. 60.

11. Ibid., p. 111.

12. Ibid., p. 174.

13. Ibid., p. 58.

14. Ibid., p. 61.

15. Zelazny, *The Doors of His Face, the Lamps of His Mouth and Other Stories* (New York: Avon, 1971), p. 122.

16. Zelazny, *Isle of the Dead* (New York: Ace, 1969), p. 52.

17. Ibid., p. 116.

18. Ibid., p. 139.

19. Ibid., p. 166.

20. Ibid., p. 102.

21. Ibid., p. 174.

22. Zelazny, *Lord of Light* (New York: Avon, 1967), p. 32.

23. Ibid., p. 52.

24. Ibid., p. 186.

25. Ibid., p. 204.

26. Ibid., p. 247.

27. Ibid., p. 206.

28. Ibid., p. 78.

29. Ibid., p. 44.

30. Ibid., p. 110.

31. Ibid., p. 303.

32. Ibid., p. 286.

33. Lack of space prevents a full discussion of other important stories such as "For a Breath I Tarry," in which the immortal machine Frost steals frozen humans and knowledge about extinct humanity from the God-machines Solcom and Divcom and rebels against the "new" gods by becoming a second Adam and regenerating the old gods (man). Similarly, Jarry Dark, virtual immortal of "The Keys to December," rebels against his world-shaping godly associates by stealing the gods' "fire" cannons and teaching the humanoid race to use them.

34. Zelazny, *Doors of His Face*, p. 172.

PART IV

BIBLIOGRAPHIES

A Checklist of Science Fiction/Fantasy Works Containing Religious Themes or Motifs

ROBERT REILLY, FRANK D. McSHERRY, JR., AND CHARLES G. WAUGH

Because definitions of *religion* and *religious* vary greatly, the compilers have attempted to list everything they regarded as reasonably included by these terms, but they cannot guarantee that the list is comprehensive. Initially, this list was composed only of works with religious themes; Frank McScherry and Charles Waugh have contributed many items that deal more specifically with the Christ motif. For the user's convenience these items are preceded by an asterisk (*). This list only includes items published through June 1983.

The compilers gratefully acknowledge the assistance of all those who have helped them collect this bibliography, especially Thomas Whitehead, Temple University Library, and David M. Rich, Syracuse University Library. Part of the work on this bibliography was made possible by a Summer Fellowship from Rider College.

Some anthologies of particular usefulness are *Flame Tree Planet*, ed. Roger Elwood (cited as *Flame*); *Strange Gods*, ed. Roger Elwood (cited as *Strange*); *Other Worlds, Other Gods*, ed. Mayo Mohs (cited as Mohs); *Perpetual Light*, ed. Alan Ryan (cited as Ryan); *God of Tomorrow*, ed. Hans Santesson (cited as Santesson); and *The New Awareness*, eds. Patricia Warrick and Martin Harry Greenberg (cited as Warrick and Greenberg). The contents of these works have been listed, citing the short title or editor's name only, as above. For stories included in an anthology, where no other editor is shown, the author of the story is also the author or editor of the collection.

*Adams, Louis J. A. "Dark Conception." *Fantasy and Science Fiction*, November 1964.

Aldiss, Brian W. *The Dark Light Years*. New American Library, 1964.

————. "Heresies of the Huge God." In *Invaders from Space*, ed. Robert Silverberg. Hawthorne Books, 1972.

————. "A Private Whale." In Ryan.

*Allen, Steve. "The Gadarene Swine." In *14 for Tonight*. Dell, 1955.

Anderson, Poul. "A Chapter of Revelation." In *The Day the Sun Stood Still*, ed. Lester del Rey. Thomas Nelson, 1972.

————. "Eve Times Four." *Fantastic*, April 1960.

————. "Kyrie." In *The Farthest Reaches*, ed. Joseph Elder. Also in *World's Best Science Fiction 1969*. Ace, 1969.

————. "The Martyr." *Fantasy and Science Fiction*, March 1960.

————. "The Problem of Pain." *Fantasy and Science Fiction*, February 1973.

*Andreyev, Leonid. "Lazarus." In *New Worlds of Fantasy No. 2*, ed. Terry Carr. Ace, 1970.

Anthony, Piers. *Macroscope*. Avon, 1969.

Arthur, Robert. "Evolution's End." In Warrick and Greenberg.

————. "Postpaid to Paradise." In *The Golden Road*, ed. Damon Knight. Simon and Schuster, 1973.

Ashby, Richard. "Act of God." *Other Worlds*, December 1951 and January 1952.

Asimov, Isaac. "Nightfall." *Astounding*, September 1941. Widely reprinted.

————. "Reason." In *I, Robot*. Fawcett Crest Books, 1950.

*Aurelio, John. "The Greatest Feat." In *Visions of Wonder*, ed. Robert H. Boyer and Kenneth J. Zahorski. Avon Books, 1981.

*Azorin, John. "The First Miracle." In *Strange to Tell*, ed. Marjorie Fischer and Rolfe Humphries. Julian Messner, 1946.

Balke, Betty T. "Apostle to Alpha." In Santesson.

*Ballard, J. G. "The Comsat Angels." *Worlds of If Science Fiction*, December 1968.

*Balzac, Honoré de. "Christ in Flanders." In *The First Complete Translation into English: Honoré de Balzac in Twenty-five Volumes*, vol. 22. P. F. Collier and Son, 1905.

Banks, Raymond. "The Short Ones." In *The Best from Fantasy and Science Fiction, 5th Series*, ed. Anthony Boucher. Ace, 1956.

Bass, T. J. *The Godwhale*. Ballantine, 1974.

————. *Half Past Human*. Ballantine, 1971.

Baxter, John. *The God Killers*. Horwitz, 1968.

————. *The Off-Worlders*. Ace, 1966.

Bear, Greg. *Hegira*. Dell, 1979.

*————. "Petra." *Omni*, February 1982.

————. *Strength of Stones*, Ace, 1981.

————. "The Venging." *Galaxy Science Fiction*, June 1975.

Beaumont, Charles. " 'The Devil, You Say.' " *Amazing Stories*, January 1951.

————. "Last Rites." *Worlds of If*, October 1955.

Beck, L. Adams. "Hell." In *The Openers of the Gate*. Cosmopolitan, 1930.

Bedford-Jones, H. "Old Man with a Staff." *Blue Book*, June 1944.

————. "Wrath of the Thunderbird." *Blue Book*, January 1939.

Benet, Stephen Vincent. "The Angel Was a Yankee." In *The Last Circle*. Farrar and Straus, 1946.

————. "Doc Mellhorn and the Pearly Gates." In *Twenty-Five Short Stories by Stephen Vincent Benet*. Sun Dial Press, 1943.

*————. "Into Egypt." In *Twenty-Five Short Stories by Stephen Vincent Benet*. Sun Dial Press, 1943.

Benford, Gregory. "Relativistic Effects." In Ryan.

Benson, Robert Hugh. *Lord of the World*. Dodd, Mead, 1907.

Bequaert, Frank. "A Matter of Organization." *Fantasy and Science Fiction*, August 1966.

Bester, Alfred. "Adam and No Eve." *Astounding Science Fiction*, September 1941.

————. "Hell Is Forever." In *The Light Fantastic*. Putnam, 1976.

————. "Will You Wait?" *Fantasy and Science Fiction,* March 1959.

Biggle, Lloyd, Jr. "In His Own Image." *Fantasy and Science Fiction*, January 1968.

————. "What Hath God Wrought." In *Strange*.

Binder, Eando. "All in Good Time." In *Signs and Wonders*, ed. Roger Elwood. Revell, 1972.

Bischoff, David F., and Christopher Lampton. *The Seeker*. Laser, 1976.

Bishop, Michael. *Catacomb Years*. Berkley, 1979.

————. *A Little Knowledge*. Berkley, 1977.

Bixby, Jerome. "The Battle of the Bells." In *Space by the Tale*. Ballantine, 1964.

————. "The Good Dog." In *Space by the Tale*. Ballantine, 1964.

————. "Trace." In *Space by the Tale*. Ballantine, 1964.

Blackwood, Algernon. "Carlton's Drive." In *The Lost Valley and Other Stories*. Eveleigh Nash, 1910.

Blayre, Christopher. "The House on the Way to Hell." In *The Strange Papers of Dr. Blayre*. Philip Allan, 1932.

Blish, James. *And All the Stars a Stage*. Doubleday, 1971.

————. *A Case of Conscience*. Ballantine, 1958.

Block, Robert, "Second Coming." In *The Eighth Stage of Fandom*. Advent, 1962.

Bond, Nelson S. "The Bookshop." In *Mr. Mergenthwirker's Lobblies and Other Fantastic Tales*. Coward-McCann, 1946.

————. "The Cunning of the Beast." *Blue Book*, November 1942. Also in Mohs.

———. "The Judging of the Priestess." *Fantastic Adventures*, April 1940.

———. "Last Inning." In *Nightmares and Daydreams*. Arkham House, 1968.

———. "The Priestess Who Rebelled." *Amazing Stories*, October 1939.

———. "Saint Mulligan." In *The Thirty-first of February*. Gnome, 1949.

———. "Uncommon Castaway." *Avon Fantasy Reader No. 11*, April 1949.

———. "Union in Gehenna." In *Mr. Mergenthwirker's Lobblies and Other Fantastic Tales*. Coward-McCann, 1946.

Bone, J. F. "For Service Rendered." *Amazing Stories*, April 1963.

———. "High Priest." In *Strange*.

———. "The Missionary." *Amazing*, October 1960.

Bonfiglioli, Kyril. "Blastoff." In *England Swings SF*, ed. Judith Merril. Ace, 1968.

*Booth, Maud Ballington. "Christ's Tree." In *Fifty Years of Christmas*, ed. Ruth M. Elmquist. Rinehart, 1951.

*Borges, Jorge Luis. "Three Versions of Judas." In *Labyrinths*. New Directions, 1962.

*Bosworth, Alan R. "Jesus Shoes." In *From Unknown Worlds*, ed. John W. Campbell, Jr. Atlas Publishing, 1952.

Boucher, Anthony. "Balaam." In *Best SF: Four Science Fiction Stories*, ed. Edward Crispin. Also in Mohs.

———. "The Quest for St. Aquin." *New Tales of Space and Time*, ed. Raymond J. Healy. Also in Mohs.

Bowen, Marjorie, "The Bishop of Hell." In *The Bishop of Hell and Other Stories*. The Bodley Head, 1949.

Bowker, Richard. "Contamination." In Ryan.

———. "Grace." *Isaac Asimov's Science Fiction Magazine*, November 1982.

Boyd, John. *The Last Starship from Earth*. Weybright and Talley, 1968.

———. *The Rakehells of Heaven*. Weybright and Talley, 1969.

Brackett, Leigh. "How Bright the Stars." In *Flame*.

———. *The Long Tomorrow*. Doubleday, 1955.

Bradbury, Ray. "Christus Apollo." In Mohs.

———. "The Fire Balloons." In *The Illustrated Man*. Doubleday, 1951. Also in Warrick and Greenberg.

———. "In This Sign." In *Looking Forward*, ed. Milton Lesser. Beechurst Press, 1953.

*———. "The Man." In *The Illustrated Man*. Doubleday, 1951.

———. "Mars Is Heaven." In *The Science Fiction Hall of Fame, Vol. I*, ed. Robert Silverberg. Doubleday, 1970.

*———. "The Messiah." In *Long After Midnight*. Knopf, 1976.

Bradley, Marion Zimmer. *Darkover Landfall*. DAW, 1972.

Brand, Jonathan. "Encounter with a Hick." In *Dangerous Visions*, ed. Harlan Ellison. Doubleday, 1967.

Brennan, Herbie. "Angel." *Analog*, January 1976.

*————. "The Armageddon Decision." *Fantasy and Science Fiction*, September 1977.

————. "Blessing in Disguise." *Analog*, March 1976.

Broderick, Damien. "The Magi." In Ryan.

*————. "There Was a Star." In *A Man Returned*. Horwitz, 1965.

Brown, Frederick. "The Angelic Earthworm." In *Angels and Spaceships*. E. P. Dutton, 1954.

————. "Answer." In *Angels and Spaceships*. E. P. Dutton, 1954.

————. "Jaycee." In *Nightmares and Geezenstacks*. Bantam, 1961.

————. "Rustle of Wings." *Fantasy and Science Fiction*, August 1953.

————. "Search." In *Angels and Spaceships*. E. P. Dutton, 1954.

————. "Solipsist." In *Angels and Spaceships*. E. P. Dutton, 1954.

Brown, Lise. "Leviathan." *Galaxy Science Fiction*, March 1969.

*Brunner, John. "Judas." In Mohs.

————. "The Vitanuls." *Fantasy and Science Fiction*, July 1967. Also in Mohs.

*Bryant, Edward. "Eyes of Onyx." In *Protostars*, ed. David Gerrold and Stephen Goldin. Ballantine, 1971. Also in Warrick and Greenberg.

Bulwer-Lytton, Edward George. "The Fallen Star." In *The Pilgrims of the Rhine*. Saunders and Otley, 1834.

————. "The Soul in Purgatory." In *Pilgrims of the Rhine*. Saunders and Otley, 1834.

Burks, Arthur J. "When the Graves Were Opened." *Wierd Tales*, December 1925. Reprinted in *Black Medicine*. Arkham, 1966.

*Burnett, Frances Hodgson. "The Little Hunchback Zia." In *The Fireside Book of Christmas Stories*, ed. Edward Wagenknecht. Bobbs-Merrill, 1945.

Campbell, John W. "All." In *The Space Beyond*, ed. Roger Elwood. Pyramid Publications, 1976.

Card, Orson Scott. *Hart's Hope*. Berkley, 1983.

————. "Holy." In *New Dimensions 10*, ed. Robert Silverberg. Harper and Row, 1980.

————. "Mortal Gods." In *Unaccompanied Sonata and Other Stories*. Dial, 1981.

Carr, A.H.Z. "It Is Not My Fault." *Fantasy and Science Fiction*, July 1960.

Carr, Terry. "If God Is God." *Vertex*, December 1974.

————. "Who Sups with the Devil." *Fantasy and Science Fiction*, May 1962.

Cartmill, Cleve. "With Flaming Swords." *Astounding*, September 1942.

Chandler, A. Bertram. *The Broken Cycle*. DAW, 1979.

————. "No Room in the Stable." *Isaac Asimov's Science Fiction Magazine*, Fall 1977.

———. "The Rim Gods." *Worlds of If Science Fiction*, April 1968.

———. "Temptress of Eden." *Future Science Fiction*, April 1959.

Chandler, G. K. *God Told Me To*. Ballantine, 1976.

Chilson, Robert. "O Ye of Little Faith." *Cosmos*, November 1977.

*Christopher, John. "Rock-a-Bye." In *The Twenty-Second Century*, Grayson and Grayson, 1954.

Clarke, Arthur C. *Childhood's End*. Ballantine, 1953.

———. "The Nine Billion Names of God." *Star Science Fiction*, January 1953. In Mohs and in Warrick and Greenberg.

*———. "The Star." *Infinity Science Fiction*, November 1955. Widely reprinted.

———. *2010: Odyssey Two*. Ballantine, 1982.

*Clarke, James Mitchell. "The Judas Touch." *Adventure*, April 1944.

Cleeve, Brian. "The Devil and Democracy." In *The Best from Fantasy and Science Fiction, Series Seventeen*, ed. Edward L. Ferman. Doubleday, 1968.

———. "The Devil and Jake O'Hara." *Fantasy and Science Fiction*, August 1968.

———. "The Devil in Exile." *Fantasy and Science Fiction*, November 1968.

Closser, Myla Jo. "At the Gate." In *Famous Modern Ghost Stories*, ed. Dorothy Scarborough. Putnam, 1921.

Cogswell, Theodore R. "Impact with the Devil." In *Deals with the Devil*, ed. Basil Davenport. Dodd, Mead, 1958.

Cole, Everett B. "Here There Be Witches." *Analog*, April 1970.

Collier, John. "After the Ball." In *The Devil and All*. Nonesuch Press, 1934.

———. "The Devil, George, and Rosie." In *The John Collier Reader*. Knopf, 1972.

———. "Fallen Star." In *Fancies and Goodnights*. Doubleday, 1951.

———. "Hell Hath No Fury." In *The John Collier Reader*. Knopf, 1972.

———. "The Right Side." In *The Devil and All*. Nonesuch Press, 1934.

*Coolen, Anton. "The Godchild of the Highwayman." In *The World's Greatest Christmas Stories*, ed. Eric Posselt. Prentice-Hall, 1950.

Cooper, Edmund. *A Far Sunset*. Walker, 1967.

Coppard, A. E. "Clorinda Walks in Heaven." In *Clorinda Walks in Heaven*, Golden Cockrel Press, 1922.

———. "Father Raven." In *Fearful Pleasures*. Arkham House, 1946.

———. "Ring the Bells of Heaven." In *The Collected Tales of A. E. Coppard*. Knopf, 1948.

———. "Simple Simon." In *Fearful Pleasures*. Arkham House, 1946.

*Coppee, Francois. "The Sabot of Little Wolff." In *Merry Christmas to You!*, ed. Wilhelmina Harper. E. P. Dutton, 1935.

Corelli, Marie. "The Distant Voice." In *Cameos*. Hutchinson, 1896.

Costello, P. F. "The Devil Downstairs." *Fantastic Science Fiction*, January 1958.

*Counselman, Mary Elizabeth. "A Handful of Silver." In *Half in Shadow*. Arkham, 1978.

Cowper, Richard. "Piper at the Gates of Dawn." In *The Custodians and Other Stories*. Gollancz, 1975.

Cox, Irving E. "A Lady in Satin." *Fantastic Universe Science Fiction*, July 1955.

*Cross, Ronald Anthony. "Water Kwatz, *Or* More Bible Suckers." In *Other Worlds*, ed. Roy Torgeson. Zebra Books, 1979.

Dallas, Paul. "Hell's Own Parlor." *Fantastic Science Fiction*, May 1957.

Dane, Clemence. "Nightly She Sings." In *Fate Cries Out*, ed. Winifred Ashton. Heinemann, 1935.

Dann, Jack. *More Wandering Stars*. Doubleday, 1981.

————. *Wandering Stars*. Harper and Row, 1974.

Davidson, Michael. *The Karma Machine*. Popular Library, 1975.

*Davis, Alice L. "The First Disciple." In *Fifty Years of Christmas*, ed. Ruth M. Elmquist. Rinehart, 1951.

Davis, Wesley Ford. "Ask and It May Be Given." In Warrick and Greenberg.

de Camp, L. Sprague. "A Sending of Serpents." *Fantasy and Science Fiction*, August 1979.

Delany, Samuel R. *The Einstein Intersection*. Ace, 1967.

del Rey, Lester. *The Eleventh Commandment*. Regency, 1962.

————. "Evensong." In *Dangerous Visions*, ed. Harlan Ellison. Doubleday, 1967. Also in Mohs.

————. "For I Am a Jealous People." In *Star Science Fiction Stories*, ed. Frederick Pohl. Ballantine, 1953.

————. "Hereafter, Inc." In *And Some Were Human*. Prime Press, 1949.

————. "Seat of Judgement." *Venture*, July 1957.

Dentiger, Stephen. "God of the Playback." In Santesson.

Dick, Philip K. *The Divine Invasion*. Simon and Schuster, 1981.

————. *Eye in the Sky*. Ace, 1956.

————. "Faith of Our Fathers." In *Dangerous Visions*, ed. Harlan Ellison. Doubleday, 1967.

————. *Galactic Pot-Healer*. Doubleday, 1969.

————. *The Man in the High Castle*. Putnam, 1962.

————. *A Maze of Death*. Doubleday, 1970.

————. *The Three Stigmata of Palmer Eldritch*. Doubleday, 1965.

————. *The Transmigration of Timothy Archer*. Timescape, 1982.

————. *Valis*. Bantam, 1981.

Dickey, Charles. "It Came to Pass." *Playboy*, August 1974.

Dickson, Gordon R. "Things Which Are Caesar's." In *The Day the Sun Stood Still*, ed. Lester del Rey. Thomas Nelson, 1972.

Dixon, Terry. "The Prophet of Zorayne." In *Strange*.

*Dozois, Gardner. "The Disciples." *Penthouse*, December 1981.

————. "The Peacemaker." *Isaac Asimov's Science Fiction Magazine*, August 1983.

*Du Maurier, Daphne. "Happy Christmas." In *Stories of Christ and Christmas*, ed. Edward Wagenknecht. David McKay, 1963.

Dunn, Philip. *The Evangelist*. Corgi, 1979; Berkley, 1982.

Dunsany, Lord. "The Club Secretary." In *Out of This World*, ed. Julius Fast. Penguin, 1944.

————. "The Demagogue and the Demi-Monde." In *Fifty-One Tales*. Elkin Mathews, 1915.

————. "The Doom of La Traviata." In *The Sword of Welleran and Other Stories*. George Allen, 1908.

————. "The Gratitude of the Devil." In *The Man Who Ate the Phoenix*. Jarrolds, 1949.

————. "A Moral Little Tale." In *Fifty-One Tales*. Elkin Mathews, 1915.

————. "Old Emma." In *The Man Who Ate the Phoenix*. Jarrolds, 1949.

————. "The Reward." In *Fifty-One Tales*. Elkin Mathews, 1915.

Duntemann, Jess. "Our Lady of the Endless Sky." *Nova*, April 1974.

*Earley, A. "And It Was Good." *Amazing Stories*, February 1962.

Easton, Thomas. "End and Beginning." *Vertex*, December 1974.

Edelstein, Scott. "Botch." In *Nameless Places*, ed. Gerald W. Page. Arkham House, 1975.

————. "The Victim." *Vertex*, August 1973.

Edmonds, Walter D. "Moses." In *The Newbery Award Reader*, ed. Charles G. Waugh and Martin H. Greenberg. Harcourt Brace Jovanovich, 1984.

Eisenberg, Larry. "The Teacher." *Galaxy*, January 1971.

Eklund, Gordon. "The Shrine of Sebastian." In *Chains of the Sea*, ed. Robert Silverberg. Thomas Nelson, 1973.

————. "Three Comedians." In *New Dimensions 3*, ed. Robert Silverberg. Nelson Doubleday, 1973.

Elkund, Gordon, and Gregory Benford. "If the Stars Are Gods." In *Universe 4*, ed. Terry Carr. Random House, 1974.

Elgin, Suzette Haden. "Lest Levitation Come Upon Us." In Ryan.

Elliot, Bruce. "The Devil Was Sick." In *Deals with the Devil*, ed Basil Davenport. Dodd, Mead, 1958.

Elliot, George P. "The Beatification of Bobbsa Wilson." In *Among the Dangs*, ed. George P. Elliott. Holt, Rinehart and Winston, 1961.

Ellison, Harlan. "The Deathbird." In *Deathbird Stories*. Harper and Row, 1975.

————. "Hitler Painted Roses." In *Strange Wine*. Warner Books, 1978.

*————. "The Place with No Name." In *Deathbird Stories*. Harper and Row, 1975.

————. "The Region Between." In *Five Fates*, ed. Keith Laumer. Doubleday, 1970.

————. "Satan Is My Ally." *Fantastic Science Fiction*, May 1957.

Elwood, Roger, ed. *Flame Tree Planet*. Concordia, 1973.

————, ed. *Strange Gods*. Pocket Books, 1974.

————. "Throwback." In *Strange*.

*Fairman, Paul W. "Witness for the Defense." *Science Fantasy 4*, Spring 1971.

Farmer, Philip J. "Attitudes." *Fantasy and Science Fiction*, October 1953.

————. "A Bowl Bigger Than Earth." In *Down in the Black Gang and Other Stories*. Nelson Doubleday, 1971.

————. "Father." *Fantasy and Science Fiction*, July 1955.

————. *Flesh*. Galaxy, 1960.

————. "Heel." *If Science Fiction*, May 1960.

————. *Inside Outside*. Ballantine, 1964.

————. "JC on the Dude Ranch." In *Riverworld and Other Stories*. Berkley, 1979.

————. *Jesus on Mars*. Pinnacle, 1979.

————. *The Magic Labyrinth*. Berkley, 1979.

————. *The Maker of Universes*. Ace, 1965.

————. "The Making of Revelation, Part I." In *After the Fall*, ed. Robert Sheckley. Ace, 1980.

————. *Night of Light*. Berkley, 1966.

————. *A Private Cosmos*. Ace, 1968.

————. "Prometheus." *Fantasy and Science Fiction*, March 1961. Also in Mohs.

————. *Strange Relations*. Ballantine, 1964.

————. *The Unreasoning Mask*. Putnam, 1981.

Fast, Howard. "Tomorrow's *Wall Street Journal*." In *The General Zapped an Angel*. Ace, 1969.

*Federer, Heinrich. "Santa Risolina." In *The World's Christmas Stories from Many Lands*, ed. Olive Wyon. Fortress Press, 1964.

Forster, E. M. "The Celestial Omnibus." In *The Celestial Omnibus and Other Stories*. Sidgwick and Jackson, 1911. Also in *The Collected Tales of E. M. Forster*. Knopf, 1948.

————. "Co-ordination." In *The Eternal Moment and Other Stories*. Sidgwick and Jackson, 1928. Also in *The Collected Tales of E. M. Forster*. Knopf, 1948.

————. "The Other Side of the Hedge." In *The Celestial Omnibus and Other Stories*. Sidgwick and Jackson, 1911. Also in *The Collected Tales of E. M. Forster*. Knopf, 1948.

————. "The Point of It." In *The Eternal Moment and Other Stories*. Sidgwick and Jackson, 1928. Also in *The Collected Tales of E. M. Forster*. Knopf, 1948.

Foster, Alan Dean. "Instant with Loud Voices." In Ryan.

*Frahm, Leanne. "Deus Ex Corporis." In *Chrysalis 7*, ed. Roy Torgeson. Zebra Books, 1979.

*France, Anatole. "The Ocean Christ." In *Golden Tales of Anatole France*. Dodd, Mead, 1927.

Fritch, Charles E. "If at First You Don't Succeed, to Hell with It." *Fantasy and Science Fiction*, August 1972.

Gallico, Paul. "The Word of Babe Ruth." In *Baseball 3000*, ed. Frank D. McSherry, Jr., Charles G. Waugh, and Martin H. Greenberg. Elsevier/ Nelson Books, 1981.

Gardner, Craig Shaw. "God's Eyes." In Ryan.

Garnett, Richard. "Duke Virgil." In *The Twilight of the Gods and Other Tales*. T. Fisher Unwin, 1888.

*Garrett, Randall. "The Briefing." *Fantastic Stories*, August 1969.

Gat, Dimitri. *The Shepherd Is My Lord*. Doubleday, 1971.

Gedge, Pauline. *Stargate*. Dial Press, 1982.

Gilbert, Daniel. "The Meat Box." In Ryan.

Gilden, Mel. "Small Miracles." In Ryan.

Gilford, C. B. "Heaven Can Wait." *Ellery Queen's Mystery Magazine*, August 1953.

Godwin, Tom. "The Cold Equations." In Warrick and Goldberg.

Gordon, Rex. *First on Mars*. Ace, 1957.

Gordon, Stuart. *Smile on the Void*. Arrow, 1982.

*Goudge, Elizabeth. "Midnight in the Stable." In *A New Christmas Treasury*, ed. Robert Lohan and Maria Lohan. Stephen Daye Press, 1954.

Grant, Charles L. "Confess the Seasons." In Ryan.

Grasty, William K. "One Afternoon in Busterville." In *Strange*.

Graves, Robert. *Watch the North Wind Rise*. Creative Age Press, 1949; Farrar, Straus and Giroux, 1982. Also published as *Seven Days in New Crete*. Cassell, 1949.

*Greth, Robert. "The Rope." In *Magazine of Horror*, July 1969.

Grove, Walt. "John Grant's Little Angel." In *The Playboy Book of Science Fiction and Fantasy*. Playboy Press, 1966.

Grubb, Davis A. *Ancient Lights*. Viking, 1982.

*Gruber, Frank. "The Golden Chalice." *Weird Tales*, July 1940.

Gunn, James. *This Fortress World*. Gnome, 1955.

———. "The Joy Ride." In *The End of the Dreams*. Charles Scribner's Sons, 1975.

———. "Kindergarten." In *100 Great Science Fiction Short Short Stories*, ed. Isaac Asimov, Martin Greenberg, and Joseph D. Olander. Avon Books, 1978.

*Hagedorn, Hermann. "The Hour of Stars." In *Stories of Christ and Christmas*, ed. Edward Wagenknecht. David McKay, 1963.

Hale, Edward Everett. "Hands Off." In *Isaac Asimov Presents the Best Fantasy of the 19th Century*, ed. Isaac Asimov, Charles G. Waugh, and Martin H. Greenberg. Beaufort Books, 1982.

Hamilton, Edmond. "Twilight of the Gods." In *What's It Like Out There? and Other Stories*. Ace, 1974.

Harness, Charles L. "Time Trap." *Astounding*, August 1948.

———. "The New Reality." *Thrilling Wonder Stories*, December 1950.

Harper, Rory. "Psycho-Stars." *Isaac Asimov's Science Fiction Magazine*, March 1980.

*Harris, Frank. "The Miracle of the Stigmata." In *The Short Stories of Frank Harris*, ed. Elmer Gertz. Southern Illinois University Press, 1975.

Harris, Gordon. *Apostle from Space*. Logos International, 1978.

*Harrison, Elizabeth. "The Legend of the Christ Child." In *Merry Christmas to You!*, ed. Wilhelmina Harper. E. P. Dutton, 1935.

Harrison, Harry. "The Streets of Ashkelon." In Santesson. Also in Warrick and Greenberg.

Hawkes, Jacquetta. *Providence Island*. Random House, 1959.

———. "The Unities." In *A Woman as Great as the World and Other Fables*. Random House, 1953.

Heard, Gerald. *Gabriel and the Creatures*. Harper, 1952.

*Hecht, Ben. "The Heavenly Choir." In *A Book of Miracles*. Viking Press, 1939.

———. "A Lost Soul." In *A Book of Miracles*. Viking Press, 1939.

———. "The Missing Idol." In *A Book of Miracles*. Viking Press, 1939.

———. "Remember Thy Creator." In *A Book of Miracles*. Viking Press, 1939.

Heinlein, Robert. "Magic, Inc." In *Waldo and Magic, Inc*. Doubleday and Co., 1950.

———. "The Man Who Traveled in Elephants." In *The Unpleasant Profession of Jonathan Hoag*. Gnome, 1959.

———. *Methuselah's Children*. Gnome, 1958.

———. *Revolt in the Year 2100*. Shasta, 1953.

———. *Stranger in a Strange Land*. Putnam, 1961.

Henderson, Zenna. *Pilgrimage: The Book of the People*. Doubleday, 1961.

———. *The People: No Different Flesh*. Doubleday, 1966.

Herbert, Frank. *Destination Void*. Berkley, 1966.

———. *Dune*. Chilton, 1965.

———. *Dune Messiah*. Putnam, 1969.

———. *Children of Dune*. Berkley, 1976.

———. *God Emperor of Dune*. Putnam's, 1981.

———. *The God Makers*. Putnam, 1972.

———. *The Heaven Makers*. Avon, 1968.

———. *The Priests of Psi*. Gollancz, 1980.

Herbert, Frank, and Bill Ransom. *The Jesus Incident*. Berkley, 1979.

Hock, Edward D. "Sword for a Sinner." In *The Judges of Hades*. Leisure Books, 1971.

———. "The Wolfram Hunters." In Santesson.

*Hodgson, William Hope. "The Baumoff Explosive." *Nash's Weekly*, 17 September 1919.

Holmes, Clara H. "In the Beyond." In *Floating Fancies Among the Weird and Occult*. F. T. Neely, 1898.

Houseman, Laurence. "The Catch of the Cherub." In *Strange Ends and Discoveries*. Jonathan Cape, 1948.

———. "The Cry of the Parrot." In *Strange Ends and Discoveries*. Jonathan Cape, 1948.

———. "The Great Adventure." In *Strange Ends and Discoveries*. Jonathan Cape, 1948.

———. "The Impossible Penitent." In *Strange Ends and Discoveries*. Jonathan Cape, 1948.

———. "Improved Relations." In *Strange Ends and Discoveries*. Jonathan Cape, 1948.

———. "The New Dispensation." In *Strange Ends and Discoveries*. Jonathan Cape, 1948.

———. "The Return Journey." In *Strange Ends and Discoveries*. Jonathan Cape, 1948.

———. "Vessels of Clay." In *Strange Ends and Discoveries*. Jonathan Cape, 1948.

Howard, James. "The Director." In *Strange*.

Hoyle, Fred. "A Play's the Thing." In *Element 79*. Signet, 1967.

———. "Pym Makes His Point." In *Element 79*. Signet, 1967.

Hughes, Richard. "The Stranger." In *A Moment of Time*. Chatto and Windus, 1926.

Irving, Washington. "The Devil and Tom Walker." In *Speak of the Devil*, ed. Sterling North and Clarence B. Boutell. Doubleday, Doran and Co., 1945.

Jacks, L. P. "All Men Are Ghosts." In *All Men Are Ghosts*. Williams and Norgate, 1913.

Jakes, John. "Crack Up." *Fantasy and Science Fiction*, September 1954.

Jameson, Malcolm. "Heaven Is What You Make It." *Unknown Worlds*, August 1943.

*Jennings, Gary. "The Relic." *Fantasy and Science Fiction*, June 1979.

Jones, Leslie. "The Devil and Mrs. Ackenbough." *Fantasy and Science Fiction*, August 1958.

Jones, Raymond F. "The Lions of Rome." In *Strange*.

*Joseph, Jim. "Come Again." *Galaxy Science Fiction*, December–January 1978.

Keizer, Gregg. "Angel of the Sixth Circle." In Ryan.

Keller, David H. "Men of Avalon." In *The White Sybil by Clark Ashton Smith and Men of Avalon by David H. Keller, M.D.* Fantasy Publications, 1935.

*Kemp, Lysander. "Silent Night." *Fantastic*, April 1955.

Kersh, Gerald. "The Epistle of Simple Simon." In *The Brighton Monster and Others*. Heinemann, 1953. Also in *Men without Bones*. Pocket Books, 1962.

*Kessel, "Uncle John and the Saviour." *Fantasy and Science Fiction*, December 1980.

Kidd, Virginia. "CholoM." In *Strange*.

Killough, Lee. *A Voice Out of Ramah*. Ballantine, 1979.

*Kilworth, Gary. "Let's Go to Golgotha!" In *Gollancz—Sunday Times Best SF Stories*. Victor Gollancz, 1975.

*Kimberly, Gail. "Many Mansions." In *Flame*.

Kipling, Rudyard. "The Enemies to Each Other." In *Debits and Credits*. Macmillan, 1926.

———. "The Man Who Would Be King." In *The Phantom Rickshaw*. H. Altemus, 1898.

———. "On the Gate, A Tale of '16." In *Debits and Credits*. Macmillan, 1926.

———. "Uncovenanted Mercies." In *Limits and Renewals*. Macmillan, 1932.

Knight, Damon. "Shall the Dust Praise Thee?" In *Dangerous Visions*, ed. Harlan Ellison. Doubleday, 1967. Also in Mohs.

*Knowles, Vernon. "The First Coming." In *Two and Two Make Five*. Newnes, 1935.

Koontz, Dean R. "The Sinless Child." In *Flame*.

Korolenko, Vladimir. "Makar's Dream, a Christmas Story." In *Strange to Tell*, ed. Marjorie Fischer and Rolfe Humphries. Julian Messner, 1946.

Kube-McDowell, Michael P. "A Green Hill Far Away." In Ryan.

Kurtz, Katherine. *Camber of Culdi*. Ballantine, 1976.

———. *Camber the Heretic*. Ballantine, 1981.

———. *Saint Camber*. Ballantine, 1978.

Kuttner, Henry. "A Cross of Centuries." *Star Science Fiction*, March 1958. Also in Mohs.

———. "The Misguided Halo." In *The Unknown*, ed. D. R. Bensen. Pyramid Books, 1963.

———. "Two-handed Engine." *Fantasy and Science Fiction*, August 1955.

La Farge, Oliver. "I'll Take Care of You." *Famous Fantastic Mysteries*, June 1952.

238   Checklist

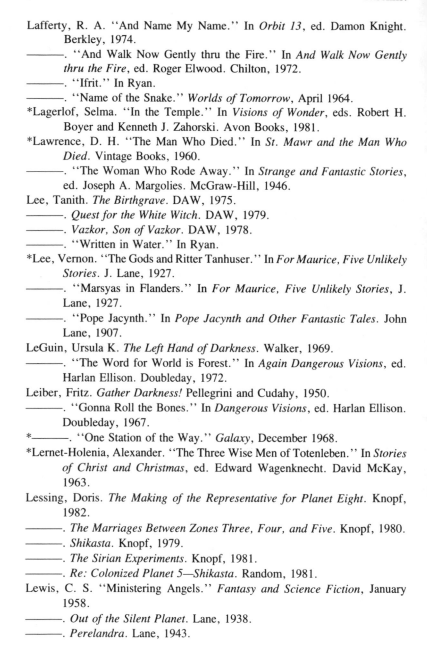

Lafferty, R. A. "And Name My Name." In *Orbit 13*, ed. Damon Knight. Berkley, 1974.

———. "And Walk Now Gently thru the Fire." In *And Walk Now Gently thru the Fire*, ed. Roger Elwood. Chilton, 1972.

———. "Ifrit." In Ryan.

———. "Name of the Snake." *Worlds of Tomorrow*, April 1964.

*Lagerlof, Selma. "In the Temple." In *Visions of Wonder*, eds. Robert H. Boyer and Kenneth J. Zahorski. Avon Books, 1981.

*Lawrence, D. H. "The Man Who Died." In *St. Mawr and the Man Who Died*. Vintage Books, 1960.

———. "The Woman Who Rode Away." In *Strange and Fantastic Stories*, ed. Joseph A. Margolies. McGraw-Hill, 1946.

Lee, Tanith. *The Birthgrave*. DAW, 1975.

———. *Quest for the White Witch*. DAW, 1979.

———. *Vazkor, Son of Vazkor*. DAW, 1978.

———. "Written in Water." In Ryan.

*Lee, Vernon. "The Gods and Ritter Tanhuser." In *For Maurice, Five Unlikely Stories*. J. Lane, 1927.

———. "Marsyas in Flanders." In *For Maurice, Five Unlikely Stories*, J. Lane, 1927.

———. "Pope Jacynth." In *Pope Jacynth and Other Fantastic Tales*. John Lane, 1907.

LeGuin, Ursula K. *The Left Hand of Darkness*. Walker, 1969.

———. "The Word for World is Forest." In *Again Dangerous Visions*, ed. Harlan Ellison. Doubleday, 1972.

Leiber, Fritz. *Gather Darkness!* Pellegrini and Cudahy, 1950.

———. "Gonna Roll the Bones." In *Dangerous Visions*, ed. Harlan Ellison. Doubleday, 1967.

*———. "One Station of the Way." *Galaxy*, December 1968.

*Lernet-Holenia, Alexander. "The Three Wise Men of Totenleben." In *Stories of Christ and Christmas*, ed. Edward Wagenknecht. David McKay, 1963.

Lessing, Doris. *The Making of the Representative for Planet Eight*. Knopf, 1982.

———. *The Marriages Between Zones Three, Four, and Five*. Knopf, 1980.

———. *Shikasta*. Knopf, 1979.

———. *The Sirian Experiments*. Knopf, 1981.

———. *Re: Colonized Planet 5—Shikasta*. Random, 1981.

Lewis, C. S. "Ministering Angels." *Fantasy and Science Fiction*, January 1958.

———. *Out of the Silent Planet*. Lane, 1938.

———. *Perelandra*. Lane, 1943.

————. *That Hideous Strength*. Lane, 1945.

Lewis, L. A. "The Tower of Moab." In *Tales of the Grotesque*. Philip Allan, 1934.

Lewitt, Shariann. "St. Joey the Action." In Ryan.

Lindsay, David. *A Voyage to Arcturus*. Macmillan, 1963.

Linklater, Eric. "Kind Kitty." In *God Likes Them Plain*. Jonathan Cape, 1935.

*Linney, Romulus. *Jesus Tales*. North Point Press, 1981.

*Locke, William J. "A Christmas Mystery." In *Stories of Christ and Christmas*, ed. Edward Wagenknecht. David McKay, 1963.

London, Jack. "The Red One." In *Selected Science Fiction and Fantasy Stories: Jack London*. Fictioneer Books, 1978.

Lovin, Roger. "Apostle." In *Flame*.

Lowndes, Robert. *Believer's World*. Avalon, 1961.

Lucas, Jay. "Black Horses." *Blue Book*, September 1937.

Lupoff, Richard A. "Musspelsheim." In *Strange*.

MacApp, C. C. "All That Earthly Remains." *Worlds of If Science Fiction*, July 1962.

McCormack, Ford. "Hell-Bent." In *Deals with the Devil*, ed. Basil Davenport. Dodd, Mead, 1958.

Machen, Arthur. "The Soldier's Rest." In *The Angels of Mons, The Bowmen, and Other Legends of the War*. Simpkin, Marshall, Hamilton, Kent, 1915.

McLean, Katherine. "Unhuman Sacrifice." In Santesson.

*MacLeod, Fiona. "The Fisher of Men." In *The Washer of the Ford and Other Celtic Moralities*. Patrick Geddes, 1896.

*————. "Muime Chiosd." In *The Washer of the Ford and Other Celtic Moralities*. Patrick Geddes, 1896.

Maddux, Rachael. "Final Clearance." In *The Best from Fantasy and Science Fiction, Sixth Series*, ed. Anthony Boucher. Doubleday, 1957.

Malamud, Bernard. "Angel Levine." *Gamma*, No. 3, 1964.

*Malzberg, Barry N. "The Annual Bash and Circumstance Party." *Fantasy and Science Fiction*, May 1979.

————. "Bearing Witness." In *Flame*.

————. "Big Ernie, the Royal Russian and the Big Trapdoor." *Fantasy and Science Fiction*, May 1978.

————. *The Cross of Fire*. Ace, 1982.

*————. "The Falcon and the Falconeer." *Fantasy and Science Fiction*, December 1969.

*————. "In the Cup." In *Signs and Wonders*, ed. Roger Elwood. Revell, 1972.

*————. "Le Croix." In *Their Immortal Hearts*, ed. Bruce McAllister. West Coast Poetry Review, 1981.

*————. "Outside." *Fantasy and Science Fiction*, January 1973.

*————. "Track Two." In *The Best of Barry N. Malzberg*. Pocket Books, 1976.

————. "Try Again." In *Strange*.

Mano, D. Keith. *Horn: A Novel and a Fable, an Adventure and a Fantasy*. Houghton, 1969.

————. *Bishop's Progress*. Houghton, 1968.

*March, William. "Mist on the Meadow." In *The Best Short Stories of 1932*, ed. Edward J. O'Brien. Dodd, Mead, 1932.

*————. "Private Edward Romano." In *Pause to Wonder*, eds. Marjorie Fischer and Rolfe Humphries. Julian Messner, 1944.

Marks, Winston. "He Stepped on the Devil's Tail." *Fantastic Universe Science Fiction*, February 1955.

Martin, George R. R. "Song for Lya." In *Song for Lya and Other Stories*. Avon, 1976.

*————. "The Way of Cross and Dragon." *Omni*, June 1979.

*Matheson, Richard. "The Traveller." *Fantasy and Science Fiction*, February 1962.

Maugham, W. Somerset. "The Judgment Seat." *Pause to Wonder*, eds. Marjorie Fischer and Rolfe Humphries. Julian Messner, 1944.

Maurois, André. "If Louis XVI Had Had a Atom of Firmness." In *If, or History Rewritten*, ed. Sir John Collings Squire. Kennikat, 1964.

————. *The Weigher of Souls*. Macmillan, 1963.

*May, Julian. "Star of Wonder." *Thrilling Wonder Stories*, February 1953.

*Merimee, Prosper. "Federigo." In *Strange to Tell*, ed. Marjorie Fischer and Rolfe Humphries. Julian Messner, 1946.

Merritt, A. *Dwellers in the Mirage*. Liveright, 1932.

————. *The Face in the Abyss*. Liveright, 1931.

————. "Three Lines of Old French." In *The Fox Woman and Other Stories*. Avon, 1949.

Merril, Judith. "The Shrine of Temptation." In *Santesson*.

Miller, Wade. "I Know a Good Hand Trick." *Fantasy and Science Fiction*, November 1959.

Miller, Walter M., Jr. *A Canticle for Leibowitz*. Lippincott, 1960.

————. "Crucifixus Etiam." *Astounding*, February 1953.

Mines, Sam. "Find the Sculptor." *Thrilling Wonder Stories*, 1946. Also in *Wonder Story Annual, 1952–1953*.

Mitchell, Edward Page. "The Cave of the Splurgles." In *The Crystal Man*. Doubleday, 1973.

*Mitchison, Naomi. "Mary and Joe." In *Nova 1*, ed. Harry Harrison. Delacorte, 1970.

*Moffitt, David. "The Scroll." *Fantasy and Science Fiction*, May 1972.

Mohs, Mayo, ed. *Other Worlds, Other Gods*. Doubleday, 1971.

Moorcock, Michael. *Behold the Man*. Avon, 1970.

*———. *Breakfast in the Ruins*. Random House, 1974.

———. *The Fireclown*. Paperback Library, 1967.

Moore, Raylyn. "Poverello." In *Flame*.

Morris, Gouverneur. "Derricks's Return." In *The Evening Standard Second Book of Strange Stories*. Hutchinson, 1937.

Morrow, James. *The Wine of Violence*. Holt, Rinehart and Winston, 1981.

Nahin, Paul J. " 'Some Things Just *Have* to be Done by Hand,' " In *Analog Yearbook II*, ed. Stanley Schmidt. Ace, 1981.

*Nathan, Robert L. "To Come unto Me." In *Stories of Christ and Christmas*, ed. Edward Wagenknecht. David McKay, 1963.

*Nelson, R. Faraday. "Nightfall on the Dead Sea." *Fantasy and Science Fiction*, September 1978.

*Nichols, Robert. "Golgotha and Company." In *Fantastica: Being the Smile of the Sphinx and Other Tales of Imagination*. Macmillan, 1923.

Niven, Larry. "The Subject Is Closed." *Cosmos Science Fiction and Fantasy*, May 1977.

Nolan, William F. "The Party." In *The Playboy Book of Horror and the Supernatural*. Playboy Press, 1967.

Norden, Eric. "The Final Analysis." In *Starsongs and Unicorns*. Manor, 1978.

O'Brien, Clancy. "A Matter of Freedoms." In *Flame*.

O'Donnell, K. M. "Oversight." In *Strange*.

Oliphant, Margaret. "The Land of Darkness." In *The Land of Darkness*. Macmillan, 1888.

———. "The Little Pilgram in the Seen and Unseen." In *The Land of Darkness*. Macmillan, 1888.

———. "On the Dark Mountains." In *The Land of Darkness*. Macmillan, 1888.

Oliver, Chad. "The Marginal Man." *Fantasy and Science Fiction*, April 1958.

Oliver, Richard. "Reprise." *Isaac Asimov's Science Fiction Magazine*, July 1982.

O'Rourke, Frank. "The Heavenly World Series." In *Baseball 3000*, ed. Frank D. McSherry, Jr., Charles G. Waugh, and Martin H. Greenberg. Elsevier/Nelson Books, 1981.

Owen, Frank. "The Blue City." In *The Wind That Tramps the World*. Lantern Press, 1929.

*Page, Thomas Nelson. "The Shepherd Who Watched by Night." In *Stories of Christ and Christmas*, ed. Edward Wagenknecht, David McKay, 1963.

*———. "The Stranger's Pew." In *The Land of the Spirit*. Charles Scribner's Sons, 1913.

Palmer, Stuart. "A Bride for the Devil." *The Magazine of Fantasy*, Fall 1949.

Pangborn, Edgar. "Angel's Egg." In *Good Neighbors and Other Strangers*. Collier Books, 1972.

———. "Pickup for Olympus." In *Good Neighbors and Other Strangers*. Collier Books, 1972.

Panshin, Alexei. "The Sons of Prometheus." In *Farewell to Yesterday's Tomorrow*. Berkley, 1975.

Paul, Herb. "The Angel with the Purple Hair." In *The Supernatural Reader*, ed. Groff Conklin and Lucy Conklin. Lippincott, 1953.

Payes, Rachel Cosgrove. "In His Own Image." In *Strange*.

Payne, Paul L. "Fool's Errand." *Thrilling Wonder Stories*, October 1952.

Pearce, J. H. "Gifts and Awards." In *Drolls from Shadowland*. Lawrence and Bullen, 1893.

Percy, Walker. *Love in the Ruins: The Adventures of a Bad Catholic at a Time Near the End of the World*. Farrar, Straus, 1971.

Perez, Isaac Loeb. "Bontche Shweig." In *Strange to Tell*, ed. Marjorie Fischer and Rolfe Humphries. Julian Messner, 1946.

Perkins, Vincent. "And One Made of Air." *Vertex*, February 1975.

Phillips, Rog. "Services, Inc." *Fantasy and Science Fiction*, June 1958.

Piper, H. Beam. "Temple Trouble." In *Paratime*. Ace, 1981.

*Pocci, [Count] Franz. "The Stranger Child." In *Favorite Christmas Stories*, eds. Frances Cavanah and Nellie H. Farnam. Grosset and Dunlap, 1941.

Poe, Edgar Allan. "The Angel of the Odd." In *The Complete Tales and Poems of Edgar Allan Poe*. Modern Library, 1938.

———. "The Duc De L'Omelette." In *The Complete Tales and Poems of Edgar Allan Poe*. Modern Library, 1938.

Pohlman, Edward. *The God of Planet 607*. Westminster, 1972.

*Porges, Arthur. "A Devil of a Day." *Fantastic Stories of Imagination*, August 1962.

———. "The Devil and Simon Flagg." *Fantasy and Science Fiction*, August 1954.

———. "The Liberator." *Fantasy and Science Fiction*, December 1953.

———. "The Rescuer." *Analog*, July 1962.

*Powys, T. F. "A Christmas Gift." In *The Fireside Book of Christmas Stories*, ed. Edward Wagenknecht. Bobbs-Merrill, 1945.

Pratt, Theodore. "Doorway to Heaven." *Fantastic Universe Science Fiction*, September 1959.

*Price, E. Hoffmann. "The Stranger from Kurdistan." In *Strange Gateways*. Arkham House, 1967.

———. "Well of the Angels." In *Strange Gateways*. Arkham House, 1967.

Priestley, J. B. "The Grey Ones." In *The Other Place*. Harper and Row, 1953.

*Pronzini, Bill, and Barry N. Malzberg. "Coming Again." *Fantasy and Science Fiction*, June 1975.

Pyle, Howard. "In Tenebris." In *Shapes That Haunt the Dusk*, ed. W. D. Howells, H. M. Alden, and Henry Mills. Harper, 1907.

*Quinn, Seabury. "Roads." In *Worlds of Weird*, ed. Leo Margulies. Jove Publications, 1965.

*Reynolds, Mack. "The Second Advent." *If, Worlds of Science Fiction*, June 1974.

———. "Your Soul Comes C.O.D." In *The Best of Mack Reynolds*. Pocket Books, 1976.

Riddell, Mrs. J. H. "Sandy the Tinker." In *Weird Stories*. James Hogg, 1882.

Riley, Frank. "Bright Islands." *If, Worlds of Science Fiction*, June 1955.

Robbins, Tod. "Who Wants a Green Bottle?" In *Silent, White and Beautiful and Other Stories*. Boni and Liveright, 1920.

Roberts, Keith. *Pavane*. Doubleday, 1968.

*Roberts, Mary-Carter. "He Descended Into Hell." *Fantasy and Science Fiction*, June 1975.

Rosmund, Babette. "One Man's Harp." In *From Unknown Worlds*, ed. John W. Campbell, Jr. Atlas Publishing, 1952.

Rosenberg, Joel. "The Emigrant." In Ryan.

Russell, Bertrand. "The Queen of Sheba's Nightmare." In *Nightmares of Eminent Persons*. The Bodley Head, 1954.

Russell, Eric Frank. "The Army Comes to Venus." In Santesson.

———. "Displaced Person." In *Somewhere a Voice*. Ace, 1965.

———. "First Person Singular." *Thrilling Wonder Stories*, October 1950.

———. "Second Genesis." In *Deep Space*. Fantasy Press, 1954.

Russell, Ray. "Ripples." *Playboy*, October 1967. Reprinted in *Sagittarius*. Playboy Press, 1971.

———. "Xong of Xuxan." *Playboy*, October 1970.

Ryan, Alan. *Perpetual Light*. Warner Books, 1982.

———. "The Rose of Knock." In Ryan.

Saki [H. H. Munro]. "The Infernal Parliament." In *The Square Egg and Other Sketches*. John Lane, 1924.

———. " 'Ministers of Grace.' " In *The Chronicles of Clovis*. John Lane, 1911.

Sambrot, William. "The Night of the Leopard." In Warrick and Greenberg.

Sanders, Winston P. "The Word to Space." *Fantasy and Science Fiction*, September 1960. Also in Mohs.

Santesson, Hans S., ed. *God of Tomorrow*. Award, 1967.

Schenck, Hilbert. "The Theology of Water." In Ryan.

Scortia, Thomas N. "Tarrying." In *Flame*.

Scott, [Sir] Walter. "Wandering Willie's Tale." In *Ghosts and Marvels*, ed. V. H. Collins. Oxford, 1924.

Sellings, Arthur. "That Evening Sun Go Down." In Santesson.

Serling, Rod. "A Stop at Willoughby." In *More Stories from the Twilight Zone*. Bantam, 1961.

Shaara, Michael. "The Book." In *Soldier Boy*. Pocket Books, 1982.

Sheckley, Robert. "The Battle." *Worlds of If*, September 1954.

———. *Dimension of Miracles*. Dell, 1968.

———. "The Victim from Space." In *The People Trap and Other Pitfalls*. Dell, 1968.

Siegal, Larry. "Another Chance for Casey." *The American Legion Magazine*, July 1950.

Silverberg, Robert. *Downward to the Earth*. Doubleday, 1970.

———. "The Feast of St. Dionysus." In *An Exaltation of Stars*, ed. Terry Carr. Simon and Schuster, 1973.

———. "Good News from the Vatican." In *Unfamiliar Territory*. Scribner's, 1973. Also in Warrick and Greenberg.

———. *The Masks of Time*. Ballantine, 1968.

———. "The Nature of the Place." *Fantasy and Science Fiction*, January 1963.

———. *Nightwings*. Avon, 1969.

———. "The Pope of the Chimps." In Ryan.

———. "Sundance." In *The Best from Fantasy and Science Fiction*, ed. Edward L. Ferman. Doubleday, 1969.

———. "Thomas the Proclaimer." In *The Day the Sun Stood Still*, ed. Lester del Rey. Thomas Nelson, 1972.

———. *To Open the Sky*. Ballantine, 1967.

Simak, Clifford D. "The Creator." *Marvel Tales*, April 1935.

*———. "The Voice in the Void." *Wonder Stories Quarterly*, Spring 1932.

———. *Why Call Them Back from Heaven?* Doubleday, 1967.

Simonds, Vance. "The Red Tape Yonder." *Fantastic Stories of Imagination*, August 1963.

Sinclair, May. "The Finding of the Absolute." In *Uncanny Stories*. Hutchinson, 1923.

———. "Heaven." In *The Intercessor, and Other Stories*. Hutchinson, 1931.

———. "Where Their Fire Is Not Quenched." In *Uncanny Stories*. Hutchinson, 1923.

Sinclair, Upton. *Our Lady*. Rodale Press, 1938.

Slesar, Henry. "The Jam." In *The Playboy Book of Horror and the Supernatural*. Playboy Press, 1967.

Smith, Cordwainer. "The Crime and Glory of Commander Suzdal." In *The Best of Cordwainer Smith*, ed. J. J. Pierce. Nelson Doubleday, 1975.

Smith, George H. "Flame Tree Planet." In *Flame*.

*Spence, Lewis. "Himsel'." In *The Archer in the Arras and Other Tales of Mystery*. Grant and Murray, 1932.

Springer, Nancy. *The Black Beast*. Pocket Books, 1982.

Stapledon, Olaf. *Star Maker*. Methuen, 1937.

Starrett, Vincent. "The Sinless Village." In *The Quick and the Dead*. Arkham House, 1965.

Stead, Christina. "The Centenarist's Tales, III." In *The Salzburg Tales*. Peter Davies, 1934.

———. "Sappho." In *The Salzburg Tales*. Peter Davies, 1934.

Stephens, James. "The Threepenny Piece." In *The Best from Fantasy and Science Fiction*, ed. Anthony Boucher. Little, Brown, 1952.

Sternbach, Richard. "The Hand." *Amazing Stories*, October–November 1953.

Stewart, George R. *Earth Abides*. Random House, 1949.

Sturgeon, Theodore. "Dazed." In Warrick and Greenberg.

———. "Fear is a Business." *Fantasy and Science Fiction*, August 1956.

———. "The Man Who Learned Loving." In Warrick and Greenberg.

———. "The Riddle of Ragnarok." *Fantastic Universe Science Fiction*, June 1955.

Suskind, Murray. "The Second Coming." *Playboy*, November 1982.

Sutton, Lee. "Soul Mate." *Fantasy and Science Fiction*, June 1959. Also in Mohs.

Swigart, Rob. *The Book of Revelations*. Dutton, 1981.

Tarkington, Booth. "Hell." In *Mr. White, The Red Barn, Hell, and Bridewater*. Doubleday, 1935.

Tem, Steve Rasnic. "Firestorm." In Ryan.

Temple, Willard. "The Eternal Duffer." In *The Saturday Evening Post Fantasy Stories*, ed. Barthold Fles. Avon, 1951.

Tevis, Walter. *Mockingbird*. Doubleday, 1980.

Thackeray, William Makepeace. "The Devil's Wager." In *Gothic Tales of Terror, Volume One*, ed. Peter Haining. Penguin, 1973.

Thomas, John B. "Return to a Hostile Planet." In *Strange*.

Thorne, Guy. *When It Was Dark*. Putnam's, 1904.

Tiptree, James, Jr. "And I Have Come upon This Place by Lost Ways." In Warrick and Greenberg.

*Tofte, Arthur. "The Mission." In *Microcosmic Tales*, ed. Isaac Asimov, Martin Harry Greenberg, and Joseph D. Olander. Taplinger, 1980.

Traven, B. "Sun Creation." *Fantasy and Science Fiction*, April 1964.

Tritten, Larry. "Playback." *Fantasy and Science Fiction*, August 1978.

*Twain, Mark. "The Diary of Adam and Eve." In *Space Mail, Vol. 2*, ed. Isaac Asimov, Martin H. Greenberg, and Charles G. Waugh. Fawcett, 1981.

———. "The Second Advent." In *Mark Twain's Fables of Man*, ed. John S. Tuckey. University of California Press, 1972.

Vaisberg, Maurice. "The Sun Stood Still." *The Original Science Fiction Stories*, November 1958.

Vance, Jack. "Temple of Han." *Astounding*, August 1948.

*Van Doren, Mark. "The Strange Girl." In *The Worlds of Science Fiction*, ed. Robert P. Mills. Dial Press, 1967.

VanScyoc, Sydney J. *Saltflower*. Avon, 1971.

Varley, John. *Titan*. Berkley, 1978.

————. *Wizard*. Berkley, 1980.

Vidal, Gore. *Khalki*. Random House, 1978.

————. *Messiah*. Dutton, 1954.

Vinge, Joan D. "Mother and Child." In *Orbit 16*, ed. Damon Knight. Harper and Row, 1975.

Vonnegut, Kurt. *Cat's Cradle*. Holt, Rinehart, 1963.

Wainwright, Ruth Laura. "Mint in D/j." *Fantasy and Science Fiction*, June 1954.

*Walpole, Hugh. "Major Wilbraham." In *The Silver Thorn*. Macmillan, 1928.

Ward, Frank. "Judgment Day." In Ryan.

Warrick, Patricia, and Martin Harry Greenberg, eds. *The New Awareness*. Delacorte, 1975.

Watson, Ian. *Deathhunter*. Gollancz, 1981.

————. "A Letter from God." *Destinies*, Winter, 1981. Reprinted in *Sunstroke and Other Stories*, Gollancz, 1982.

Weinreb, Nathaniel Norsen. "Devil Play." In *Baseball 3000*, eds. Frank D. McSherry, Jr., Charles G. Waugh, and Martin H. Greenberg. Elsevier/ Nelson, 1981.

*Welbore, M. W. " 'Rejected of Men.' " In *Some Fantasies of Fate*. Digby, Long, 1899.

Wellen, Edward. "The Book of Elijah." *Fantasy and Science Fiction*, January 1964.

*Wellman, Manly Wade. "On the Hills and Everywhere." In *Who Fears the Devil?* Arkham House, 1963.

————. "Young-Man-with-Skull-at-his-Ear." In *Worse Things Waiting*. Carcosa, 1973.

Wells, H. G. "In the Abyss." In *Science Fiction A to Z: A Dictionary of the Great S.F. Themes*, ed. Isaac Asimov, Martin H. Greenberg, and Charles G. Waugh. Houghton Mifflin 1982.

————. "The Story of the Last Trump." In *The Short Stories of H. G. Wells*. Ernest Benn, 1927.

————. "A Vision of Judgment." In *The Country of the Blind and Other Stories*. T. Nelson, 1911.

Wetjen, Albert Richard. "The Strange Adventure of Tommy Lawn." *Adventure*, 15 March 1927.

Wharton, Edith. "The Fulness of Life." *Scribner's Magazine*, December 1893.

White, Ted. "Vengeance Is Mine." *Fantastic Stories*, June 1977.

Wilde, Niall. "A Divvil with the Women." *Fantasy and Science Fiction*, January 1960.

Wilde, Oscar. "The Selfish Giant." In *The Happy Prince, The Selfish Giant, and Other Stories*. Octopus Books, 1980.

Wilhelm, Kate. *Let the Fire Fall*. Doubleday, 1969.

Williamson, Jack, and Frederick Pohl. *Starchild*. Ballantine, 1965.

Willis, Connie. "Samaritan." In *Starry Messenger: The Best of Galileo*, ed. C. C. Ryan. St. Martins, 1979.

Willoughby, Barrett. "The Devil-Drum." In *The Best Short Stories of 1925*, ed. Edward J. O'Brien. Small, Maynard, 1926.

Wilson, F. Paul. "Be Fruitful and Multiply." In Ryan.

*Wolfe, Gene. "La Befana." *Galaxy Science Fiction*, January–February 1973.

*Wooster, John J. "And on the Third Day." *Fantastic Stories of Imagination*, November 1963.

Wright, S. Fowler. "Choice." In *The New Gods Lead*. Jarrolds, 1932.

Wylie, Philip. "The Answer." In *The Post Reader of Fantasy and Science Fiction*. Doubleday, 1964.

Wyndham, John. "Confidence Trick." In *Tales of Gooseflesh and Laughter*. Ballantine, 1956.

Yep, Lawrence. "My Friend Klatu." In *Signs and Wonders*, ed. Roger Elwood. Revell, 1978.

Yermakov, Nicholas. "Hamburger Heaven." In Ryan.

Young, Robert F. "Added Inducement." *Fantasy and Science Fiction*, March 1957.

———. "Chrome Pastures." *If Science Fiction*, April 1956.

———. "The Deep Space Scrolls." *Amazing Stories*, May 1963.

———. "A Drink of Darkness." In *The Worlds of Robert F. Young*. Simon and Schuster, 1965.

———. "Minutes of a Meeting of the Mitre." *Fantasy and Science Fiction*, October 1965.

———. "Promised Planet." *If Science Fiction*, December 1955.

*———. "The Quality of Mercy." *Fantastic Universe Science Fiction*, April 1955.

*———. "Robot Son." *Fantastic Universe Science Fiction*, September 1959. Also in Santesson.

*———. "Time Travel, Inc." *Super-Science Fiction*, February 1958.

*———. "To Touch a Star." *Worlds of If Science Fiction*, April 1970.

Younger, William. "The Angelus." In *A Century of Horror Stories*, ed. Dennis Wheatley. Hutchinson, 1935.

Zebrowski, George. "Heathen God." *Fantasy and Science Fiction*, January 1971.

———. "Interpose." *Infinity*, May 1973.

————. *The Omega Point*. Ace, 1972.

Zelazny, Roger. "Creatures of Light." *If, Worlds of Science Fiction*, November 1968.

————. *Lord of Light*. Doubleday, 1967.

————. "A Rose for Ecclesiastes." *Fantasy and Science Fiction*, November 1963. Widely reprinted.

————. "The Salvation of Faust." *Fantasy and Science Fiction*, July 1964.

————. *This Immortal*. Ace, 1966.

Zelazny, Roger, and Philip K. Dick. *Deus Irae*. Doubleday, 1976.

Secondary Works
Dealing with Religion
in Science Fiction

ROBERT REILLY

Abernethy, Francis E. "The Case for and against Science Fiction." *Clearing House* 34 (April 1960), 474–77.

Anderson, Susan A. "Evolutionary Futurism in Stapledon's Star Maker," *Process Studies* 5 (Summer 1975), 123–28.

Bayley, Barrington J. "Science, Religion and the Science Fiction Idea; or, Where Would We Be without Hitler?" *Foundation* 17:50–57.

Blish, James [as William Atheling]. "Cathedrals in Space." In *The Issue at Hand*. Advent, 1973.

Bossay, Lyssa Dianne. "Religious Themes and Motifs in Science Fiction." Ph.D. dissertation, University of Texas at Austin, DAI, 40:5857A.

Bradbury, Ray. "The God in Science Fiction." *Saturday Review* 10 (December 1977), 36–38, 43.

Bradham, Jo Allen. "The Case in James Blish's *A Case of Conscience*." *Extrapolation* 16 (December 1974), 67–80.

Brady, Charles J. "The Computer as a Symbol of God: Ellison's Macabre Exodus." *The Journal of General Education* 28:55–62.

deWohl, Louis. "Religion, Philosophy, and Outer Space." *America*, 24 July 1954, 420–21.

Dilley, Frank. "Multiple Selves and the Survival of Brain Death." In *Philosophers Look at Science Fiction*, ed. Nicholas D. Smith. Nelson-Hall, 1982.

Dimeo, Steven. "Man and Apollo: A Look at Religion in the Science Fantasies of Ray Bradbury." *Journal of Popular Culture* 5 (Spring 1972), 970–78.

250   Robert Reilly

Disch, Thomas. "Science Fiction as a Church." *Foundation* 25 (June 1982), 53–58.
Freibert, Lucy M. "World Views in Utopian Novels by Women." In *Women in Utopia: Critical Interpretations*, ed. Nicholas D. Smith and Marleen Barr. University Press of America, 1983.
Heard, Gerald. "Science Fiction, Morals and Religion." In *Modern Science Fiction: Its Meaning and Its Future*, ed. Reginald Bretnor. Advent, 1953; 2d ed. 1979.
Hilton-Young, Wayland. "The Contented Christian." *Cambridge Journal* 10 (July 1952), 603–12.
Kessler, Carol Farley. "The Heavenly Utopia of Elizabeth Stuart Phelps." In *Women in Utopia: Critical Interpretations*, ed. Nicholas D. Smith and Marleen Barr. University Press of America, 1983.
Ketterer, David. "Covering *A Case of Conscience*." *Science Fiction Studies* (July 1982), 195–214.
———. *New Worlds for Old*. Indiana University Press, 1974.
King, J. Norman. "Theology, Science Fiction and Man's Future Orientation." In *Many Futures, Many Worlds*, ed. Thomas D. Clareson, 237–59. Kent State University Press, 1977.
Kreuziger, Frederick A. *Apocalypse and Science Fiction: A Dialectic of Religious and Secular Soteriologies*. Scholars Press, 1982.
Lantero, Erminie Huntress. "What Is Man? Theological Aspects of Contemporary Science Fiction." *Religion in Life* 38 (Summer 1969), 242–55.
Lewis, C. S. "On Science Fiction." In *Of Other Worlds: Essays and Stories*, ed. Walter Hooper, 59–73. Harcourt, Brace and World, 1966.
McDonnell, Thomas P. "The Cult of Science Fiction." *Catholic World* 178 (October 1953), 15–18.
Merritt, James D. "She Pluck'd, She Eat." In *Future Females: A Critical Anthology*, ed. Marleen S. Barr. Popular Press, 1982.
Moskowitz, Sam. "Religion: Space, God and Science Fiction." In *Strange Horizons*, 3–21. Charles Scribner's Sons, 1976.
Murphy, Carol. "The Theology of Science Fiction." *Approach* 23 (Spring 1957), 2–7.
Pauly, Rebecca M. "The Moral Stance of Kurt Vonnegut." *Extrapolation* 15 (December 1973), 66–71.
Phalan, J. M. "Men and Morals in Space." *America* 113 (9 October 1965), 405–7.
Plank, Robert. "The Place of Evil in Science Fiction." *Extrapolation* 14 (May 1973), 100–111.
Platzner, John. "The Mystification of Outer Space: Pseudo-Mysticism and Science Fiction." *Studia Mystica* (California State University) 1:44–51.
"Pop Theology: Those Gods from Outer Space." *Time*, 5 September 1969, 64.

Ready, Karen, and Franz Rottensteiner. "Other Worlds, Otherworldliness: Science Fiction and Religion." *The Christian Century* 5 (December 1973), 1192–95.

Reilly, Robert. "The Discerning Conscience." *Extrapolation* 18 (May 1977), 176–80.

Rose, Lois, and Stephen Rose. *The Shattered Ring: Science Fiction and the Quest for Meaning.* John Knox, 1970.

Rothfork, John. "Grokking God: Phenomenology in NASA and Science Fiction." *Research Studies*, 44:101–10.

———."Science Fiction as a Religious Guide to the New Age." *Kansas Quarterly* 10 (Fall 1978), 57–66.

Smith, Nicholas D., and Fred D. Miller, Jr., eds. *Thought Probes.* Prentice-Hall, 1980.

Stapleford, Brian. *A Clash of Symbols.* Borgo, 1979.

———."Immortality." In *The Science Fiction Encyclopedia*, 307a–c. Ed. Peter Nicholls, Doubleday, 1979.

———."Religion." In *The Science Fiction Encyclopedia*, 493b–96a, ed. Peter Nicholls, Doubleday, 1979.

———."The Science Fiction of James Blish." *Foundation* 13:12–24.

Sturgeon, Theodore. "Science Fiction, Morals and Religion." In *Science Fiction, Today and Tomorrow*, ed. Reginald Bretnor, 98–113. Harper and Row, 1974.

Ward, Hiley H. *Religion 2101 A.D.* Doubleday, 1975.

Woodman, Tom. "Science Fiction, Religion and Transcendence." In *Science Fiction: A Critical Guide*, ed. Patrick Parrinder, 110–30. Longman, 1979.

Zebrowski, George. "Introduction: Whatever Gods There Be: Space-time and Deity in Science Fiction." In *Strange Gods*, ed. Roger Elwood. Pocket Books, 1974.

Index

Contributors

ELIZABETH M. ALLEN holds a Bachelor of Journalism from the University of Texas at Austin and an M.A. in English from Baylor University. Formerly a newspaper reporter, she is now Chairman of the English Department at Rosebud-Lott High School. She has published several articles and presently is working on a children's fantasy novel.

MARTHA A. BARTTER is a science fiction writer who is teaching science fiction and working for a Ph.D. at the University of Rochester.

NANCY TOPPING BAZIN, Associate Professor of English and Director of Women's Studies at Old Dominion University, is the author of *Virginia Woolf and the Androgynous Vision*. She has also published articles on Woolf, Lessing, Wharton, Lawrence, androgyny, and women's studies. She is on the editorial board of the *Doris Lessing Newsletter* and has recently participated in two faculty development projects in Third World studies funded by the U.S. Department of Education.

ANDREW J. BURGESS, who has taught religious studies at Case Western University and Cleveland State University, now serves as Assistant Professor of Philosophy and Chairman of the Religious Studies Program at the University of New Mexico. He is the author of *Passion, "Knowing How," and Understanding: An Essay on the Concept of*

Faith, as well as articles on the philosophy of religion in the works of Kierkegaard, Wittgenstein, and Brentano.

ALEXANDER J. BUTRYM is Associate Professor of English at Seton Hall University, where he has taught, except for a stint as a technical writer, since 1961. He holds a Ph.D. in English from Rutgers University. In addition to science fiction, he teaches courses in Medieval and Renaissance literature and in technical writing. His particular areas of interest in science fiction are the ethics of scientists, the characterization of scientists as heros, and style and "literary flavor" in popular literature.

EDGAR L. CHAPMAN is Associate Professor of English at Bradley University. He was educated at William Jewell College and Brown University, where he wrote a doctoral dissertation on Renaissance comedy. He has published articles in various journals including *Mythlore* and *Texas Studies in Literature and Language*, and an article on Philip K. Dick in *The Salem Survey of Science Fiction*. His book on Philip José Farmer was published in 1982 by Borgo Press.

JOSEPH V. FRANCAVILLA teaches English at the State University of New York at Buffalo. A member of both SFWA and SFRA, he has published fiction and articles in *Ethos*, *Leighdt*, *Cinéfantastique*, and Robert Silverberg's anthology *New Dimensions 10*. He is currently writing a science fiction novel, a critical book on Kafka and Poe, and is editing a book about popular literature.

ADAM J. FRISCH is Assistant Professor of English at Briar Cliff College. He holds degrees from the universities of Michigan, Washington, and Texas and has taught courses in dramatic literature and science fiction at both Memphis State University and the University of Texas at Austin. He is the author of "Language Fragmentation in Recent Science-Fiction Novels" in *The Intersection of Science Fiction and Philosophy* (Greenwood Press, 1983). His interest in science fiction dates back to his first disappointments with a real telescope at age eight.

FRANK DAVID KIEVITT received his B.A. from Seton Hall University and his M.A., M. Phil., and Ph.D. from Columbia University. At present he is Assistant Professor of English at Bergen Community College. He has published articles dealing with religion and literature, and the eighteenth-century British novel in *Mid-Hudson Language Studies* and *Renaissance and Renascences*.

FRANK D. McSHERRY, JR., is a commercial artist who does illustrations and book jackets. In addition, he writes mystery stories for *Mike Shayne Mystery Magazine* and critical-biographical articles in both the science fiction and the mystery fields. With Martin Greenberg and Charles G. Waugh he has edited *Baseball 3000*, a science fiction anthology for young adults.

JOSEPH MARTOS, who has taught at both De Paul University and Briar Cliff College, holds degrees in philosophy and theology. He has recently written a book on the relation between sacraments and religious experience. His interest in science fiction dates back to the 1950s when, in his own words, "Heinlein, Asimov, Clarke, and others started me thinking about many of the things that until then I had naively believed and implicitly accepted."

DAVID M. MILLER, Associate Professor of English at Purdue University, teaches Milton, science fiction, and creative writing. Among his publications are *The Net of Hephaestus; John Milton: Poetry*; and *Frank Herbert*. Professor Miller has also written several critical essays on J.R.R. Tolkien.

DIANE PARKIN-SPEER is Associate Professor of English at Southwest Texas State University. She teaches and does research in the fields of speculative fiction and English Renaissance literature, particularly Reformation thought.

RICHARD L. PURTILL, Professor of Philosophy at Western Washington State College, has published eleven books, including six textbooks, three trade nonfiction, and two fantasy novels. The most recent of these is *C. S. Lewis's Case for the Christian Faith*. His current research interests include philosophy of religion, "mythopoetic" fantasy, and ancient and modern Greece.

WILLIAM A. QUINN received his Ph.D. in English from Ohio State University and is currently Assistant Professor at the University of

Arkansas. He has reviewed science fiction scholarship for *Style* and is co-author of *Jongleur*, a book on rhymecraft in Middle English romance.

ROBERT REILLY is Professor of English at Rider College. A medievalist by training, he has devoted most of his recent critical effort to science fiction. He has published articles in *Medieval Studies* and *Extrapolation*.

KATHERIN A. ROGERS received her B.A. and M.A, in philosophy from the University of Delaware, where she now teaches part-time. She received her Ph.D. from the University of Nortre Dame, where she specialized in medieval philosophy, particularly St. Anselm of Canterbury. She lives in Newark, Delaware, with her husband Mark, an artist and writer, and their two daughters.

PATRICIA S. WARRICK is Professor of English at the University of Wisconsin–Fox Valley. Her undergraduate degree is in chemistry and her M.A. and Ph.D. are in English. She has published essays in *Critique, Science Fiction Studies*, and *Extrapolation*. Coeditor of a number of anthologies, she has also written *The Cybernetic Imagination in Science Fiction*. She is currently finishing a book-length study of the fiction of Philip K. Dick.

CHARLES G. WAUGH is Professor of Psychology and Communications at the University of Maine at Augusta. His major areas of academic interest include social influence and interpersonal communications, but his real love is science fiction, of which he has been a fan and collector for more than 25 years. He has published approximately 30 articles and coedited more than 40 anthologies.